The RIDDLE of
KONNERSREUTH

By the Same Author

IN ENGLISH:

The Philosophy of Evil (New York: The Ronald Press Co.).
The Enigma of the Hereafter (New York: Philosophical Library).

IN FRENCH:

La psychophysique humaine d'après Aristotle, Préface de J. Chevalier (Paris: Alcan, Coll. Histor. des Grands Philosophes).
L'âme et le corps d'après Spinoza (Paris: Alcan, Coll. Histor. des Grands Philosophes).
Spinoza et le panthéisme religieux (Paris: Desclée de Brouwer, Bibliothèque Française de philosophie).
Le problème du mal (Rio de Janeiro: Desclée de Brouwer, Bibliothèque Française de philosophie).
La réincarnation des esprits (Rio de Janeiro: Desclée de Brouwer, Bibliothèque Française de philosophie).
Une stigmatisée de nos jours (Paris: Lethielleux).
Au coeur du Spinozisme (Paris: Desclée de Brouwer, Bibliothèque Française de philosophie).

IN LATIN:

Psychologia Metaphysica (Romae: Univers. Gregoriana).
Aristotelis De Anima libri tres. Graece et latine (Romae: Univers. Gregoriana).

IN POLISH:

Wedrowka dusz (Warszawa: Jezuici).
Reinkarnacja dusz w swietle filozofji moralnej (Kraków).
Metody badań zjawisk nadprzyrodzonych (Kraków: Jezuici).
Konnersreuth w swietle nauki i religji (Kraków: Jezuici).
W pogoni za Nieskonczonoscia (Kraków: Jezuici).

IN PORTUGUESE:

Psicologia Experimental (Rio de Janeiro: Univers. Cat.).
A psicoánalise (Sao Paulo: Univers. Cat.).
Transformismo Antropologico (Sao Paulo: Livraria Academica).
Em busca de Deus (Sao Paulo: Livraria Academica).
A reincarnaçao dos espiritos (Livraria Academica).

IN SPANISH:

El problema del Mal (Buenos Aires: Huarpes).
La reincarnación de los spiritos (Buenos Aires: Huarpes).
En busca de Dios (Buenos Aires: Huarpes).

The RIDDLE of KONNERSREUTH

A Psychological and Religious Study

By PAUL SIWEK, S.J., Ph.D., S.T.D.

PROFESSOR AT FORDHAM UNIVERSITY

Translated by IGNATIUS McCORMICK, O.F.M.Cap.

PROFESSOR AT MARY IMMACULATE FRIARY

GLENCLYFFE-GARRISON, N. Y.

THE BRUCE PUBLISHING COMPANY

MILWAUKEE

Imprimi potest:
ADRIAN HOLZMEISTER, O.F.M.CAP.
Minister Provincial, Providence, R. I.

Nihil obstat:
JOHN A. SCHULIEN, S.T.D.
Censor librorum

Imprimatur:
✠ ROMAN R. ATKIELSKI
Administrator, sede vacante, archidioecesis Milwauchiensis

Die 24 auguste, 1953

.

Letter of Archbishop Carinci

SACRED CONGREGATION OF RITES

ROME, April 8, 1952

VERY REVEREND FATHER SIWEK,

I HAVE read with attention your book *Une stigmatisée de nos jours.* I admired therein your impartial and objective presentation of the facts of the case, as well as your carefully considered judgment on the various marvelous phenomena which are found in Theresa Neumann. Not a few of these are, from a scientific viewpoint, of the natural order, and a few indeed are at present of doubtful origin. You do not come out with a final judgment for or against these latter, as, alas, so many superficial writers have done. Although unqualified in logic, pathology, psychology, or theology they issue opinions with exceeding levity, and, if they are Catholics, believe that they are promoting the interests of God and of the Church, either by denying the supernatural or by attributing all, or almost all, the phenomena to a supernatural cause.

The Church, herself a supernatural society, necessarily admits the possibility and the existence of supernatural facts. But she demands certain, not doubtful, evidence for them. She wishes to possess the truth, not mere probability, no matter how great the latter may be. Such is the rule followed by the Sacred Congregation of Rites when there is question of judging the facts presented as miracles in causes of the beatification or canonization of servants of God. The present Holy Father, moreover, has determined to intensify the scientific investigation (which up to now was conducted by at least three doctors in every case of marvelous healing) by creating a medical

v

council. This council discusses, with complete freedom, the independent and written statements of two physicians who, as far as possible, are specialists. The collective opinion of the council, drawn up in writing by eight or nine experts, finally affords moral certainty for the competency of the aforesaid judges. Even then it sometimes happens that the Sacred Congregation requests further clarifications from the medical council.

This manner of procedure shows the great precautions taken by the Church to exclude all doubt and to bring out clearly the truth of divine intervention in facts presented as miraculous.

For this reason your book, which is a critical, physiological, psychological, logical, and theological study of the facts of Konnersreuth, offers a precious contribution to the study of analogous cases and is a model of its kind. Furthermore, it will be of great utility to all physicians, whether Catholic or non-Catholic; to the latter because it will reveal much data hitherto unknown to them, and, if they be of good faith, will dissipate many misunderstandings and prejudices; to the former because it will encourage them to write freely and express their opinions without any fear of incurring the stigma of unbelief, provided only that they are mindful to remain on a strictly scientific plane. Your book, finally, will be of advantage to all readers, for it will show them clearly that the Church, and in particular the Sacred Congregation of Rites, is a friend of truth and uses every means to attain to it. Nor does she hesitate to withhold her recognition of the miraculous from facts which suggest the slightest doubt concerning their natural origin.

Through this work, then, your reverence has earned the gratitude of science, of the Church, and especially of the Sacred Congregation of Rites.

Please accept my congratulations and thanks,

Devotedly yours,

✠ ALFONSO CARINCI, *Archbishop of Seleucia*
Secretary of the Sacred Congregation of Rites

Translator's Preface

"Of the making of many books there is no end," wrote Solomon nearly three thousand years ago. His complaint might well apply to the case of Theresa Neumann. Hardly any other living person has been the subject of so many and such greatly varied books and articles. Why then add to the number?

In answer to that question, we might say that it is because, first of all, Theresa is still living and the extraordinary phenomena that have made Konnersreuth world famous are still taking place. Moreover, a study of their current development is always fascinating. Second, because, while any number of critical studies have appeared in Europe, the English reading public until recently has made acquaintance with only one side of the problem. Practically all the books and articles published in this country have accepted without question the supernatural origin of her cures, visions, ecstasies, stigmatization, and fasting. When Hilda Graef published her criticisms in 1951 her book had the effect of a bombshell on most American Catholics.

Audiatur et altera pars — "Give heed also to the other side" — is an axiom of modern as well as of ancient Roman law. The Catholic Church not only encourages, but on occasion demands, a most searching and critical investigation of alleged supernatural occurrences.

Father Siwek is exceptionally qualified for this investigation and his work deserves a careful and unprejudiced study. He is not only an eminent authority in theology and philosophy, but also has devoted years of study, under Pierre Janet and others, to the strange phenomena which constitute the field of psychopathology and parapsychology. His interest in the Konnersreuth case dates back almost to its inception.

The translator, of course, assumes full responsibility for the English rendering of French and German scientific terms, except where such terms are found in quotations from works already published in English.

IGNATIUS McCORMICK

Capuchin Friary
Garrison, N. Y.

Author's Preface
to the English Edition

THE present work is more than a mere translation of my book *Une stigmatisée de nos jours;* it is a new and enlarged edition. The original French version has been carefully revised, corrected in several places, and some explanatory notes have been added. Some ideas, barely sketched in the French text, have been more fully developed, and some new problems, which have presented themselves since the book's first appearance, have been introduced, and so forth. With all these changes, however, the *substance* of the book, together with its general tenor, its guiding thought, and its *method* have not been changed.

There is no dearth of fascinating accounts of the Konnersreuth phenomena in English. Far from it. For the most part, however, these accounts offer nothing more than personal impressions garnered by the various authors upon visiting Konnersreuth. They do not set out to give us a *scientific explanation* — in fact, some of the writers explicitly disclaim any such intention. And the few historical details they present add nothing of importance to what has already been recorded by older writers, notably L. Witt and Fr. Gerlich.[1]

We must keep these facts in mind if we are to avoid being misled. A number of people consider those who have seen Theresa Neumann and who have conversed with her as "authorities" on the Konnersreuth problem, and accept naïvely whatever these assert regarding the *nature* of the phenomena which

---

[1] L. Witt, *Konnersreuth im Lichte der Religion und Wissenschaft,* 2 ed. (Waldsassen, 1927); Fr. Gerlich, *Die stigmatisierte Therese Neumann von Konnersreuth* (München, 1929).

occur. Such a credulous attitude is certainly not according to the mind of the Church. Whenever there is question of determining whether a cure is to be attributed to natural forces or to a supernatural intervention of God, the Church does not rely on the "impressions" of eyewitnesses. She looks to the judgment of experts, who, in this case, would be competent physicians. They are the ones who must judge whether the alleged cure really exceeds the natural powers of the organism.[2]

Now if, in addition to remarkable cures, we find (as at Konnersreuth) phenomena of the *psychic* order (visions, revelations, the gift of tongues, etc.), are we not obliged to consult authorities in the field of *psychology?* Such a procedure would seem to be recommended by logic and elementary common sense.

Nor is this all. Whenever there is question of phenomena touching matters of *Catholic faith* we must seek the views of authorities competent in the field of religion, that is to say,

---

[2] This alleged cure must be attested by reliable witnesses. These witnesses, however, can be different from the physicians who are to pronounce judgment on the character of the cure. Nor are the latter obliged to see personally the individual who is said to be "miraculously" cured. The essential thing for them is to get reliable documents on the cure under consideration.

What we have said contradicts those (and they are legion) who categorically deny any right to judge scientifically the case of Konnersreuth to all those who have not "seen" Theresa Neumann or have not "spoken" with her. It is in virtue of this principle that H. Fröhlich denied Dr. Deutsch the right to give his opinion on Theresa Neumann, since "he had not been in Konnersreuth" (*Konnersreuth Heute* . . . [Wiesbaden: Credoverlag, 1950], p. 64). They forget that the reliable documents on Theresa Neumann are commonly known. They were carefully collected especially by L. Witt and Fr. Gerlich. There remains little to be found that could change our opinion on Konnersreuth.

We shall go even further. We are hesitant in admitting any information from Konnersreuth which is *in contradiction* with the documents mentioned above. The experiments made by several scholars (e.g., by J. Philippe) show very curious and important deformations which our remembrance experiences under the influence of time. It is for this reason that we personally prefer L. Witt to Fr. Gerlich, and both to J. Teodorowicz. Therefore if, for example, we find in Witt the assertion that Theresa Neumann had, in her childhood, a great devotion to the passion of Christ, and a quite opposite observation in Teodorowicz, we uphold Witt. Before Witt's book was published it was read to Theresa and carefully corrected according to her suggestions, which at that time were fresh. Teodorowicz's book, on the contrary, was composed many years later. Moreover it is more a panegyric than a history. It has been pointed out by Professor J. Lhermitte and Professor Dom Aloys Mager, O.S.B., that it lacks critical objectivity.

theologians. Once the medical and psychological experts have decided that a given event cannot be explained naturally, they must make place for the theologian who will examine it in the light of criteria provided by the doctrine and history of the Church.

All these considerations show clearly how cautious we must be concerning the pronouncements of those who would settle the Konnersreuth problems by means of "intuition" or mere impressions. A certain physician (T. M.), with whom we are personally acquainted, once assured us that he was able to diagnose illnesses by a short-cut method — by simple intuition. All our efforts to correct his notions were fruitless. One day he was called to examine a very sick woman. Relying on his intuition, he ordered the patient to the mountains. When she arrived there she was seized with new and violent attacks. Summoned once more, the physician next sent her to the seashore where she could breathe the fresh sea air. She obeyed at once, but her condition became more critical. A medical student who happened to be nearby examined her, found her suffering from acute diabetes, and sent her immediately to a hospital. Prolonged treatment saved her life.

Some time ago we attended a conference at which a speaker (A. K.) assured his audience in all sincerity that by means of his "intuition" he could "read the thoughts of chance passers-by in the street." Any psychologist with even a rudimentary knowledge of recent experiments on emotional expression would smile at such a pretension. His technique had even less foundation than the hasty diagnostic methods of our physician friend.

Among the publications on Theresa Neumann which have appeared in English, that of Hilda Graef[3] certainly is the best. A specialist in ascetico-mystical theology, she examines Theresa's spiritual life and her external deportment in the light of the teachings of eminent theologians. It must be admitted that Theresa fares rather badly by this yardstick. In addition,

---

[3] *The Case of Therese Neumann* (Westminster, Md.: The Newman Press, 1951).

Miss Graef has published a number of documents which cast suspicion on the famous stigmatic. The conclusions she draws are far from favorable to the supernatural character of the Konnersreuth phenomena.

While acknowledging the great merit of Miss Graef's work, we have chosen a very different approach to the problem. Whenever some extraordinary event is encountered in the life of Theresa Neumann we ask the question: "Can this phenomenon be accounted for by natural forces?" If it can be explained in this way, we accept it as a natural occurrence, normal or abnormal. If the phenomenon cannot be attributed to natural forces, then it must be due to some supernatural power. But to what kind of supernatural power? Good or evil? Divine or diabolical? For a solution to this *last* question we must have recourse to the moral criteria offered by "mystical theology." We must carefully inquire whether the phenomenon is productive of moral good or evil for Theresa. Does it help her advance in virtue, or does it rather retard her? Does it fill her with sentiments of genuine love for God, or does it attach her to the world and its pleasures? and so on.

After all, the virtue of the individual is not of paramount importance in deciding the supernatural (as against the natural) character of such phenomena. Theologians assure us that one may be endowed with authentic supernatural charisms without possessing great moral virtue. What is more important here is the use which the subject makes of his alleged supernatural gifts. *Ex fructibus eorum cognoscetis eos* — "By their fruits you shall know them."

The method outlined above simply makes use of the principle of "intellectual restraint," also called "the principle of economy." It means that when we set out to account for some phenomenon, we must begin with the simplest hypothesis. In other words, we should appeal to a supernatural cause *only when the insufficiency of natural causes has been proved.*

As can be seen, we do not neglect or underestimate the criteria of mystical theology. Rather, we choose to use them in a different way than some other writers. Instead of beginning the study with theological criteria, we introduce them only after we have proved that the phenomenon in question actually surpasses the forces of nature. The practical result of this method is apparent when there is question of determining the nature of the extraordinary phenomena found in the lives of certain saints. Their heroic virtue, their holiness, gives us more or less assurance that the phenomena do not originate with the evil spirit. But are they from *God* or from *nature?* To solve this problem we must look to scientific criteria (physiological, psychological, etc.). Only in this way can we exclude a possible natural origin of the phenomena. Those who start with theological criteria are generally content, at least in practice, to remain within these norms. We often hear them remark: "I am not concerned that these phenomena might also be explained naturally. They are, nonetheless, part of a supernatural plan." Such reasoners trifle with the word *supernatural.* They seem to forget that there is nothing in the world that cannot be called "supernatural" in this sense of the word. *Diligentibus Deum omnia cooperantur ad bonum* — "For those who love God all things work together unto good"; yes, everything — poverty and wealth, sickness and health, disgrace and honor, failure and success. But when we inquire whether a vision be "supernatural," is this the meaning we have in mind?

One final word about the method we choose to employ. Let us suppose that a physiological and psychological investigation should lead to the conclusion: "The phenomena can be explained very well by natural forces." What possible reason would we then have to advance to theological (mystical) criteria? This should be borne in mind by the reader. But we must not anticipate.

The problem of Konnersreuth has lost nothing of its *timeliness.* The marvelous events narrated in this book are still taking place. Even the horrors of war were not able to halt them or even alter them. And pilgrims continue to stream into Konnersreuth from all over the world.

The timeliness of the problem, however, stems more from its significance. No one can determine this significance a priori. A careful investigation of the facts is of supreme importance. And here we emphasize the necessity of a correct *method* of investigation.

What method of investigation must be employed? An explanation of what we believe to be the correct method is precisely the purpose of this book. Consequently our study will transcend the limited spatiotemporal framework in which this particular problem is found. Let us not forget that the case of Theresa Neumann is not an isolated one in the history of the Church. Such phenomena reoccur periodically. At the present time more and more instances occur each year. What we have to say on the subject of Theresa Neumann may help in evaluating similar cases. This is the "timeliness" we have principally in mind.

We wish to express our heartfelt thanks to Father Ignatius McCormick, O.F.M.Cap., of the Capuchin Seminary, Garrison, N. Y., for having made this study of the Konnersreuth phenomena accessible to the English reading public. The reader can judge and appreciate for himself the merits of his translation. What has impressed us personally is the exactness with which he has rendered all the nuances of our thought. His work gives the lie to the old saying: *Traductor, traditor* — "A translator is a traitor."

Nor can we pass over in silence the valuable services rendered by the Capuchin seminarians who prepared the manuscript for publication. Above all, we are indebted to the Capuchin superiors, Very Reverend Fathers Cyprian Abler and Adrian Holzmeister, without whose generosity and co-operation this book could not have been published.

Contents

Contents

PART I
The Facts

Introduction

NOT far from the Czechoslovakian frontier lies the little Bavarian town of Waldsassen. Artists and art lovers have visited the place from time to time to admire the beauty of the old Cistercian church. Since the beginning of Lent, 1926, however, the influx of visitors to this sector of Bavaria has taken on the proportions of pilgrimages. One can find among them distinguished scientists as well as ignorant countryfolk, members of the clergy, and laymen from all walks of life. Waldsassen is no longer the goal of their journey. This is merely the place where they get off the train to take an automobile or bus to Konnersreuth.

What is the attraction? Konnersreuth has nothing to offer in the way of artistic beauty. Neither does it offer any inducement to people in search of livelihood, boasting neither factories nor mines. Konnersreuth is only a small village (population, about 950), off the beaten path. The nearest railroad station is about four and one-third miles distant.

What attracts the crowds to this place is the mysterious fascination exercised upon the human mind by the intrusion into this world of the life beyond, of the infinite, of which we have spoken elsewhere.[1] Konnersreuth is said to be a predestined spot. There God deigns to raise the veil of mystery which hides Him from human eyes. There He permits men to touch with human hands, so to speak, the supernatural world, of which faith tells us only obscurely and in fragments.

Sensational reports from Konnersreuth were heard around the

---

[1] *Em busca de Deus* (Sao Paulo: Livraria Academica, 1944); translated into Spanish in 1945. This book has also been published in Polish.

3

world and had a profound effect on souls to whom World War I had exposed the bankruptcy of naturalism and who in consequence felt a pressing need for God. It was not surprising, then, that among the pilgrims who made their way to Konnersreuth we found mingled together Catholics and Protestants, believers and atheists, Jews and nonreligionists. On some Fridays as many as two and three hundred automobiles, with some 5000 passengers, would arrive at the little village. Scarcely were the cars parked in the public square than the pilgrims rushed toward the one center of attraction, the parental home of Theresa Neumann.

Originally the house consisted of a single story. However, after the throngs of the curious and the souvenir seekers had inflicted considerable damage on the building, Theresa's father repaired it and converted the attic into living quarters. One of these attic bedrooms is now Theresa's. It is a simple room, scrupulously clean, not too small but with a low ceiling. The room has two windows; on one sill stands a bowl of goldfish and on the other, a cage of songbirds.

CHAPTER 1

Theresa's Childhood

ACCORDING to official records, Theresa Neumann was born on April 9, 1898. (Her mother insisted that the date was April 8.) She is the eldest of ten children. Her parents were simple countryfolk who earned their living partly by farming a few acres and partly by tailoring. They enjoyed the respect of their neighbors, being known for their honesty, sound common sense, and their strong attachment to their religion, a trait characteristic of the Bavarian people.

Her parents gave Theresa a thoroughly Christian upbringing. They taught her to love her Catholic faith and to fulfill its obligations faithfully. Like other Bavarian families, the Neumanns assembled each morning and evening for prayer in common, which was recited aloud. Grace before and after meals was never omitted. On Sundays and holydays they attended holy Mass and Vespers. During divine service Mr. Neumann kept a close watch over his children, and any one of them who failed to behave with proper decorum could be sure of an exemplary punishment. Once back in the house, the culprit would be obliged to recite the Rosary, kneeling on a block of wood.

The children were trained from early childhood to habits of obedience and thrift. If one of them happened to receive a tip from a customer he was expected to place it in the little savings bank placed on his father's sewing machine. In this way the family accumulated a small reserve. When the need for cash made itself felt, the father would ceremoniously open the bank and withdraw as much of the savings as was required. The children could then take a certain noble pride in the consciousness that they too were contributing to the upkeep of the household.

Those who were acquainted with Theresa as a child cannot recall any strange events worthy of recall. She suffered from intestinal worms during her first and second year, and this condition left her somewhat irritable and nervous. Moreover, she was subject to frequent attacks of vertigo which prevented her from joining her playmates in climbing trees.[1]

The family was by no means well to do, but, thanks to the industry and economy of the parents, the children never lacked their daily sustenance.

Today Theresa reminisces with evident pleasure on those early days passed in the healthy environment of a good home. She delights in telling of her happiness when she received a beautiful doll as a present. She was then three years old. Her joy, unfortunately, was short-lived, for she soon discovered that the doll's body was stuffed with sawdust. Disgustedly she ripped the cloth, emptied out the sawdust, and threw the limp form under the table. Apropos of this event Theresa herself remarks that it was impossible for her to derive any pleasure from lifeless objects. On the other hand, she was fascinated by flowers, young animals, and especially by birds. However, she had an insurmountable aversion for long-haired animals. Gerlich tries to explain this by the fact that her mother, shortly before the birth of Theresa, had been frightened by a woolly animal. A rather fantastic explanation! It is far more probable that the aversion resulted from some terrifying experience which she herself experienced as a child. But we have no reliable evidence of any such experience.

Father Naber, the pastor of Konnersreuth, gave Theresa her first catechism lessons on September 15, 1909. From this

---

[1] This detail is not without interest. Vertigo is often a sign of a neurasthenic disposition, according to Charcot and his school. This type of vertigo does not cause the patient to fall to the ground. It is not a true disturbance of equilibrium. It is rather a feeling of a void in the head and of weakness in the limbs which seem to sink under the weight of the body. Cf. Pierre Janet, *Névroses et Idées fixes,* Vol. II (Paris: Alcan, 1924), pp. 83–84; Vol. I, 1925, pp. 219–220.

time on he became her spiritual director. He assures us that he noticed nothing remarkable about the girl, except perhaps a greater assiduity in sustained work than usually found in children of her age.

After school she was accustomed to write down in notes all that she had learned about her religion. These notes would be of immense importance at the present day, since they would throw considerable light on her early spiritual life. Unfortunately, they were burned in 1927 when the parental home was renovated.

Theresa loved to page through illustrated books, to read and reread her catechism and prayer book. Strangely enough, she always derived the same satisfaction in doing this. We shall find similar examples of stereotypy in her Friday ecstasies. But we must not anticipate.

She also enjoyed paging through the *Notburg*, a periodical published for Catholic servant girls, the illustrated monthly review *Rosenhain*, as well as the *Messenger of Divine Love*, published by the Salesian Fathers at Munich to foster devotion to St. Francis de Sales and St. Theresa of the Child Jesus. Among other books read by her at this time were the *Imitation of Christ*, Goffine's *Catholic Manual*, St. Francis de Sales's *Introduction to a Devout Life*, and St. Thérèse of Lisieux's autobiography. The latter work especially made a deep impression on her mind. From it she learned the doctrine of "spiritual childhood" and felt a keen desire to imitate the way of simplicity.

Whenever she read, heard, or meditated about the passion of our Saviour she wept bitterly. Even from her earliest childhood — her biographer asserts — she had an unusually tender devotion to the passion. During her school days she often used her recess periods to make short visits to the church with a school companion, where she meditated on the sufferings of Christ.

In 1912, that is, when Theresa was 14 years old and had completed her elementary schooling, she was employed as a servant by a wealthy neighbor, Max Neumann.

This situation would not have been particularly difficult, but

World War I broke out soon after, and practically all the farm hands were called into the army, leaving the burden of working in the fields to the women. Theresa was gifted with a robust constitution and showed a decided preference for physical work even as a child, to the extent of despising such feminine occupations as embroidering, knitting, and the like. During the war years she rendered invaluable service to her employer: plowing, harrowing, threshing, even carrying 150-pound bags of grain on her shoulders. She never complained. No amount of physical work could break her spirit — so long as the weather was fine. An overcast sky usually put a damper on her otherwise gay disposition.

She did more than her share, being always willing to assume some of the duties assigned to her two sisters who by this time also worked for Max Neumann. As their elder sister she felt herself obliged to watch over and protect them.

During this period of her life Theresa gave evidence of great strength of character. One day while working in the barn loft she was annoyed by a farm hand who tried to make violent love to her. She struggled free and jumped down to the threshing floor. She took more drastic means with another amorous swain. Angered by his importunity she finally agreed to an evening rendezvous. She came armed with a whip handle and applied it v'gorously to the back of her unfortunate admirer.

She had one compelling ambition at this time, to enter a missionary order and consecrate her life to the conversion of the African Negro. Only the insistence of her mother, who had to bear the whole burden of the household after her father left for the front, persuaded Theresa to postpone her project until after the war.

CHAPTER 2

Illness

FIRST SYMPTOMS

On March 10, 1918, at 7:30 in the morning, a sudden fire broke out in the buildings of a neighboring farm. Theresa was terrified. As she herself says, she was filled with horror (*ein heftiger Schrecken*). When she had regained her self-control she ran to the home of her parents, which was not far from the fire. Her father, home on furlough, was still asleep. She roused him with shouts of "fire! fire!" Then, driven partly by curiosity, partly by a desire to be of some assistance, she ran back to the scene of the fire. "The sight of the burning sheaves and the sound of the rafters crashing in flames," she told Gerlich years later, "made me tremble like a child meeting St. Nicholas."[1] However, she quickly controlled her emotions and helped lead the livestock from the stables to a safe place. As she ran back and forth to lend help wherever she could she met her employer who asked: "Where are you running? Our own farm is in danger." Theresa then hurried to her room to save her best clothing. Meanwhile the fire was spreading across the fields and threatened the home of Max Neumann. The household and servants organized a bucket brigade to wet down the building. Herr Neumann climbed to the roof, while Theresa stood on a stool and handed up pail after pail of water to him. We must note a few circumstances here. The pails were passed to Theresa from her left. She seized the handle with her right hand and, supporting the weight with her left, lifted the pail

[1] L. Witt, *Konnersreuth im Lichte der Religion und Wissenschaft*, 2 ed., Part I, p. 36.

over her head to her employer. The latter, becoming tired of the constant bending to grasp the pails, complained sharply that Theresa was not lifting them high enough. "I'm doing all I can," she kept repeating.

Theresa worked like this for two hours, her stomach empty and her whole body bathed in perspiration, without paying any attention to herself. She had worked just as hard many times before at the plow. She did not feel at all fatigued. But suddenly a pail slipped from her hand and clattered to the ground. She felt that she "could do no more. I felt a sudden pain in my back as if something had pinched me."[2] The pain caused her to lose her balance, but she managed to lean against the wall of the building for an instant and thus avoid falling. Her legs seemed to have become numb, as if they had "gone asleep" and become a dead weight. She tried to go to her room to change her clothes, which by this time were drenched, but she could not do so, for it was impossible for her to climb the stairs. And yet, still wearing her wet garments, she went to the stable to feed the cattle! Here she discovered that she could not bend her body even to pick up an empty basket. Then she remembered that she had not eaten breakfast, but all efforts to eat only brought on nausea and vomiting. The pain in her back, instead of slackening, grew more severe each moment; it spread over her entire body. She seemed to experience knifing pains in the region of her spine. Realizing that she should have absolute rest, and not being able to climb the stairs to her room, she managed to hobble, in a half crouch, to her parents' home.

To her mother's anxious questioning Theresa could only answer: "I don't know what is the matter with me. I have a pain in the back, and I can't do anything. I feel as if I were tied with a rope." She reclined on a bench beside the stove and after a few hours felt considerably better. She then returned to the home of her employer and climbed the stairs to her room.

She had not, however, recovered from the attack. She suffered

---

[2] Fr. Gerlich, *Die stigmatisierte Therese Neumann von Konnersreuth*, Vol. I, pp. 18–20.

pains in her back and around her waist to such an extent tha
she seemed to lose all sensation in her abdomen and could not
retain any food except barley gruel and liquids. When she
walked her body was inclined to the left and her steps faltered.
Of course she could not do heavy work. Several days' rest
brought no improvement in her condition; she lost weight
perceptibly.

Despite her afflictions she did not remain idle, but devoted
herself to lighter tasks, especially since her employer was com-
plaining about her "laziness" and some gossip was beginning to
make the rounds in the village. April arrived; a month which
meant weeks of continual and arduous labor for the farm hands.
Theresa was compelled to help along. One day she went down
to the cellar to prepare seed potatoes. She filled a sack with
potatoes and slung it over her shoulders. She says it was not
very heavy, only fifty pounds! When she started to climb the
stairs, having advanced only three or four steps, her legs suddenly gave way and she fell backward, striking her head against
the stone ledge and losing consciousness for several minutes.
She lay there, her head covered with blood, until her sister,
worried when Theresa did not return to the field, found her at
the foot of the cellar steps. Her sister raised Theresa up and
helped her reach the yard. She had a violent headache and
experienced a piercing pain in her eyes, which seemed about to
"burst from their sockets." Seeing her in this condition, her
employer excused her from further work in the field and told
her to return to the house and chop up straw. This, too, was
impossible. Finally someone helped her to her mother's home,
where she was confined to bed for a week.

New and disagreeable symptoms now made their appearance,
among them loss of sphincter control. Nevertheless, as soon as
the pain in her back diminished, she got up and helped her
mother with the housework. But once again she overestimated
her strength. Spasms of coughing and pains in her chest left
her in a weakened condition. She could not fasten her dress or
even tie her apron without suffering violent pains in her back.

Worst of all, her character seemed to undergo a transformation. Formerly she was happy and serene; now she became melancholy and irritable. Everything annoyed her and provoked such fits of temper that she became unbearable to her family (*schwererträglich*).

AT THE HOSPITAL

Finally Theresa's parents decided to place her under medical treatment. On April 23, 1918, she was admitted to the hospital at Waldsassen.

Days and weeks passed and there was no improvement in her condition. On the contrary, each day her condition became worse. The pain in her back and around her heart subsided somewhat, but she suffered agonizing spasms from the slightest stimulus. If she merely extended her arm toward her bed table, or if she attempted to pick up her slipper from the floor, or turn her head to look out the window she would be seized with a violent spasm. Her fingers would tremble and contract convulsively inward toward the palms of her hands, and soon her whole body would be shaken and become rigid as a stick. These attacks were always accompanied by a complete loss of consciousness.

Dr. Goebel, the physician in charge of the hospital during Dr. Otto Seidl's military service, could find no remedy for this disorder. What further aggravated the situation was Theresa's strong dislike for the doctor from her very first meeting with him. She could not give a reason for her dislike, and refused to co-operate with him. She volunteered no information, and answered his questions evasively or incompletely. She said nothing about the pain in her back or about her strange sensation of being "tied with a rope." She told him that her bowel movements were infrequent, but was silent concerning other important symptoms, such as her loss of sphincter control. Dr. Goebel prescribed some sedatives and a tonic, ordered absolute rest in bed, and put her on a strict diet. It was this last which caused the greatest hardship for the patient. Tormented by hunger pains, she had food brought in secretly, and even thought seriously of escaping from the hospital. Convinced that, under such conditions, hospitalization would be of no benefit, Dr. Goebel finally agreed to her discharge.

Thus she returned home on June 10, 1918, without any marked improvement. In fact, her symptoms were sensibly aggravated. Menstruation ceased completely. Her whole body was at times shaken by such violent spasms that even strong doses of morphine would not relieve her pain.

HOME AGAIN

When she returned to her own home, Theresa again tried to help with the housework, but she found herself too weak. One day while on a ladder she fell backward and struck her head on the floor. Another time, leaning over a milk pail to lift it, she lost her balance. She had similar experiences pulling weeds in the garden, plucking a goose for a neighbor, and even buttoning her skirt. At length her condition became such that any bending or muscular effort would bring on convulsions and contortions, always accompanied by loss of consciousness. Since she could not raise herself from the ground she sometimes lay for hours before help arrived.

Every accident in which she struck her head intensified the pains in her head and eyes, which began with her first fall. Meanwhile her vision seemed gradually to be failing. First she experienced difficulty in reading; then various pathological symptoms appeared, such as flickering lights or black dots whirling about in the visual field; she had difficulty in discerning the faces of people and even the outlines of objects. Finally, on May 17, 1919, emerging from a long and severe convulsive attack, she discovered she was completely blind. This new affliction caused no immediate concern to her parents. They thought it would be temporary, especially since her eyes presented a normal appearance, except for an unusual dilation of the pupils and a marked diminution of sensibility, particularly in the left eye, to the extent that Theresa could put her finger to the cornea without any discomfort. Only when the blindness persisted did her parents consult Dr. Seidl. When the doctor wished to examine her eyes to ascertain whether there was any organic lesion, he attempted to raise her to a sitting position. At that moment, however, she suffered another convulsive seizure and lapsed into unconsciousness. Unable to examine his patient in such a condition, Dr. Seidl left without discovering the cause of the blindness.

About this time, too, Theresa suffered anesthesia of the entire left side of her body. She was completely deaf in her left ear, and, according to her own account, also in her right ear for two weeks. She could recognize her parents and friends only by physical contact. The presence of her parents had a beneficial influence on her; it was a sort of talisman. She could not bear to be touched by a stranger. During the doctor's visits she constantly held her mother's hand.

For a period of three months, Theresa likewise suffered from several paralytic attacks in her left arm. The genesis of this affliction is very instructive. Attempting one day to feed a tame pigeon with which she played during the time of her blindness, she leaned too far out of bed. When she was unsuccessful in trying to regain her position, she screamed, and fell into her usual convulsive fit. When she regained consciousness she found it impossible to move her left arm; it was paralyzed. The doctor applied electric treatments, but without result.

There were still more afflictions in store for Theresa. Toward Christmas of 1922 she experienced a violent pain in her throat which made it impossible for her to swallow. Theresa gives the following account of this disorder. A student of theology, suffering from an ailment of the throat, was in danger of being dismissed. When Theresa heard about it she earnestly prayed that God would cure the seminarian and allow her to suffer in his stead. Shortly thereafter Theresa began to experience the symptoms in her throat. She felt as if her throat were wounded, and, sometimes, when coughing or gargling, she spat blood.

This illness prevented her from taking nourishment. Any

attempts to do so resulted immediately in nausea and a sense of choking. In the course of time a large abscess formed in her throat, making it difficult for her to swallow even a few drops of water. Thus, since March, 1923, her daily nourishment was reduced to a few teaspoonfuls of gruel or barley mash. During the two weeks preceding Holy Saturday in 1925 Theresa did not take so much as a drop of water; and since the Feast of the Transfiguration in September, 1927, her only nourishment has consisted of six to eight drops of water, taken after receiving Holy Communion.

The physician who was consulted on this matter is reported to have said that the impossibility of taking solid food or liquids resulted more from the paralysis of a muscle of the esophagus than from any chronic indisposition of the stomach. But if this be true, how explain the fact that Theresa can swallow her saliva in a perfectly normal manner during the intervals between the separate visions of her Friday ecstasies?

When we consider Theresa's abstinence from all nourishment, we cannot overlook the following fact: up to 1927, that is, during the period when Theresa was still receiving some little nourishment, at least in liquid form, her weight fell off, slowly but steadily. From the time that she abstained from all food (except Holy Communion and a few drops of water), however, her weight remained constant (about 110 pounds). During her ecstasies, which are always accompanied by copious hemorrhages, her weight drops sharply; but within the next few days it is restored!

To present a complete picture of the sufferings of Theresa, we must add that, since 1919, she has had several very painful gastric ulcers and six or seven boils in her armpits. Since the month of October, 1918, when she became bedridden, her body was covered with sores and abscesses which distressed her until May, 1925. Remedies of every kind were applied to these sores without obtaining a definitive cure. As soon as one sore would be cleared, another would break out.

Theresa suffered likewise from constant coughing and pains in her side, which were caused, she claims, by her failing to change her wet garments on the unforgettable day of the fire. This cough — aggravated by colds which she contracted on several occasions — was so violent that onlookers feared that she would choke to death.

In a word, the life of Theresa was nothing but one continuous span of suffering. More than once her life was despaired of; more than once the parish priest, Father Naber, administered the last rites. Her father, however, was far from sharing these apprehensions; he even tried to convince his daughter that what she lacked was not so much good health, but energy and will power. Theresa herself tells us this.[3]

Such was the physical condition of Theresa Neumann. Our picture, however, would not be complete without an observation of her psychological state. The latter was well calculated to render her physical sufferings most acute. As we have remarked, Theresa, formerly lively and jovial, became, after her illness, melancholy, taciturn, suspicious, and exceedingly irritable. When the doctors examined her she anxiously observed their gestures, their facial expressions, and the sound of their voices in an effort to learn their diagnosis. When Dr. William Burkhardt, of Hohenberg, examined Theresa's spinal column, she noticed that he shrugged his shoulders, which gesture she interpreted as a sign of despair. It made an extremely painful impression on Theresa, as she herself acknowledges. Even today her eyes fill with tears in telling of it. And when Doctor Burkhardt told her that her illness might last a long time she became very despondent.

Another day, when almost the entire Neumann family was ill with the grippe, Theresa tried to divine, from the doctor's tone of voice, what he thought about the condition of each patient. When he repeated the same sentence to each one: "You'll soon get over it," she thought he was convinced that she herself would not recover. She felt bitterness toward the doctor and showed it by mimicking his tone of voice. During this period Theresa confesses to a "passionate desire to be cured." For this

---

[3] L. Witt, *op. cit.*, I, p. 53.

reason she implored the doctors to restore her health. To such pitiful manifestations of the instinct of self-preservation there would follow long intervals of discouragement, despair, and bitterness. It was very difficult for her to resign herself to the prospect of being bedridden. She would have to suffer much more; she would have to listen to the counsels of her spiritual father, of her parents and friends before she would be able to master her passionate desire to live, and be able to resign herself to the will of God. After she accepted the will of the heavenly Father, she regained her peace of soul. Sufferings, as such, are not sources of delight for Theresa. She bears them patiently, supported by the memory of Him who triumphed over the world on the cross.

With supernatural trust in God, Theresa's natural nobility of soul was likewise restored, the nobility she showed in time of good health when she reserved for herself the hardest work in order to spare others. We see this nobility reawakened now in Theresa offering herself as a victim in place of a seminarian, in Theresa making a novena of prayer that God might relieve her father of a painful attack of rheumatism and transfer it to herself.

CHAPTER 3

Signs and Wonders

IN THE preceding chapter we have centered attention on the dark side of Theresa's life — her suffering, physical and mental. There is another side, however, one of light and consolation. Associated with her painful experiences are numerous extraordinary phenomena which she regards as special divine favors, and on account of which she is able to endure her afflictions not merely with resignation but with peace and joy.

Throughout her life she sees continual evidence of God's particular providence in her regard; His paternal hand may cause her tears, but it also wipes them away. She sees herself, a poor servant girl, become the center of attention not only for simple folk but for ecclesiastics and savants from all over the world. Konnersreuth has become a magnet attracting pilgrims from every country of Europe and America. Indeed, is she not aware that many people unhesitatingly proclaim her a saint and even give her the title of "blessed"? Does she not know that some of the people press around her during divine service hoping to snatch a hair from her head as a relic, or even to touch her with medals, rosaries, and prayer books? She cannot ignore the fact that hundreds of thousands have made long journeys to visit her, to recommend themselves to her prayers, to seek guidance in some difficult problem, or to ask for information concerning missing loved ones. She is aware that several hundred books and brochures, in many different languages, have been published about her, and that articles in periodicals appear unceasingly.

It will not be difficult to understand such an enthusiastic cultus when we examine the signs and wonders that have filled the life of Theresa.

MARVELOUS CURES

Recovery of Sight

On April 29, 1923, Thérèse of Lisieux, a Carmelite nun who died in 1897, was solemnly proclaimed "blessed" in St. Peter's Basilica, Rome. That very day, at six in the morning, Theresa Neumann's father entered his daughter's room to tell her that he was going to get some medicine for her. After her father left, Theresa fell asleep. While she slept she seemed to hear something scratching at her pillow, close to her ear. She woke up suddenly, opened her eyes, and for the first time in four years saw her own hand clearly! Overcome with joy, she rapped on the wall to summon her mother. Instead of her mother, one of her sisters entered, and Theresa, failing to recognize her, asked: "Who are you?" "Why, I'm Zenzl," her sister answered, somewhat puzzled. Theresa recognized her voice immediately. During the four-year period Zenzl had grown up and changed so much that her sister did not recognize her features. Theresa then told the good news: she could see perfectly — her blindness was gone! And with the blindness she was relieved of the terrible head pains which had tormented her so cruelly. Her other sufferings remained for two years longer: the pain in the spine, frequent convulsions, malfunctioning of the bladder and bowels, throat trouble, painful bed sores, and finally a discharge of pus and blood from her eyes.

Cure of a Foot Wound

After one of her convulsive attacks in the late summer of 1924, Theresa noticed that the lower part of her left leg, which had previously been paralyzed, was now permanently contracted beneath her right leg. As a result of constant pressure and friction a festering wound soon appeared on the inner surface of her left ankle which remained for six months.

On May 3, 1925, the sufferer prayed to Blessed Thérèse of the Child Jesus, asking for at least some improvement, if not a complete cure. She made her plea with all the more fervor, for she wished to relieve her mother who was worried about the

possibility of amputation.[1] Filled with confidence in a supernatural intervention on the part of Blessed Thérèse, she managed
to slip three rose petals which had been touched to the tomb
of the virgin of Lisieux between the folds of the bandage when
it was being changed. Shortly thereafter she felt a strong itching
sensation in the wound and then all pain disappeared. Later,
when her sister removed the bandage, the wound was covered
over by a tender bluish pellicle.[2]

Cure of the Spine

May 17, 1925, was a day filled with tender emotion for Theresa
Neumann. It was the canonization day of her heavenly patron,
Blessed Thérèse of the Child Jesus. Helpless on her bed of
pain, she could at least assist in spirit at the splendid ceremonies
which were taking place in St. Peter's.

That same day she began a novena in honor of the new saint.
She took her beads to pray the Rosary, but when she reached
the second decade she was astonished to behold a light infinitely
more brilliant and more beautiful than that of the sun, yet not
harmful to her eyes. Her first reaction was to cry out in fear.
When her parents came running to her side, Theresa, who
seemed to have lost consciousness, asked them in an appealing
tone: "Where is the parish priest?" Then, her face beaming
with indescribable joy, her arms stretched before her, her eyes
fixed on some invisible object, she bowed her head respectfully,
as if to salute some distinguished person. Evidently she was
conversing with someone. Then she raised up her head and
shoulders and slowly sat upright in her bed for the first time
in six years! A few moments later she lay down again, still
beaming with happiness. Gradually her ecstatic expression faded
and she began to weep bitterly. The wondrous vision had disappeared, and she found herself once more in Konnersreuth,
bedridden. She picked up the stick which she used to strike on
the wall whenever she wanted to summon one of the family,

[1] L. Witt, *Konnersreuth im Lichte der Religion und Wissenschaft*, I, p. 82.
[2] *Ibid.*, I, p. 83; Fr. Gerlich, *Die stigmatisierte Therese Neumann von Konnersreuth*, I, p. 84.

although at the moment the entire family, and the parish priest, were standing around her. The priest then asked her: "Resl [familiar for Theresa], where were you just now?" She answered: "I can sit up now! I can walk!" And, in fact, she left her bed, and with the help of her father took several steps around the room.

Only then did she tell what she had seen during her ecstasy. A mysterious light had appeared to her and she heard a friendly voice ask: "Resl, would you like to be cured?" Theresa answered: "Health or sickness, death itself, are all one for me — just what God wills." The voice continued: "Resl, wouldn't you be happy to enjoy a little relief?" Theresa answered: "I am satisfied with whatever God sends me: the flowers, the birds, or even some new suffering; that would be a change. But my greatest happiness is my loving Saviour." The voice replied: "Today you are going to enjoy a little favor: you will be able to sit up. Try it, I will help you." At the same time Theresa felt someone take her right hand and lift her up. When she lay down again she experienced a sharp pain in her back, but the voice continued: "You are to suffer still more, and no remedy will afford you any relief. But do not fear! I have helped you till now and I will continue to help you. It is only through suffering that you will be able to realize your vocation as a victim soul, and in this way help the priests. Many more souls are saved by suffering than by the most brilliant sermons, as I have written. *And henceforth you will be able to walk.*"

Theresa told her family that she no longer felt any pain in her back, and that she wished to have her back examined. Sister Regintrude did so immediately and, to her great surprise, found the spinal column perfectly normal and the back sores completely cured.

News of this cure reached Dr. Seidl, and he lost no time in coming to see for himself. Having certified the cure, he could only remark that it was very "remarkable" (*auffallend*).[3]

From this time on the mysterious light and the voice reap-

---

[3] L. Witt, *op. cit.*, I, pp. 99–100.

peared to Theresa many times. They roused the courage of the sufferer, advised her concerning her life, solved her doubts, soothed her sufferings, and finally granted her new cures.

At midnight on September 30, 1925, the anniversary of the death of St. Thérèse of Lisieux, while Theresa was reciting a litany in honor of her patroness, the light appeared and the voice told her that she would now be able to walk without any assistance.[4] The voice added, however: "Your external suffering will cease; but you must undergo another suffering more cruel. Encourage people to place all their trust in God!" Theresa then asked whether she was really being guided by a heavenly voice, or whether she was the victim of some illusion. By way of response she heard the following words: "Obey your spiritual director implicitly and confide everything to him. You must seek to die to self more and more. Always remain simple as a child." The next day Theresa went to church unassisted.

Cure of Appendicitis and Pneumonia

During the night of November 6, 1925, Theresa underwent a severe mental struggle which left her bathed in perspiration. She awoke later than usual and did not have time to change her underwear, now soaked in perspiration, before going to church. Since it was a chilly day Theresa believed she had caught cold, because a few hours later she felt so weak that she was obliged to lie down. Soon thereafter she experienced abdominal pains and suffered such nervous weakness that she could not even open her eyes. This condition lasted three days, and finally her parents decided to call Dr. Seidl. He came at about 6 p.m. on November 13 and, upon examination, diagnosed acute appendicitis. He recommended an immediate operation as the only means of saving Theresa's life. Her parents opposed the idea of surgery, believing that their daughter was too weak. They yielded only when Father Naber, the village pastor, succeeded in persuading them that under the circumstances the advice of

---

[4] Since May 17, 1925, she could walk only with someone's support or with a cane.

the doctor was certainly a manifestation of God's will. Preparations were made to transfer Theresa to the hospital. Meanwhile she was "squirming like a worm," as Father Naber later reported to Witt.[5]

If her physical pain was severe, her mental anguish was equally as great. "As for me," she related to Witt, "it was all the same. But the pitiful cries of my mother rent my heart." Was not this the time to call upon her great protectress who had once promised to "aid her in the future"? She asked Father Naber, and he encouraged her to follow her inspiration. He applied a relic of St. Thérèse to the affected area and the entire family began to pray for her recovery. Theresa herself prayed earnestly: "Everything is all right with me . . . but, you understand, St. Thérèse, how my mother is suffering." Suddenly she raised herself a little in bed and opened her eyes, which up to then had been tightly closed. Her face radiant with happiness, she stretched out her hands as if trying to touch something. Then she placed her hands over the painful area and at the same moment felt herself cured. Asked by Father Naber about her experience, she said that a marvelous light had appeared to her surrounding a hand, white and delicate like that seen in pictures of St. Thérèse of the Child Jesus. Then she heard the following words: "Your complete resignation and your joy in suffering pleases us. That men may realize a superior power is working here, you will not have to undergo an operation. Arise, go to the church and render thanks to God, immediately, immediately! You still have much to suffer, but you have no need to fear. Do not be afraid of interior trials. . . ."

Theresa's mother objected to her going to the church, because of the cold weather. An appeal was made to Father Naber, and he decided: "If St. Thérèse has come to help you, let us go immediately!" And Theresa, accompanied by all present, went to the church where she spent 20 minutes in thanksgiving.

One year later, November 19, 1926, Theresa was cured in a

---

[5] L. Witt, *op. cit.*, I, p. 138; Gerlich, *op. cit.*, I, pp. 97, 113.

most unexpected manner of an attack of pneumonia. In this instance, too, her recovery was attributed to supernatural intervention.

VISIONS AND STIGMATA

The Lent of 1926 marked a new stage in the life of Theresa Neumann, for from this period date the great Friday visions.

She had been confined to bed for some time, because of extreme weakness and a violent headache caused by an abscess in her ear which could not be lanced until Holy Saturday. She felt so ill that, according to her own words, she "could hardly pray all during Lent, or make the Way of the Cross." She was scarcely able to repeat mentally the words: "Our Divine Saviour has suffered much more for us." Her mind was so affected that she no longer knew the day of the week. If her mother told her, she would ask again in a few minutes. As she told Witt, she was not able to retain anything in her memory.[6]

In this condition she was resting in bed the Thursday night of March 4, 1926, when suddenly she saw Christ before her. He was kneeling amid the rocks, flowers, and trees in the Garden of Olives. Near Him were the three Apostles sitting down, leaning against the rocks, utterly fatigued, though not asleep.[7] Jesus was undergoing His agony in the garden. While she was contemplating with deep emotion the sufferings of the Saviour and sharing in His agony, she suddenly felt a pain in her left side, so penetrating that she thought she was going to die. At the same time she felt something warm trickling down her body. It was blood. The blood continued to ooze until the next day around noon.

A week passed without further occurrence, but Theresa continued in her state of mental prostration and suffered from a violent headache. The next Thursday night while she was lying in bed, "without thinking of anything," she once more witnessed the agony in the garden, and early Friday morning the scourging

---

[6] L. Witt, *op. cit.*, I, p. 179.
[7] F. von Lama, *Therese Neumann von Konnersreuth*, Karlsruhe, 1929, p. 23.

of Jesus; this vision was accompanied, like the preceding, by a flow of blood from her left side.

The third week, in identical circumstances, she saw the Saviour crowned with thorns; the following week she accompanied Him on the way of the cross, and, finally, during the night between Holy Thursday and Good Friday she witnessed the entire sacred passion.

With the help of one of her sisters Theresa succeeded in hiding the wound in her side from her family. But on Good Friday her ecstasy was so profound and her mind so absorbed in the spectacle of the sufferings of Christ that the stigmatization could no longer be concealed. That same day, for the first time, drops of blood mingled with pus flowed from her eyes, and the wounds of the Saviour appeared on her hands and feet.

Theresa's parents, having no further doubt as to the nature of her suffering, sent for Father Naber. As soon as he entered the room he said: "In the name of holy obedience, I command you to show me the wounds in your hands and feet!" What he saw struck him so forcefully that he had great difficulty in maintaining his composure.

From that time Theresa has borne the stigmata continuously. This is, perhaps, the most sensational of all the wonders of Konnersreuth. Anyone visiting Konnersreuth from Sunday to Thursday may see Theresa walking through the village, wearing a simple black dress, a white kerchief over her hair, her hands covered with mittens. Her pace is slow and hesitant, for she must walk on tiptoe. These stigmata are no mere ornaments; they are meant to be a participation in the suffering of our Lord, as Theresa knows very well. Consequently she must endure a continual pain in her hands, feet, and side as well as in the eight scars which formed around her head during the Friday ecstasies. At first, all the wounds bled during every Friday ecstasy. In the course of time some of them have ceased to bleed.

Some circumstances of this occurrence deserve special mention. Theresa's parents, frightened at the sight of blood flowing from her hands and feet, decided to consult Dr. Seidl. The latter examined the wounds carefully, spread some salve over them, and bandaged them, with an assurance that they would soon disappear. He had scarcely left the house when Theresa felt intolerable pain in her hands and feet. The bandages were removed immediately. When, three days later, the physician made another visit to the Neumann home he found the stigmata in the same state as previously. He once more applied his salve, but this time, before leaving the house, he insisted that the bandages be not removed without his permission, promising to return in a few days. But the same scene was repeated; and to spare Theresa further suffering her family removed the bandages a few hours after the doctor's departure.

Theresa then had recourse to St. Thérèse, her heavenly patroness. She did not ask her to be cured of the wounds, but only to be enlightened as to what attitude she should take toward them. Shortly after this prayer, on April 17, 1926, that is two weeks after her stigmatization, the wounds in the hands and feet ceased bleeding and a pellicle formed over them. Only during the ecstasies do they revive somewhat, take on a rose tint, and become soft; a few days are sufficient to restore their normal condition. In the beginning the stigmata appeared only on the back of the hands and feet. The soles of the feet and the palms of the hands showed no abnormality except unusual sensitivity to the least pressure. On Good Friday, 1927, the stigmata made their appearance on the inner surfaces also, but they are not so large as those on the dorsal surface.

While the stigmata on the hands and feet have become dry, all the others continued bleeding more or less copiously during the ecstasies. The wound in the side, about three and a half centimeters long and one centimeter broad, becomes continually deeper, according to Theresa. She even affirms that in the course of time it will become visible on her back "just as with Christ, who was pierced through with a lance." The marks of the "crown of thorns" were formed on November 5, 1926. During her usual Friday ecstasy she witnessed the soldiers press the crown of thorns on the Saviour's head and at the same time felt a piercing pain in several parts of her own scalp. Three wounds appeared. Five others developed later to complete the crown which to this day encircles her head.

Every Friday morning, when Theresa witnesses the mock crowning of our Saviour, the wounds in her head revive and impress eight patches of blood, like so many roses, on the white veil which covers her head.

The blood which flows so abundantly from the stigmata is only an external sign of the internal experiences of Theresa. Motionless on her bed of suffering, insensible to all external stimuli, Theresa assists at a drama of life and movement. Beneath all external appearance of lethargy there is hidden a refined sensibility and the most delicate emotional life. If she is unconscious of all that is taking place around her in Konnersreuth, it is because she has been transported to ancient Jerusalem. Indeed, she cannot properly be said to be "meditating" on the passion of Christ, as we might do in our prayers; no, she sees it, as we might look at pictures in a museum. She actually hears Jesus, Peter, Pilate, and the others speaking. She feels in her own body all the torments they inflict on Jesus. Thus the cross carried by the Saviour weighs heavily on her too. She suffers from the broiling Palestinian sun when Jesus leaves the shady streets of Jerusalem to cross the open country to Calvary. She puts out her arm to protect Him from blows, or to help raise Him from a fall, but seeing the uselessness of her efforts she drops her arms in a gesture of sorrowful resignation and despair.

Her greatest suffering during these visions is the failure of her efforts to save Jesus or at least to be of help to Him. At a given time she will raise her hands to her head and groan; this is an attempt to protect the brow of Jesus from the thorns which are being driven into it, or at least to draw out some of them. During the "scourging" her whole body becomes tense, and then doubles over; clearly, she is feeling the lashes which the executioners are raining upon the body of Christ. At the "carrying of the cross" she suddenly raises her right hand as if to appeal for help, but then she manifests keen disappointment.

She has seen Simon of Cyrene in the crowd and urges him to assist Jesus; but since he does it with such bad grace, his help is too meager. For this reason Theresa is disappointed. When Jesus is crucified she crosses her legs and her whole body shudders in agony at each stroke of the hammer. The words of forgiveness: "Father, forgive them, for they know not what they do," are accompanied by a compassionate movement of her head. The cursing of the bad thief, who mocked Jesus, fills her with indignation and elicits a vigorous gesture of condemnation. But this sentiment does not last long. Her countenance suddenly softens into a beatific smile when she hears Jesus say to the good thief: "Amen, Amen I say to you this day you shall be with me in paradise." Thereupon Theresa can be observed to moisten her lips with her tongue; she opens and closes her mouth before some proffered drink. It is not hard to see that she is suffering the thirst which tormented Jesus on the cross, and that she tastes the sponge dipped in vinegar.

At this point onlookers see a spectacle that fills them with horror. Theresa's bloodshot eyes expand enormously as if they were sounding the infinite abyss of Christ's suffering, penetrating the very depths of His tortured soul. Over her pale and emaciated face, now streaked with blood from eyes to chin, spreads an unspeakable sorrow, an abandonment that cannot be described. Her body stiffens and falls backward while her head rests on her right shoulder; her hands are joined on her breast; her face is like alabaster, lined with the blood from her eyes; her body lies there without motion and hardly breathing — a veritable corpse!

The Friday ecstasy is over. It has lasted thirteen successive hours from Thursday midnight until 1:00 p.m. on Friday. It should be noted, however, that the ecstasies do not always begin punctually. Sometimes they commence at 10:45 p.m., sometimes after eleven, or a few minutes before midnight.

The most characteristic trait of this phenomenon is its suddenness. When the time has arrived Theresa lapses into silence, even in the midst of a lively conversation; her eyes fixate on some distant object invisible to those around her. The vision has seized her; it is a true *raptus*.

The very posture of her body is peculiar. Neither lying nor sitting, she maintains a sort of intermediate position, so fatiguing that it would challenge the strength of a trained athlete.

When the first vision — that of Christ in the Garden of Olives — has begun, all the other scenes recorded in the Gospels follow infallibly in proper order. They do not constitute one continuous spectacle. Rather, the story of the passion is broken down into some fifty individual episodes. In other words, fifty distinct scenes unfold before Theresa, fifty "stations" of the sacred passion, we might say. The duration of each varies from two to fifteen minutes. Once a scene has occupied the attention of Theresa, neither shouting nor shaking can distract her.

Coming out of her trance Theresa is only vaguely aware that she is no longer in Jerusalem contemplating the passion of Christ, but in her own bedroom. Only then does she begin to react to stimuli from the world of sense, enter into contact with those around her, and answer their questions. However, she does not immediately enjoy complete presence of mind, being still dominated by the scenes at which she had just been a witness.

This mental condition is known as "absorption" (*Zustand des Eingenommenseins*) or "infantile state," for it resembles that of a four-year-old child. It is characterized by a narrowing of consciousness and an incapacity for higher mental synthesis. Even such simple notions as *brother, sister,* become unintelligible. In this condition Theresa does not know what is meant by *bishop* or *pope*. If someone speaks to her, she asks, sometimes repeatedly, "Who are you?" Even her mother has had to identify herself: "It is I — your mother." But Theresa connot repeat the word *mother*. She can only pronounce the first syllable: *Mu (Mutter)*. When Theresa is finally made to understand questions concerning her vision she answers, but in a very low voice. The questioner must place his ear close to her lips to hear what she says. Her answers are not always very clear. She cannot recall any proper name, indicating the participants of the passion by short expressions relating mainly to external characteristics. Thus St. John is always called "the young man"; Herod, "the red man"; Pilate, "the one who has no hair on his head or on his face"; Caiphas, "the mocking man with the long white beard," and so for the others.

She not only forgets names, but is ignorant of the role played by the various actors. For example, she describes Judas as "the man who was affectionate toward the dear Saviour." She refuses to see him as a traitor. He loves Jesus, she insists; did he not kiss Him? And no one can convince her that she is in error.

Pontius Pilate awakens great sympathy in Theresa. Did he not try to deliver Jesus from the hands of the Jews? On the other hand, she cannot endure St. Peter, who cut off the ear of Malchus and thus spilled the first human blood in the drama of the passion. She labels him contemptuously: "The ear cutter" (*Ohrwaschelabschneider*).

During the state of absorption she is incapable of the simplest arithmetic problems. To express the idea that the cross was composed of four parts she must say that she sees "one part, one part, one part, one part." "Very well," said Father Naber, "the cross of Jesus was made of four parts." "Four? I don't know," answered Theresa, and once more she will enumerate the parts one by one.

On another occasion Father Naber, at the request of Bishop Waitz, asked Theresa the question: "How many devout women accompanied Jesus on the way of the cross?" She answered: "One, one, one . . . Oh, I can't count them. They are very many."

What is more remarkable is the fact that Theresa has no idea of the final outcome of the passion. While in her infantile condition following the vision of the arrival at Mount Calvary, she said excitedly to Dr. Wutz, who she thought was present in the procession: "Run quickly to the Mother of Jesus and tell her that Resl says they have set Him free. . . . They made Him carry the wood only for use in a building!"

In this condition she no longer knows her catechism. She forgets also many details concerning herself. In the infantile state following her vision of the Resurrection (in 1928) she happened to touch her own stigmata. Feeling the sudden pain she asked in amazement: "Did I receive these while I was asleep?"

The state of infancy is regularly followed by another very different mental condition which is called the state of "exalted repose" (*erhobener Ruhezustand*). We shall discuss this state in a later section.

The passion of Jesus Christ is not the only object of Theresa's visions. During her ecstasies she has witnessed the birth of our Lord, His Transfiguration, the Assumption of the Blessed Virgin, the finding of the holy cross, the descent of the Holy Spirit upon the Apostles, the stigmatization of St. Francis of Assisi, the martyrdom of St. Lawrence, and various scenes in heaven and in purgatory.

THE GIFT OF TONGUES

Another remarkable feature of Theresa's visions must be mentioned here. The various persons she sees in ecstasy during the passion do not speak German, her own mother tongue, but a language which certain orientalists have identified as Aramaic. This is an important point. Aramaic was, in fact, the language spoken in Palestine at the time of Jesus, and anyone really present at the passion would have heard this language used. Such a witness would not understand the meaning of the words. The only exception would be the Pentecostal sermon of the Apostles which every man understood in his own language (cf. Acts 2:6–11). Now all this fits in exactly with Theresa's experience. She understands St. Peter's sermon, but she does not understand the words spoken during the passion of Christ. An orientalist, Dr. Wutz, had to tell her the meaning of the word *galapa* (traitor), which she heard at the moment Judas kissed Jesus in the Garden of Gethsemani. The same scholar interpreted for her the words of the Archangel Gabriel, which she heard during a vision of the Annunciation, on March 25, 1927. She had the same experience when she heard words spoken in Latin, Portuguese, and other languages.

CLAIRVOYANCE

As we said above, the state of infancy in Theresa is normally followed by a condition called the state of exalted repose. After ten or fifteen minutes in the state of infancy, Theresa subsides into a kind of sleep which restores her strength. She relaxes comfortably on cushions, almost motionless, her hands crossed on her breast, her eyes generally closed. Sometimes, but rarely, she will get out of bed and speak in a lively manner. These two states are so different that it is impossible not to distinguish them. In the state of infancy Theresa is evidently exhausted, depressed, sad; she speaks only of herself and of the vision she has just experienced; her speech is hesitant; she asks others what she must do; she uses the Bavarian dialect; she cannot recall proper names; abstract concepts are meaningless for her; and she is incapable of any mental synthesis. In the state of exalted repose, on the contrary, she feels refreshed and happy; she talks in a majestic tone of voice; she speaks good German and makes use of turns of speech unusual in her ordinary life; abstract concepts and mental synthesis afford no difficulty; her attention is no longer centered on herself or her visions; Theresa then takes an interest in other people, gives them advice, answers their questions without any hesitation or even reflection.

It is during this latter state that Theresa gives evidence of a remarkable gift of clairvoyance. Here are a few examples.

When, in October, 1927, Theresa was told that someone wished to speak to her, she replied: "Let him come in. I have something to tell him." When the visitor had entered, Theresa, without even opening her eyes, declared: "This man does not love our Lord, and our Lord does not love him" (*mag nicht*). And she proceeded with a pitiless revelation of the man's misdeeds committed while a Communist in Russia.

Another time a young man who seemed to her to be proud and arrogant happened to lean against her bed. Summoning all her strength she said very forcibly that there was someone in her room whose life was displeasing to our Lord. At this unexpected censure the young man turned pale and made a hasty exit.

Many a pilgrim who came to her for advice received her answer before he had had a chance to ask his question. Once, before a letter was read to her, she revealed who the author was and also the contents of the letter. At the very moment when Pius XI was imparting a special blessing to herself and to Father Naber (May 3, 1928) she said to the latter: "The Holy Father is giving us his blessing now."

When Father Agostino Gemelli, O.F.M., was about to leave Konnersreuth for Rome Theresa told him that he would see the Holy Father on Saturday, not on Thursday as he was expecting. Her prediction was fulfilled.

For some persons she painted a faithful picture of their interior state. This was the experience of Dr. Gerlich (September 16, 1927), Bishop Schrembs, of Cleveland (December, 1927), and a nun from Marienbad. She told Dr. Aloysius Mager, of Salzburg, details of his own life that could not have been revealed to her by a third party.

Her powers of clairvoyance are said to be particularly striking when there is question of distinguishing between blessed and unblessed articles, between authentic and spurious relics of the holy cross or of the saints. When she is in ecstasy she can recognize a priest by touching his fingers with which he holds the consecrated Host. Once when the relic of St. Thérèse of Lisieux was presented to her she exclaimed: "Oh, I know her very well. She has come to me several times." Another time, when Father Naber touched her with a hair of Catherine Emmerich, she said: "Oh, poor girl, she had much to suffer, just as I." Again, when Father Naber applied a reliquary to her mouth, she declared: "There is something here of the girl whose neck was severed (St. Cecilia), also something of St. Teresa, but a great St. Teresa" (St. Teresa of Avila).

A young man asked Father Naber to find out from Theresa what vocation he would best be fitted for. She replied that he would enter a seminary in six months. Another time she warned that something would happen to the engine of an automobile. Both predictions came true.

FASTING

We have already touched briefly on the mystery of Theresa's fasting. Stricken with a disorder of her throat, toward the end of 1922, it was impossible for her to swallow any solid food. Her diet thenceforth was limited to purées and liquids. In the course of time she had to abstain from even this type of food. Since the Feast of the Transfiguration, 1926, it is claimed that she has taken no nourishment at all, except a spoonful of water after her daily Communion. Since September, 1927, even the spoonful of water after Holy Communion has been discontinued.

Before closing this section, we would like to remind the reader that the extraordinary phenomena we have related are not a matter of past history. They are taking place now, and continue to arouse an interest which neither the disasters of the recent war nor the present world troubles can quench. Books and pamphlets about the famous stigmatic continue to pour from the presses; the influx of visitors from all parts of the world shows no sign of diminishing. During the months immediately following the cessation of hostilities, and again during the Holy Year of 1950, Konnersreuth was thronged.

Among the distinguished visitors who honored Theresa Neumann with a visit was Bishop J. Gawlina, chaplain-in-chief of the Polish troops. He stopped at Konnersreuth on a Friday in August, 1945, a little after 3:00 p.m. Theresa was resting in the parish house after her ecstasy. The white cloths which covered her head and her left side were soaked with blood. At a given moment the pastor signaled for the Bishop (who was dressed as an ordinary priest) to touch Theresa's hand. Opening her eyes she looked at her visitor and said: "Oh, you are a bishop. May the Saviour be with you! As I see, you work very hard and travel all over the world. You are struggling with your ideas and your responsibilities. But courage! All will end well. You and your men will return home. All will end well, for you have someone in heaven who prays much for you. Another Polish bishop came here; he was in exactly the same place as you are, and later he wrote a book about me . . . he is already in heaven." After a short pause the stigmatic added: "Our people [the Germans] have treated your men [the Poles] very badly. Our people were bad, but those from the east [the Russians] are no better, for they are enemies of the Saviour. What are they looking for in your country? Let them go back to where they came from." Then she asked for news of the Holy Father, whom she is accustomed to see twice a year in her visions.

This interview shows that the phenomena of Konnersreuth have undergone no sudden change. The Friday ecstasies, the visions, clairvoyance, and all the rest take place today just as we have described them. The only exception is that on Good Friday, 1951, the stigmata did not bleed during the ecstasy, but this will be discussed in a later chapter.

PART II

A Critical Study of the Facts

.

CHAPTER 4

Various Explanations

THE paramount problem of Konnersreuth revolves around the question: Do we find here the voice of God speaking to humanity by means of miracles, or can the phenomena be explained in terms of natural forces? The question is not without importance, for if the events are really divine signs, miracles, then the faith of Christ, of which Theresa Neumann is such a zealous apostle, gains new proof of its truth, a proof all the more valuable inasmuch as it is immediately evident to the senses. That is why the "problem of Konnersreuth" has become a "religious problem." We are not surprised, consequently, to find here the same variety of opinions and theories that we usually find when religious problems are under consideration.

THE THEORY OF FRAUD

First of all, there are those who see in the phenomena of Konnersreuth merely cheap deception. This was the attitude taken by certain communist and socialist editors toward the close of 1927, when they published some sensational "revelations" by a Mrs. Gusti Fink, under the title of *The Saint of Konnersreuth Finally Unmasked.* According to her account, Theresa had illicit relations with a certain magician, L. Loewenich. When he abandoned her she went to Bamberg and gave birth to a child on January 7, 1926 (1920). Later she returned to Konnersreuth and began her career as a wonder-worker. An official inquiry, conducted by the Bamberg police, proved Mrs. Fink's "revelations" to be a vicious calumny. Nevertheless, the editors refused to retract, and Theresa's parents were forced to take the matter to court. The editors were found guilty of libel and punished.[1]

But the advocates of the imposture theory are not always so blatant. Many limit themselves to casting a suspicion on the authenticity of the phenomena. Such a suspicion is quite respectable. Indeed, the authorities in ascetico-mystical theology warn us not to begin an examination of alleged marvels until we have demonstrated their historic authenticity. Church history offers many instances of ecstasies, visions, stigmata, levitations, and inedia (fasting), which were merely inventions of some unscrupulous devotees. Magdalena of the Cross, who lived in Cordova in the sixteenth century, succeeded in deceiving the royal court of Spain, bishops, cardinals, and even the Spanish Inquisition with her fictitious ecstasies and levitations. In the nineteenth century a certain Sabina S. convinced many people that she never partook of food. In reality she subsisted on dry almonds and crusts of bread which she kept hidden in her "holy box." Cardinal Albitius (seventeenth century) tells us that during his lifetime more than twenty persons were condemned by the Holy See for faking supernatural phenomena. Recently there was a tremendous imposture in Lipa (Batangas, the Philippines). It was organized by "Teresita," a Carmelite postulant, and some nuns. During some years (1948–1951) they deceived credulous people by fictitious messages from the Blessed Virgin, visions, and especially by "miraculous petals" which were asserted to have fallen from heaven. These examples should warn us to be on our guard against fraudulent prodigies. The first question to be answered with regard to Konnersreuth is: "Are the alleged facts real, or can they be ascribed to fraud?"

We are convinced that not all the Konnersreuth phenomena must be doubted. Those who have made careful investigations are of the same opinion. Dr. M. Naegle, a university professor, calls the marvels "an irrefutable fact" (*eine unleugbare*

---

[1] The men convicted of libel were: R. Schaible, editor of *Freiheit;* B. Schmidt, editor of the *Nord-Bayerische Volkszeitung;* Josef Rademacher, editor of the *Freie Presse;* Hans Pilot, editor of the *Blick im Osten.*

Tatsache).[2] Father Wunderle, a professor at the University of Würzburg, is "profoundly convinced that no greater injustice could be done to this girl than to suspect her of premeditated simulation or, in general, of any deliberate fraud."[3] "We would be definitely unfair to Theresa," says Dr. Boehm, "to attribute these events to deceit."[4] Dr. Reissemann declares emphatically: "We must definitely put aside any suspicion of dishonesty."[5] The eminent professor of psychiatry at the University of Erlangen, Dr. G. Ewald, affirms that any doubt as to the authenticity of the phenomena of Konnersreuth would be an insult to science.[6] "I do not believe there is any fraud, not only because the girl has made an excellent impression on me . . . but because she has been under the observation of the Catholic clergy for such a long time," testifies Dr. von Weisl.[7] For Dr. Hollsteiner, another university professor, such a doubt would be simply "ridiculous."[8]

For many years Theresa has had to endure the closest scrutiny on the part of thousands of visitors, many of whom came for the express purpose of exposing her supposed trickery. They attempted to involve her in some compromising situation. They watched her as she took her walk, when she went to church, and even in her own home. They have seen her in ecstasy and listened to her ordinary conversation. Despite all their efforts, they have not been able to bring to light any unequivocal evidence of premeditated deception. Finally, the four hospital nuns who, at the command of the bishop and under the supervision of Dr. Seidl, kept watch over Theresa from July 13 to July 28, 1927, could find no trace of premeditated fraud.

Whoever wishes to brush aside all these testimonies in order to cling to a theory of imposture would logically be forced to conclude that we are faced here with a most ingeniously organized

---

[2] *Deutsche Presse,* Prague, No. 187, July 25, 1926.
[3] *Die Stigmatisierte von Konnersreuth,* 2 ed., Eichstätt, 1927, p. 11.
[4] *Tiroler Anzeiger,* No. 1, Jan. 3.
[5] *Kölnische Zeitung,* No. 537, Sept. 14, 1927.
[6] *Die Stigmatisierte von Konnersreuth,* München, p. 35 *n.*
[7] *Vossische Zeitung,* No. 198, Aug. 19, 1927.
[8] *Reichspost,* Vienna, No. 354, Dec., 1926.

conspiracy, involving not only Theresa herself and her parents, but the whole village of Konnersreuth and its spiritual leader, Father Naber. The inhabitants of Konnersreuth do not derive any considerable material profit from having an ecstatic in their midst. It is true that several families of the village rent furnished rooms to tourists, but at a price so low that the visitors are amazed. It is not the good people of Konnersreuth who exploit the extraordinary phenomena centered about Theresa Neumann, but rather certain Berlin periodicals, especially the *Konnersreuther Sonntagsblatt* (a weekly) and the *Konnersreuther Zeitung,* which feature detailed accounts of the "miracles" and lavish extravagant praise upon Theresa and her associates. The village folk of Konnersreuth have nothing to do with this sensational journalism.

Nor have the parents of Theresa realized great material gains as a result of their daughter's gifts. On the contrary, according to certain authors, they have sustained losses. For one thing, they are frequently obliged to interrupt their work to take care of the countless visitors who flock to their home. Then, too, they have had to repair the stairs several times which were in bad condition due to the constant tread of feet.

We are far from denying the statements of these authors. We would add, however, that the Neumann family has certainly enjoyed some remuneration for their trouble. Father J. S., about to leave for Konnersreuth, was entrusted with a sealed envelope by a certain Madame N. who insisted that he deliver it in person to Theresa Neumann. He carried out his commission on January 10, 1946, telling Theresa that the food tickets (*Fleischmarken*) in the envelope were for "her poor." Theresa took the envelope and exclaimed joyfully: "I am delighted! I will give the food tickets to my parents." In 1938, a Viennese lady told the Bishop of Ratisbon that only the nineteen visitors who brought packages were admitted by the family to see Theresa. She herself and another person who had brought no packages were sent away. When she returned a week later with a special permit issued by the Bishop of Ratisbon[9] she was received (though not very willingly) by the family. Theresa, however, would not say a word to her. Reporting this occurrence to the Vicar-General, the lady remarked: "Ah, now I understand" (*Ja, nun kenne ich mich aus*). We might add that Theresa owns a house in Eichstätt, given because of her charisms.[10]

These facts need no further comment. They show that, all in all, the Neumann family has no reason to complain of the losses they suffer because of their numerous visitors.

One final witness in favor of the authenticity of the wonders of Konnersreuth is eminently worthy of a hearing. Father Naber enjoys the complete confidence of Theresa. He is her spiritual father and confessor. He sees her every day, for she spends many hours at the parsonage. To imagine that, in these circumstances, Theresa has been able to hide all her "tricks," we would have to believe either that Theresa is guilty of diabolical malice or that the good priest is a senseless idiot. Theresa would have to live a continual lie: she receives Holy Communion every day, has frequent edifying conversations with Father Naber and other devout persons, and several times has been anointed and prepared for death.

There is no doubt that Theresa has her faults, moral imperfections. Even her most ardent defenders admit this without hesitation. One of them writes: "At the outset . . . I sound the note that I am by no means representing Theresa as a model of perfection, as a saint; she has her imperfections and weak-

[9] At this time, the Bishop was no longer issuing permits as a general rule. Consequently, the others came to Konnersreuth without permits. Similar cases are not rare. Elisabeth M. Brennan alludes to them in her pamphlet, *Visits to Theresa Neumann* (New York: The Paulist Press, 1936), p. 3: An Austrian woman, she says, "urged me to go to Konnersreuth, saying that she was confident that I could see Theresa, even though I did not have the strictly required letter of permission from either the Vatican or the local Bishop." And she was really received by Theresa to whom she gave "a little silver locket, containing a strand of hair" of St. Thérèse of Lisieux (*ibid.*, p. 12). She presented her also with other "numerous" gifts (*ibid.*, p. 25).

[10] This story was told to the author on October 17, 1951, by Father M. Waldmann, professor of moral and mystical theology at the major seminary of Ratisbon. We could cite other instances, but the above is sufficient for our purpose.

nesses."[11] They note especially a certain lack of charity and movements of impatience. "I myself," says the same writer, "without being observed by her, have noticed some impatience that she showed toward a certain person."[12] Those writers who have adopted a critical attitude toward the phenomena of Konnersreuth go further. A distinguished Hungarian priest (L. J.) writes in his Memoirs that he had come to Konnersreuth with a solid faith in the supernatural character of the events he was about to witness, but was forced to admit bitterly that he could not find in Theresa "the great respect which the saints showed to priests, the servants of God." He adduces several instances to show that she is "not very humble." She spoke discourteously to him and showed an irritation that was hard to explain. His experience shattered his favorable preconception of Konnersreuth and he could no longer see anything supernatural there.[13] Father Bruno of Jesus and Mary, O.C., editor of the *Études Carmélitaines,* had a similar unpleasant experience. At the time of his visit to Konnersreuth, Father Naber gave him permission to give Holy Communion to Theresa, provided she consented. But Theresa refused, insisting that Father Naber give her Communion. Father Bruno was only allowed to be present at the reception of the Sacrament. "He can be quite satisfied," said Theresa, "this in itself is a great concession."[14]

Father De Hover, one of her enthusiastic admirers, declared publicly that Theresa "could never endure Father Wunderle," the distinguished Catholic savant. A friend of the present writer (Father J. S.), after a long conversation with Theresa, related some very harsh, and certainly unjust, remarks which she directed against a Catholic priest who had published a critical study of Konnersreuth. Theresa suffers keenly, he added, when

[11] Teodorowicz, J., *Mystical Phenomena in the Life of Theresa Neumann* (St. Louis: Herder, 1947), p. 12.
[12] *Ibid.,* p. 27.
[13] His article, published in the Catholic magazine *Papi Közlöny* (1930), aroused great interest in Hungary. It has been translated into German under the title, *Meine Beobachtungen in Konnersreuth.*
[14] *Études Carmélitaines,* Oct., 1936, p. 165. Cf. Hilda Graef, *The Case of Therese Neumann,* p. 119.

she realizes that all do not worship her. His evidence is all the more convincing, since he himself was considered among her "worshipers." As we stated previously, Theresa, in her ecstasies, speaks of Judas as the "man who had affection for the dear Saviour." Hearing these words from the mouth of Theresa, Dr. Wutz, in the presence of Herr von Aretin, remarked: "Oh, Theresa, I think you are a little stupid today." She answered, "And I think you are even more stupid."

Many people are scandalized at the willingness of Theresa to show her stigmata to visitors, even when they do not express a desire to see them. Father J. S. wrote (February 25, 1947) that in the course of a conversation with Theresa, she had of her own accord offered to show her stigmata. He was greatly surprised at this. Gerlich, an outstanding apologist of Konnersreuth, states that in her ecstatic state she advised some nuns to construct a convent, even though their superiors had forbidden it.[15] Father Westermayr, professor of mystical theology at Freising, affirms that in her ecstasies she has at times given advice, in the name of Christ, which was unethical. He adds that he was forced by theological criteria to abandon his previously favorable attitude toward the events of Konnersreuth.[16] Finally, it is commonly asserted that in her ecstasies she sometimes publicizes the serious faults of others. Archbishop Teodorowicz writes: "Where she is convinced that there is no honest attitude to the Konnersreuth events, she becomes stern and hard, inexorably hard, to those who doubt, as well as those who believe in these happenings. She treats such people with repugnance."[17] But such an attitude exposes Theresa to the danger of committing many an injustice, for her idea of an "honest attitude to the Konnersreuth events" is much too narrow. Anyone who doubts her, or who even wishes to study

---

[15] *Die Stigmatisierte Therese Neumann von Konnersreuth,* München, Vol. I, p. 312.

[16] "Konnersreuth in der theologischen Kritik," *Augsberger Postzeitung,* Sunday supplement, No. 28, 12, July, 1930.

[17] *Op. cit.,* p. 40. Archbishop Teodorowicz's book has been described as "an apology, and not, as one would have preferred, an exposé, a piece of research," cf. *Études Carmélitaines,* Oct., 1936, p. 154.

her case without preconceived opinions, exposes himself to her antipathy. Of this we have had unquestionable evidence.[18]

Archbishop Teodorowicz relates that, "On one occasion in 1931, when a gentleman who witnessed her ecstasy left her room, I heard her cry out: 'Foolish fellow, he asks himself in his soul if there is a Saviour. . . !'" Such sentiments are very harsh. The doubter was at least deserving of some pity and should have been helped in his predicament. On another occasion a school teacher who had taught catechism for thirty years came to Konnersreuth to ask Theresa for her prayers and to seek consolation in her affliction — she was on the verge of complete blindness. Accompanied by one of her friends, she happened to meet Theresa in the cemetery and approached her.[19] Theresa received them in the worst possible manner. She accused the women bitterly of wishing her ill, of persecuting her. And without listening to their explanation, she said: "Go away! I don't want to know anything about you. You are not my friends."[20] The next day (June 24, 1950), the unfortunate teacher wrote to Theresa to tell her that "her anger and her bitter words had caused serious scandal and had caused them to lose all faith in her."[21]

Several writers who have studied the phenomena of Konners-

---

[18] In passing, let us note the difference between Theresa Neumann and St. Teresa of Avila. The devotion of the saint to her spiritual director, Father Dominic Bañez, is well known. In his letters of 1574 and 1575, he himself speaks of his manner of directing the saint. "I showed myself very firm and severe toward her. The more I humiliated her, the more she sought my advice, feeling all the more secure in submitting her soul to a confessor she believed learned. She has always sought the advice of the most learned men. She told me more than once that she felt her soul more at peace when she consulted a learned doctor, even though he were not a man of deep prayer or profound spiritual life, provided he was well versed in natural and theological science. 'For,' she says, 'devout men, because of their very kindness and gentleness toward persons given to spiritual things and prayer, lead them more easily into error, than directors who, while possessing only an ordinary knowledge of spirits, judge things in the light of reason and faith.'"

[19] Father Naber had arranged for them to visit Theresa that day at 11 a.m.

[20] *"Machen Sie, dass Sie fortkommen; ich will nichts von Ihnen wissen; Sie sind nicht meine Freunde."* I have read a copy of the letter written by the two ladies (through the courtesy of Dr. Waldmann).

[21] *"Aber Ihre Art, Ihr Zorn, Ihre wutschnaubenden Worte haben grosses Ärgernis erregt und in uns den Glauben an Sie vollständig zerschlagen."*

reuth from a religious point of view have expressed their surprise that Theresa is so neglectful of voluntary mortification, that she is so desirous of comfort, that she spends so little time in church, under the pretext that she does not want to be a "devotee" (*eine Betschwester*), that she loves to chat with agreeable companions, that she shows scant reverence for certain prayers of the Church, particularly the Breviary, that she is so willing to be photographed and distributes her picture and autograph by the thousands, and the like.[22]

Though we are far from blind to Theresa's failings, we are still convinced that she is too good a character to be a "deliberate impostor" of all her marvelous phenomena. As for Father Naber, while he is neither a savant nor a learned theologian, he is a good, simple country priest. He sees her daily and in the most varied circumstances. Is it possible that he has not discovered any trace of deceit? He speaks to her frequently, and has heard her confession regularly for many years. He directs her in her spiritual life and discusses all her problems with her.

Archbishop Teodorowicz tells us that Father Naber does his best to discover the truth concerning the events of Konnersreuth. For example: "He has given her various tests to find out whether the ego or the human will plays a part in her ecstasies and visions."[23] These "tests" which Archbishop Teodorowicz believes to be "entirely in accord with critical scientific methods"[24] would cause a professional psychologist to smile. They are not, for that reason, without significance. They show that the parish priest does not ignore the question of authenticity and that he approaches the phenomena in a spirit of criticism, albeit of a very elementary sort.

It is our contention that the theory that *all* the phenomena of Konnersreuth can be explained as deliberate fraud seems to be untenable. Whether some of them can be attributed to sub-

---

[22] Cf. Graef, *op. cit.*, pp. 130–157 and *passim*. We touched on many of these difficulties in our study of 1933. See also Elisabeth M. Brennan, *op. cit.*, p. 15.

[23] *Op. cit.*, p. 47.

[24] *Ibid.*

conscious or semiconscious subterfuge is a different question, and we shall consider this aspect in a later section.

Not all critics of Konnersreuth believe that Theresa is guilty of deceit. There are many who admit the authenticity of the facts, but claim that they must be explained by *natural forces*. For them, miracles are simply impossible, being events contrary to the laws of nature. But if the events of Konnersreuth are contrary to nature they are not worthy of serious attention on the part of a scientist.

This is not the place to enter upon a detailed discussion of the naturalistic theory. We will merely point out that it shares the weakness of the theory of imposture, inasmuch as it is contrary to scientific method. Indeed, on what grounds are such critics certain of the impossibility of the supernatural? "Scientific method," they answer, "does not permit us to allow for any supernatural occurrences in nature." But this stand, common enough among materialistic scientists, betrays a regrettable confusion of ideas; it identifies a purely methodological principle with a dogmatic assertion. It is understandable that a physicist, for example, when he investigates the cause of a given fact, must not suppose a priori that it is unattainable by his scientific techniques. He must not suppose that his research will perhaps at any moment be interrupted by some supernatural forces. Such a presupposition would discourage any scientific research. Rather he is bound to assume, for the sake of method, that the phenomenon under study can be explained by natural causes. In short, he must adopt the *methodological* principle that natural events have natural causes. But by what right does he elevate a purely *methodological principle* to the rank of a *dogmatic explanation* of the facts?

Whenever a physicist, a psychologist, or a physiologist is confronted with facts which defy explanation in terms of his particular science, the only rational attitude must be: The facts in question cannot be ascertained by *my instruments*. When he reacts by *denying their existence,* he draws a conclusion unwarranted by the premises and acts contrary to scientific method.

That an atheist should deny the supernatural should cause no astonishment. Indeed, if all reality is restricted to the material universe, then God does not exist, or is identified with Nature itself; then also any breach of physical laws is unintelligible, because such a breach postulates the existence of a power capable of acting upon nature from without and interfering with its normal activity. In other words, it postulates a supernatural force, a personal God.

But it is difficult to understand the position of a *theist* who manifests an obstinate prejudice against anything that savors of the supernatural. There is inconsistency here. Indeed, the theists admit that the entire universe owes its origin to the creative action of almighty God. They admit that the Creator, though inaccessible to our bodily senses, makes Himself known to us through the works of His hands. When man makes use of his reason he readily discovers different relations of things, which show him that he is not a world but only a part of the world, that far from acting as an autocratic master, he must respect the rights of other parts of the cosmos, and especially the rights of the Creator. In this manner, God "speaks" to every human being throughout the course of life, and manifests His will. This voice sounds for all humanity to hear from the dawn of its existence in an unchangeable manner — as unchangeable as the essential order of things, which constitutes the foundation of the *norms of morality.*

Yet the very unchangeableness and consistency of the voice of God, as heard in the laws of nature, may leave the human intelligence unresponsive. Just as a miller may become so accustomed to the noise of the mill wheel that he will sleep soundly so long as it turns, but awaken the moment it stops, so a man may sleep mentally as long as the great cosmic machinery functions regularly and may awaken only when made aware of some interruption. Such an interruption will be like thunder from a clear sky. It arouses wonder. But his wonder takes the form of anxiety — it poses a problem. Now the only way of escaping from his anxiety is to solve the problem. In this way, a man will be once more responsive to the voice of God.

Can anyone who admits the existence of a personal God deny His power to intervene in the course of nature? But if he admits this, he admits the possibility of miracles, for a miracle is nothing else than some observable fact which surpasses the powers of nature, and which God utilizes to manifest His will to man. A miracle always has some *supernatural* purpose. God does not work miracles to correct mistakes in Nature. If He did, He would be like an unskillful craftsman who must continually repair his products.

What has been said shows that a categorical denial of the supernatural on the part of a man who believes in a personal God has its source in philosophical confusion. Some such confusion seems to be the only explanation of the attitude taken by those who, believing in God, nevertheless reject a priori the authenticity of the events of Konnersreuth, because to accept them would be to admit the possibility of miracles.

People often ask: "What would God want to tell us in the sufferings of the poor peasant girl of Konnersreuth, in her bloody tears, in her stigmata?" The answer is not difficult. He would remind us of the value of suffering, the necessity of sacrifice, and the loving kindness of our Saviour. Such a goal agrees perfectly with the fundamental ideas of Christianity and corresponds admirably to the needs of our own times. Our age is characterized by materialism and naturalism which deprive men of a true sense of values and cause them to seek only sensual satisfaction. The voice of Konnersreuth would recall humanity to its forgotten supernatural ideal and remind us of our eternal destiny.

THE CATHOLIC CHURCH AND KONNERSREUTH

Rotes Echo, a German communist paper, once accused the Catholic hierarchy of concocting the whole business at Konnersreuth for the purpose of enhancing its own prestige. The author of the article "Konnersreuth Humbug" (*"Volksbetrug von Konnersreuth"*) was sued for libel, convicted, and fined 600 marks. This salutary example effectively silenced any further attacks on the Catholic hierarchy in connection with the marvels of Konnersreuth.

Unfortunately juridical punishment can correct only external behavior; it cannot correct erroneous ideas. This can be done only by a clear presentation of the whole attitude of the Catholic Church toward Theresa Neumann.

To this day the Church has not "solved" the riddle of Konnersreuth in any *dogmatic* decision, nor will she do so in the future. The Church issues dogmatic decisions only on the content of the revelation which was confided to her care by Jesus Christ. Now this content is, according to the Church, complete. The evolution of dogma does not consist in any positive *increase* of the revealed truths but only in their fuller elaboration, deeper understanding, and practical application to the needs of the time.

What about private revelations? The Catholic Church does not *condemn* them a priori, provided they are not contrary to faith. She does not prohibit belief in them if they are really conducive to real piety. The person to whom the revelation is given will, of course, be obliged to accept what is communicated in the revelation by an act of "divine faith." Others will accept it as the word of God only in so far as the recipient of the revelation can *prove* its authenticity. Both the wisdom of God and the dignity of man require this. God does not oblige the intelligence arbitrarily, nor will He violate the laws of its nature. As Master of all, He requires that each creature serve Him according to its proper nature. From man, a rational creature, He asks a reasonable service — *rationabile obsequium.*

The most eloquent illustration of this admirable divine tact with respect to humanity is the conduct of Jesus Christ Himself. He did not force an act of faith in Himself. He did not demand that men accept His divine mission on His word only. "If I bear witness concerning myself, my witness is not true. . . . If

I glorify myself, my glory is nothing. . . . The Father himself, who has sent me, has borne witness to me. . . . I am not alone, but with me is he who sent me, the Father. And in your Law it is written that the witness of two persons is true."[25]

Let us apply these criteria to Konnersreuth. For a reasonable acceptance of the supernatural origin of the events happening there, the witness of Theresa Neumann *alone* does not suffice. Another witness is necessary. God Himself must in some way guarantee that He is really the Author of the phenomena.

If God were to work a miracle, as He did at the tomb of Lazarus,[26] all our doubts about Konnersreuth would vanish. Lacking such an obvious sign, we must undertake a long and *critical examination* of the facts to see whether or not they definitely exceed the power of natural laws.

But even if the supernatural character of the facts should be established beyond reasonable doubt, our certitude would be only historical or human certitude. The facts in question would never become articles of "Catholic faith." For this reason any person rejecting private revelations would neither fall into formal heresy nor commit a sin against faith.

The "confirmation" which the Church sometimes gives to private revelations does not contradict what we have said. The Church, when approving private revelations, merely states that they contain nothing contrary to faith or morals.[27] We can readily understand why the Church permits the supernatural events narrated in the Breviary and Martyrology to be submitted to historical criticism. Moreover, the Church herself is continually revising such accounts.

"Everyone knows," says Cardinal Pitra, "that we are entirely free to believe or not to believe private revelations, even when

---

25 Jn. 5:31; 8:54; 5:37; 8:16–18.

26 Cf. Jn. 11.

27 If a person whose process of canonization is to be started has left some writings about his visions or revelations, the Sacred Congregation of Rites sends these to the Holy Office for examination. If they are found to agree with Catholic faith and morals, they are returned to the Congregation of Rites with the marking: *Nihil obstat.* It is this judgment, a negative one to be sure, which will normally remain on the writings.

they are most authentic. If the Church confirms them, they become only probable, not certain. At any rate, they should not serve to solve any historical question, the problems of physics, philosophy, or theology, which are disputable among scholars. One can differ in his opinion concerning these revelations even after they are confirmed. . . ."[28]

Benedict XIV, in his celebrated treatise, *De Servorum Dei Beatificatione et de Beatorum Canonizatione,* raises the question: "What are we to think of the private revelations which have been confirmed by the Holy See, for example, the revelations of St. Hildegarde [accepted, at least in part, by Eugene III], those of St. Brigid [approved by Boniface IX] and those of St. Catherine of Siena [confirmed by Gregory IX]?" He replies: "There is no duty, nor even a possibility, of accepting them by an act of Catholic Faith. One can admit them only by an act of human faith according to the rules of prudence which present them to us as probable."[29]

Whenever the Church employs a private revelation in her liturgical worship or in private devotion, the association is merely *historical.* In other words, the revelation as such is taken simply as the *occasion* for the approval of a devotion or institution of a feast. The true foundation is always the deposit of Catholic faith committed to the care of the Church. Some practical examples may serve to illustrate the point.

In June, 1899, Leo XIII solemnly consecrated the human race to the Sacred Heart of Jesus. The historical occasion for this act was a revelation granted to a nun of the Sacred Heart. The revelation was only an occasion, not the real foundation for the Pontiff's action. That foundation he took from Catholic theology. Consequently, in his official documents, he never alluded to the alleged revelation in any way.

Urban IV was certainly influenced by the revelations granted to St. Juliana of Liège when he instituted the Feast of Corpus Christi. Yet, in the bull establishing the feast (1264), he bases

---

[28] *Livre sur Ste. Hildegarde,* p. xvi.
[29] Book III, Chap. 53, n. 15. Cf. *ibid.,* Book II, Chap. 32, n. 11.

his decision solely on theological grounds. Only toward the close of the document does he mention the revelations of the nun (died in 1258), and then only in a cursory manner.

The attitude adopted by the Church toward private revelations is an instance of her attitude toward supernatural occurrences in general. G. Dumas, a liberal Protestant, correctly states that the Catholic Church "is far from showing an absolute reverence toward them. . . . It knows very well that . . . the stigmata have appeared in many persons who were not necessarily recommended for purity of life."[30] The reserve shown by the Church toward anything that savors of the extraordinary is based not only on her practical sense and age-old experience, but also on her very conception of the supernatural life of grace. One can be holy without evidencing any extraordinary phenomena, because holiness consists in the love of God and a complete dedication of oneself to His service. On the other hand, it is possible for a person to possess supernatural charisms without being holy. Their possession, in itself, does not make the possessor a better person. The principal purpose of charisms is the good of others, the benefit of the Church, the increase of faith. Whenever extraordinary events are reported, the Church's first reaction is to urge prudence.

This cautious attitude of the Church should serve as a norm for the faithful. We are afraid, however, that many people, carried away by their enthusiasm for phenomena which they do not understand, have rendered Theresa Neumann a cultus which the Church reserves for her canonized saints.[31] They write letters asking her to solve a great variety of problems — religious, practical, even scientific; they seek her help in recovering lost objects; ask advice about dividing their estates. Those

---

[30] "La stigmatisation chez les mystiques chrétiens," *Revue des Deux Mondes,* t. 39, Paris, 1907, pp. 206–207. Dr. Antoine Imbert-Goubeyre, writing in 1898, cites 321 known cases of stigmatization. Of these, only 62 have been beatified or canonized. See his study: *La Stigmatisation.*

[31] Dom Mager, O.S.B., Father Wunderle, Father Westermayr, as well as Catholic doctors, for example, J. Deutsch, H. Heermann, A. Brenninkmeyer, and many others have deplored this.

who dare to caution them are accused of "denying the miraculous and all supernatural facts."[32]

The practice of questioning Theresa concerning hidden or future events[33] degrades the dignity of supernatural phenomena, makes Konnersreuth another Delphi with its Pythia, placing it on the level of a consultation office for the next world, such as the spiritualistic seances which are a real blot on our times and a serious social danger. These impatient believers think they are promoting the cause of the Church in this way. In reality, they alienate souls from her. Many people, looking on their conduct as reflecting the doctrine of the Church, will have none of it.

The Bavarian bishops, at their meeting in Freising in September, 1927, asked the faithful not to form any hasty judgments on the supernatural character of the events taking place at Konnersreuth. Subsequently on October 4, 1927, the Bishop of Ratisbon issued an order "suspending for a time all visits to Konnersreuth." On October 29 of the same year, the vicar-general of Ratisbon, in a circular letter to his people, expressed his urgent desire that all visits to Konnersreuth cease. Finally,

---

[32] Dom Mager writes in the *Katholische Kirchenzeitung,* May 5, 1932:
"All those who do not accept inane methods in examining the phenomena of Konnersreuth are accused publicly of denying the possibility of miracles. . . . I experienced this myself." Similar views were expressed by Dr. Brenninkmeyer and Father Westermayr. Cf. *Katholische Kirchenzeitung,* Aug. 30, 1931.

[33] It is unfortunate that these cases are so frequent. One instance is sufficient to prove our point: One day an Italian physician came to visit me in Rome to ask whether he should write once more to Theresa Neumann. The answers he had received from her, through Father Naber, to certain questions proposed in his first letter were entirely too vague. Here are the questions he asked: (1) Had God granted him pardon of his sins? (2) How should he divide his estate? (3) What should he do to convert his brother, who had fallen into atheism? (4) Should he undergo an operation which some specialists had advised?
Archbishop Teodorowicz cites another incident which is equally as bizarre: "A Sister Superior had put on a slip of paper the questions that she wanted to ask Theresa during her ecstatic state. . . . There were about twenty questions . . . in connection with the most varied and delicate affairs, state of health, sickness, recovery, grace of vocation, advice about mystic states of prayer, spiritual direction. . . . On the Sister's list was a question that was to decide for or against a vocation" (*op. cit.,* pp. 404–405). The Archbishop adds that the Sister "showed him this paper" (*ibid.,* p. 404). We are surprised that he found nothing reprehensible in her conduct.

in September, 1928, the Bishop reserved to himself the exclusive right to grant permission to visit Theresa Neumann, and on December 10, 1937, published an official statement declaring that the Church disclaimed any responsibility for the phenomena of Konnersreuth. This is truly a shining example of pastoral wisdom.[34] Can the same be said for the local pastor, Father Naber?

Before answering the above question, we must remember that the events of Konnersreuth are not of the type encountered in everyday life. Accordingly, they can be handled properly only by a spiritual director of exceptional intellectual and moral qualities. A spiritual guide, who might be excellent for run-of-the-mill cases, might well be beyond his depth when there is question of directing a Theresa Neumann. He would have to be, above all else, a man of strong character, one who would not allow himself to be led by the person he is supposed to direct. He would have to keep in mind supernatural purposes exclusively, and carefully avoid all that might savor of the sensational or spectacular. He must never go into raptures over his penitent's experience, at least not in her presence. Above all he must ground her in the practice of ordinary solid virtue which is not subject to illusions, especially in humility and mortification.[35]

Anyone who spends even a short time at Konnersreuth cannot help but notice the powerful influence exercised by Theresa over her spiritual guide. It seems that the good Father is so dazzled by Theresa's remarkable gifts that he does not dare contradict her. He obeys her wishes faithfully. Members of the so-called "Konnersreuth circle," friends of Theresa, are far from denying this statement. "The pastor listens to Theresa's voices," writes Archbishop Teodorowicz, "because he knows from experience that they do not err," just as the King of France obeyed the voice that spoke to the Maid of Orleans.[36]

---

[34] The Bishop of Ratisbon gave further proof of pastoral wisdom when L. Witt, the pastor of Münchenreuth, published a book on Theresa Neumann without the required ecclesiastical approbation. The Bishop notified his people that the book was forbidden.

[35] Cf. St. John of the Cross, *The Ascent of Mount Carmel,* Book II, Chap. XVIII.

[36] *Op. cit.,* p. 84.

In her ecstasies Theresa often foretells future events to Father Naber and tells him "in the most exact manner" how he is to conduct himself. She tells him how he is to direct her, which visitors he should admit and which he should refuse, and the like.[37] She has entrusted him with a "mysterious secretariate" (the expression is taken from Teodorowicz[38]). And the pastor devotes himself wholeheartedly to the task confided to him.

A significant circumstance mentioned by the same author is that Theresa in her normal condition does not remember what she says in her ecstasies. She cannot recall any of the directions given to Father Naber. Consequently, on coming out of her trance, she sometimes asks things which are in conflict with the orders she gives while in the ecstatic state. Father Naber does not heed these later commands, for he feels obliged to follow faithfully her ecstatic commands.[39]

Father Naber also assumes the role of intermediary between Theresa and those around her. As such, says Teodorowicz, he shares all her difficulties and complications, which unfortunately are not lacking. He takes charge of Theresa during her ecstasies as well as in the course of her daily life just as if she were his own daughter.[40] He is the one who interprets the details of the ecstasies for the benefit of visitors. When I visited Theresa, Father Naber stood at the door reading letters, now and then glancing at Theresa and informing me of the exact moment of the passion at which I was assisting. He knows exactly the course of her ecstasy, he understands the meaning of the least details of her facial expressions and explains them marvelously. Nay more, he explains to Theresa herself many of her own visions. Thus he told her that the young man whose martyrdom she had witnessed was St. Lawrence, that on other occasions she had the good fortune to behold the Blessed Virgin, St. Stephen, and so forth; she herself seems not to have known it. But we will return to this point later.

Father Naber also relays to Theresa questions confided to

---

[37] *Ibid.*, p. 48.
[38] *Ibid.*, pp. 48, 272–273.
[39] *Ibid.*, p. 48.
[40] *Ibid.*, p. 45.

him either orally or in writing by visitors. He also asks for details of her visions, questions her on the eternal fate of certain deceased persons, and looks to her for the solution of pressing problems.

A few more facts will suffice to illustrate the role played by the pastor in the drama of Theresa Neumann. On September 30, 1927, Father Leiber, S.J., prepared to offer Mass at St. Thérèse's altar in the Konnersreuth church. Seeing the altar covered with flowers, he requested the sacristan to remove them. The sacristan answered: "We cannot do that. The flowers have been placed there on an order received by Theresa Neumann during a revelation. The pastor came here yesterday at ten o'clock to see whether the command had been carried out." Father Leiber had to offer Mass at another altar.[41]

On another occasion one of our friends, in company with some other priests, was waiting in the sacristy at Konnersreuth for an opportunity to offer Mass. Suddenly the pastor entered and announced: "Theresa will not have her vision of the passion today. Last night she had an ecstasy during which the Voice told her that she would be spared her sufferings because today is the Feast of St. Thérèse, that she must rest, rest well. For this reason, Theresa will not receive visitors until three o'clock this afternoon. . . . My dear Fathers, you must excuse me, but I cannot act contrary to the will of Jesus Christ." Having said these words, he went into the church to make the announcement.

We have seen what occurred at the time she was cured of appendicitis. Theresa asked her mother to bring her clothes so that she might go to the church, for so she had been commanded by the Voice of the vision. Her mother opposed this strange idea; it was late and it was very cold outdoors (the date was November 13). Theresa insisted. The question was put to the pastor, who answered: "Since St. Thérèse, who came here to cure you desires it, let us go immediately to the church." A little procession of about ten persons formed around Theresa and they went

---

[41] Father Leiber himself told me of this incident when we were both professors at the Gregorian University (1933). Cf. also Teodorowicz, *op. cit.*, pp. 82–83.

to the church for a *Te Deum*. All of Konnersreuth, aroused by the news of the miraculous cure, hastened to the Neumann home. There Theresa recounted the details of her "miraculous" cure till late in the night.

Dr. Seidl, wishing to cure the stigmata of Theresa's hands and feet, spread a salve (aluminum oxide) on them and covered them with a bandage. When he had gone, Theresa said that the treatment was causing her intense suffering. Soon she was on the verge of a fainting spell. The pastor ordered the bandages to be removed immediately. This scene was re-enacted on two occasions.

We have already seen the steps taken by Father Naber to verify the reality of the stigmatization of her hands and feet. Theresa herself tells us that his first sight of the stigmata left him speechless, so great was his emotion.

It is likewise attested that the good pastor, in his parochial sermons, describes certain scenes from the life of Jesus according to the visions of Theresa Neumann, and that in her very presence. Father Szpetnar had occasion, on the Feast of the Ascension, to hear a sermon preached by Father Naber "according to the vision" seen by Theresa that same morning. Theresa, seeing Jesus ascend on high, exclaimed (said the pastor): "With you, with you!" (*Mit, mit!*)[42] He also encourages people "to ask Theresa to let them see her stigmata"[43]

Father Leiber deplores the widespread publicity given to Theresa's ecstatic sufferings.[44] The same opinion was expressed more forceably by the Hungarian priest whom we mentioned previously, Dr. Ewald, professor of psychiatry, and by many others.[45] Father Wunderle insists on the necessity of introducing more "peace" to Konnersreuth.[46] To all these justifiable criticisms one more is added: Why, in Theresa's presence, is the conversation always centered about her extraordinary phenomena?

[42] Stanislas Szpetnar, *Praca i Powsciagliwosc*, 1930, p. 113.
[43] Elisabeth M. Brennan, *op. cit.*, p. 15.
[44] "Konnersreuth," *Stimmen der Zeit*, Vol. 114, 1928, p. 178.
[45] *Die Stigmatisierte von Konnersreuth*, München, 1927, p. 34.
[46] *Die Stigmatisierte von Konnersreuth*, Eichstätt, 2 ed., 1927, p. 80.

Why are her stigmata so constantly exposed to admiration? If Theresa were really humble, should she not imitate St. Francis of Assisi who guarded the secret of his stigmatization so jealously? A number of priests have received a very poor impression from the way she constantly directs the conversation to herself and her extraordinary phenomena.

All that was said so far is clear evidence that the method of spiritual guidance practiced at Konnersreuth leaves much to be desired. It is certainly contrary to the teaching of the great doctors of the Church, notably to that of St. John of the Cross. This is a serious accusation, and demands proof. Let us examine a few passages from the writings of the Doctor of Mysticism.

"The spiritual director," we read in *The Ascent of Mount Carmel,* "must be . . . careful not to make his penitent narrow-minded by attaching *any importance* to these supernatural visitations. . . . Yea, rather let him *wean* him from all visions and locutions, and guide him into the liberty and darkness of faith, where he shall receive of the abundance of the spirit, and consequently the knowledge and understanding of the words of God."[47] In another chapter, the holy Doctor speaks of "the evils that may happen to the penitent on the one hand, and his director on the other, should they be *too credulous* in the matter of visions, even if these visions come from God."[48] Directors "with little discretion" have fallen more than once "into great errors . . . together with their penitents . . . thereby verifying the words of our Lord: 'If the blind lead the blind, both fall into the pit' " (Mt. 15:14).[49] "If the spiritual director be a man who has a weakness for revelations, who is impressed by them, and feels in them a sort of pleasurable satisfaction, he must communicate, without intending it, the same feelings to the mind of his penitent."[50] St. John treats such a director with extreme severity; he calls him *sensualis homo*.[51]

---

[47] Translated by David Lewis (London: Baker, 1928), Book II, Chap. 19, n. 13.
[48] *Ibid.,* Chap. 18, n. 1. Cf. also nn. 3, 4.
[49] *Ibid.,* Chap. 18, n. 1.
[50] *Ibid.,* Chap. 18, n. 6. Cf. also Chap. 16, n. 13.
[51] *Ibid.,* Chap. 19, n. 13.

What attitude, then, does St. John demand of a spiritual director in charge of persons who are favored with visions, revelations, and the like? "We must never rely on them, nor encourage them, yea, rather, we must *fly from them*, without examining whether they be good or evil. . . . He who *makes much of them* mistakes his way, and exposes himself to the great danger of delusion, and at least places a *great obstacle* on his road to true spirituality."[52] "The more it makes of such things, the more the soul strays from the perfect way."[53] "Besides, when the soul perceives itself subject to these extraordinary visitations, *self-esteem* very frequently enters in. . . . For this reason, then, we must *always reject* and *disregard* these representations and sensations. For even if some of them were from God, no wrong is offered to Him."[54] Indeed, "all corporal visions or affections of any other senses — the same is true of all other interior communications, if from God — effect their chief object *at the moment of their presence, before* the soul has time to deliberate whether it shall entertain or reject them. . . . It is therefore expedient that the soul should *close its eyes* and reject them, come they *whence they may*. . . . It is good to *shut our eyes* against these visions and to be afraid of them *all*. . . . Many, alas, there are who enter the battle of the spiritual life against the beast, who do not cut off even the first head, by self-denial in the sensual objects of this world. Others, more successful, cut off the first, but *not the* second, that is, the visions of the senses of which I am speaking."[55] "It is now clear that these visions and apprehensions of sense cannot be the means of the divine union, for they bear no proportion to God."[56] "If we dwell upon them, we shall never reach the goal of our spiritual perfection, union with God."[57] "Visions and phenomena of this sort" are the occupations "of a child. . . . That soul which ever

---

[52] *Ibid.*, Chap. 11, n. 2.
[53] *Ibid.*, Chap. 11, n. 3. Cf. also Chap. 29, n. 4.
[54] *Ibid.*, Chap. 11, n. 4.
[55] *Ibid.*, Chap. 11, n. 6.
[56] *Ibid.*, Chap. 11, n. 8. Cf. also Chap. 12, n. 5; Chap. 16, n. 7.
[57] *Ibid.*, Chap. 12, n. 7. Cf. Chap. 16, nn. 7, 8. Chap. 29, n. 4, states: "They may prove a great hindrance to the divine union."

clings to these, and which never detaches itself from them, will never cease to be a child, as a child will it always speak, understand, and think of God, because relying on the outward veil of the senses, which is childish, it will never attain to the substance of the spirit, which is the perfect man. And so the soul ought not to admit revelations *with a view to its own spiritual growth* even though God should send them. For the infant must abandon the breasts if it is to become accustomed to more solid and substantial food."[58] "We must therefore not rely upon visions, nor accept them at once, *even when we know that they are revelations,* answers, or words of God."[59] "In renouncing them with humility and fear, there is neither imperfection nor selfishness, but rather disinterestedness and emptiness of self, which is the best disposition for union with God."[60] Moreover, in acting this way, "we are thereby delivered from the risk and labor of discerning between good and bad visions, and of ascertaining whether the angel of light or darkness is at hand. The attempt to do so is not profitable at all, but rather a waste of time, an occasion of many imperfections and delay in the spiritual journey."[61]

But what are we to do if we receive a *particular command* in a vision? St. John answers as follows: "Remember . . . that we must never do of our own head, or accept anything told us in these locutions without *great deliberation*. . . . The real and secure teaching on the subject is, *not to give heed to them,* however plausible they may be, but to be governed in all *by reason,* and what the *Church* has taught and teaches every day."[62]

Let us illustrate the doctrine of the holy Doctor by a concrete example. Someone (generally a woman) comes to me and says: "Our Lord has told me in a vision that He is displeased with your impatience in class." What must I do? I must say (though not in her presence): *"Mea culpa, mea culpa,"* and make an

[58] *Ibid.,* Chap. 17, nn. 6, 7.
[59] *Ibid.,* Chap. 18, n. 8.
[60] *Ibid.,* Chap. 17, n. 8.
[61] *Ibid.,* Chap. 17, n. 9.
[62] *Ibid.,* Chap. 30, n. 5.

effort to correct myself. As a matter of fact, I know "through reason and faith" that impatience is displeasing to God. Consequently any investigation of the alleged vision would be a sheer waste of time. But let us suppose that the person in question tells me: "Our Lord wants you to promote such and such a devotion among your students." I would then consider seriously whether such a devotion is *according to the spirit of the Church,* whether it is advantageous for souls, and so forth. If I can answer affirmatively, I will set out to accomplish what has been commanded. But I will do so, not *because* the command came to me by means of a *"revelation,"* but because "reason and faith" urge me to do so. The alleged revelation would be merely an "occasion" for me, and not really a "cause."[63]

Let us note here that the popes have acted in this manner. Indeed, Leo XIII consecrated the whole world to the Sacred Heart on the urging of Mother Mary of the Divine Heart, who said she received such a commission in a revelation. However, the Holy Father did not base his decision on the revelation granted to this nun. The decree promulgated on the occasion of the dedication appeals to theological arguments. Pius IX gives us an even more striking example in this matter. Mother Appoline Andriveau wrote one day to the Pope communicating the message which she received from God, indicating that he must: (1) introduce the Scapular of the Passion into the Church, and (2) dedicate one day, during the Octave of Easter, to meditation on the passion of Christ. The Pope immediately introduced the scapular without even inquiring into the authenticity of the nun's revelation. He definitely rejected her second request, for he judged it contrary to the spirit of the Church.

Those of a different opinion, however, will not give up easily. They adduce the doctrine of other saints, especially that of St. Teresa of Avila. Dom Mager, O.S.B., deals with this objec-

---

[63] St. Teresa, when speaking of herself, says: "Never has this person regulated her conduct on what was inspired to her during a prayer [a revelation]. Moreover when her confessors told her to do the contrary, she obeyed them without the least repugnance" (Second Letter to Fr. Rodrigues Alvarez).

tion. "The proclamation of St. John of the Cross as Doctor of the Church has marked a turning point in mystical theology. Henceforth we have a sure guide, confirmed by the Church, in the problems of mysticism. Today we can say that the teachings of St. John on essential points of mystical theology is that of the Church herself. Consequently, if there should be any real conflict between St. John of the Cross and St. Teresa in these matters, a true son of the Church can no longer hesitate for a moment as to which of the two he is to follow. Pope Pius XI, when in 1926 he gave the Church the Doctor of Mysticism in the person of Saint John of the Cross, has already shown him his duty."[64]

But is it true that there is any real conflict on this question between St. John of the Cross and St. Teresa? We do not think so. These two saints approach the "mystical problem" from two different angles. St. Teresa, as Father Garrigou-Lagrange, O.P., notes, did not have in mind a theological treatise, but a *description* of the mystical life; she looked upon it as a fact which could be recognized by certain "signs." She did not set herself to determine its nature, or the immediate principles from which it flows. She did not distinguish sufficiently between what is essential and what is merely accidental to mysticism. On the other hand, St. John of the Cross, theologian that he was, carefully distinguished between the two.[65] His doctrine on visions, revelations, locutions, and the like, is based on St. Thomas' treatise on prophecy.[66]

The teaching of St. John of the Cross, adds the late Father Richstätter, S.J., is "shared by other great mystics: St. Ignatius, St. Philip Neri, St. Thérèse of Lisieux, St. Alphonsus Liguori."[67]

In the light of the above, it is evident that there is a sharp divergence between the doctrine of the great doctors of the

---

[64] "Aus der mystischen Literatur der Gegenwart," 52, Literary Supplement of the *Augsburger Postzeitung*, 1928, Nos. 36, 37.

[65] R. Garrigou-Lagrange, O.P., *Perfection chrétienne et contemplation selon Saint Thomas d'Aquin et Saint Jean de la Croix*, 1923, p. 576.

[66] *Ibid.*, p. 538.

[67] "Der Kirchenlehrer der Mystik," *Stimmen der Zeit*, Vol. 119, p. 200.

Church and the ascetico-mystical ideas prevalent at Konnersreuth. Archbishop Kasper, of Prague, once wrote of Father Naber: "A model of piety, patience, sacrifice, and zeal for the honor of God: this is the impression we received of the pastor of Konnersreuth."[68] We are happy to agree that we received the same impression of Father Naber when we visited Konnersreuth. Nevertheless, we would like to see him show a little more firmness and less acquiescence in guiding his spiritual daughter. Then we would have greater assurance that the phenomena of Konnersreuth are not flowers from his own garden.[69]

The defenders of Konnersreuth tell us that Father Naber must play the role of "intermediary" between Theresa and her surroundings. We are not questioning this role, but we believe that he should first of all be an "intermediary" between her and God. He ought to make clear to this simple country girl what St. John of the Cross and the other great doctors of the Church have to say about visions and similar charisms. He should cease discussing her visions with her at length, cease plaguing her with endless questions about them, and, above all, he should not accept the office of *mysterious secretariate*. Such a duty would be more befitting a member of her family. He ought to maintain better control over his feelings when confronted with the stigmata and not betray his veneration in her presence. He should by no means deliver sermons "according to the visions" of Theresa, especially when she is in the congregation. When Theresa persisted, against the wishes of her mother, in going to the church immediately after her cure of appendicitis, he would have done well to have imposed some delay on his spiritual daughter, if only to test her virtue. It is well known how strongly

---

[68] *Eindrücke über Konnersreuth,* p. 33.

[69] Why do we no longer see the "classical" types of hysteria which flourished at La Salpêtrière in Charcot's time? The answer is simple: they are no longer *cultivated.* There is no show because there is no audience. In Charcot's day, savants crowded into the Salpêtrière to admire the wonderful hysterical types. The young women had a perfect setting for their exhibitions, took advantage of it, often unconsciously, and became accomplished artists. Today such hysterical patients are locked up, subjected to occasional electric shocks with the threat that if they don't behave themselves better they will get stronger doses of the same medicine.

the masters of the spiritual life exalt such obedience. He was in a position to do so especially since the heavenly voice should have said (September 30, 1925): "Obey your confessor blindly and confide everything to him. You must die to yourself more and more." Moreover, there was no special reason to remove the salve placed on her hands by Dr. Seidl. The doctor told Theresa's parents expressly that the salve was absolutely harmless, and could cause no distress to the patient. The pain she experienced was evidently imaginary.

Here is another astonishing fact. On April 1, 1926, the pastor of Konnersreuth wrote an article on the cures and stigmatization of Theresa Neumann for the *Waldsassener Grenzzeitung*. The bishop of the diocese, Dr. von Henle, learned for the first time of the extraordinary events at Konnersreuth from the account in this newspaper. This fact, attested to by serious authors, needs no comment.[70]

---

[70] Cf., for example, Hilda C. Graef, *op. cit.*, p. 46.

CHAPTER 5

Healings

CURE OF BLINDNESS

FIRST in point of time was Theresa's recovery from blindness. This cure took place April 29, 1923, and forms the first link of the long chain of marvelous events which we have described; it serves, so to say, as the point of departure for a study of the "problem of Konnersreuth." Consequently it deserves our closest attention.

Theresa Neumann and her family ascribe the cure to the supernatural intervention of St. Thérèse of the Infant Jesus — to a true miracle.[1] This belief is shared by many others. Is such a conviction well founded?

In order to admit any fact as miraculous, two conditions must be fulfilled: (1) It must be established *with certainty* that the alleged event really occurred (*veritas historica miraculi*). To establish the actuality of the event we must make use of the methods of historical criticism, exactly as for other events of history. (2) It must be proved beyond a doubt that the event surpasses the forces of nature (*veritas metaphysica miraculi*).

If one of these conditions is lacking there can be no question of a miracle. Benedict XIV says: *Quando est res dubia, cum non sint multiplicanda miracula, sanatio in eo rerum eventu naturalis*

---

[1] The day after the cure Dr. Seidl came to see Theresa. "What's new?" he asked. "Everything is fine, I can see now," she answered. "How did that happen?" asked the doctor. Before Theresa could answer, her mother exclaimed: "Yesterday Thérèse of the Child Jesus was beatified. She it is, we feel, who has cured her." "Yes, that could be," was Dr. Seidl's reply. L. Witt, who recorded the doctor's statement, warns us against reading more into the doctor's words than they actually contain.

erit censenda — "When the matter is doubtful, since miracles are not to be multiplied, the cure must be considered natural."[2]

There are, consequently, two problems to solve: first of all, is it *certain* that Theresa Neumann was really *blind?* In other words, was her "blindness" the result of serious lesion in her organs of sight (*si caecitas proveniat ab laeso prorsus organo videndi*).[3]

The first fact to be noted is this: No doctor ever diagnosed such serious damage to her eyes. This statement cannot be denied. One day Dr. Seidl, summoned by the Neumanns, tried to get Theresa to sit up so that he might examine her eyes. Suddenly she was seized with a convulsive attack and lost consciousness, her body becoming completely rigid (this occurred whenever she attempted any exertion). The doctor was unable to examine her eyes.

The fact that Theresa's blindness was never diagnosed by a medical examiner would not constitute, in itself, an insurmountable difficulty, if the injury to her visual organs would have been easily discernable to competent witnesses. Damage to the organ of sight would then be sufficiently demonstrated. As it was, however, only a careful medical examination conducted by an experienced physician could have discovered any injury to Theresa's eyes, for during the whole duration of her "blindness," her eyes appeared perfectly normal except for considerable dilation of the pupils. Those who came to visit her could not see anything abnormal about her eyes. This observation was also made by Father Kunz, S.J., who had come to bring her Holy Communion. We can understand, then, why her parents showed no particular concern when Theresa, after a particularly violent nervous seizure, told them for the first time that she was blind. They believed that this blindness would pass away just as the attack which had occasioned it. It was only when the affliction persisted that they thought of calling the doctor to

---

[2] *Opera*, t. IV; *De Servorum Dei Beatificatione et de Beatorum Canonizatione,* Book 4, Chap. 8, n. 8.

[3] *Ibid.*, Book 4, Chap. 2.

find out what had happened to those eyes which appeared so normal.

Benedict XIV agrees with Matta that blindness can sometimes occur "without the faculty of vision being destroyed." Certain persons "afflicted with blindness for a long time (*a multo tempore obcaecatos*) were cured suddenly as a result of an accident."[4] Those who have the duty to pronounce on miraculous cures of blindness must be especially careful when there is question of amaurosis (decay of sight without perceptible external signs).[5] Such blindness may be accounted for by a simple "withdrawal of the animal spirits leaving the eye through the optic nerves." In modern terminology, we would say that the blindness is "functional." Such a disorder, continues Benedict XIV, "in the opinion of all doctors (*medici omnes omnino*)" is present when "sight is lost without any apparent lesion in the eye" (*visus abolitus sit nulla apparente in oculis noxa*).[6] One woman afflicted in this manner was cured "by a violent fever," another by "prolonged fasting" (*ope pertinacis inediae*).[7] To admit a miraculous cure of blindness, therefore, the physicians (*medici et periti*) must first of all prove beyond doubt (*evidentibus probationibus*) the *fact* of the blindness and its "cause."[8]

No such proof has been offered in the case of Theresa Neumann. Therefore it is not known whether her blindness was of organic or functional origin.

Let us consider other circumstances of the cure, however, in order to find some clues which will allow us to abandon the *negative* attitude we have been obliged to take. All four doctors who attended Theresa Neumann in the course of her various afflictions (Goebel, Hitzelsberger, Frank, and Seidl) noted that her eyes reacted satisfactorily to appropriate stimulation, that the pupillary reflex was normal when light was applied to

---

[4] *Ibid.*, Book IV, Chap. 9 (ed. 1749, p. 140).
[5] *Ibid.* The word is from the Greek ἀμαυρόω, meaning *to darken*.
[6] *Ibid.*, p. 142.
[7] *Ibid.*, p. 143.
[8] *Ibid.*, p. 147.

the eyes. All of which militates against any serious injury to the organ.[9]

The conclusion must be that it is impossible to prove that Theresa was really blind. The *veritas historica facti* has not been convincingly established. This is enough to reject the cure as miraculous.

But there are other facets to the problem which bear investigation, notably the highly interesting question: How explain the onset of the blindness suffered by Theresa Neumann for more than four years, and how explain its disappearance? In seeking an answer, a choice of method is not without importance.

Fritz Gerlich, in his famous study of Theresa Neumann,[10] condemns most energetically all who make use of "psychoanalytic methods" (he probably meant "psychological methods") in order to explain the cures of Theresa Neumann. The only method he will admit is that proper to the natural sciences (*naturwissenschaftliche Methode*), a method which supposes a mechanical equivalent between cause and effect. Here is how we are to understand the problem according to such a method. The repeated falls suffered by Theresa Neumann in the course of her illness, which began on the day of the fire, produced partial hemorrhaging either in the visual center or in the retinas; this hemorrhaging was the real cause of her blindness. A cure would be necessary to clear the residue left by the hemorrhage. Now this clearing took place suddenly and completely. Consequently, we must see, in this cure, the miraculous intervention of God.

What must we think of this opinion? The method recommended by Gerlich would be excellent if man were nothing but a mineral or a purely physical being; then the *mechanical equivalence* between cause and effect would be perfect. But man is a "psychophysical" being. Causes of a strictly psychic nature can produce physical effects in the human organism.

Evidence for this fact is available from the psychology of the motor force of imagery, of the emotions, of suggestion, and

---

[9] Cf. H. Heermann, M.D., in *Theologie und Glaube,* Paderborn, 1932, Part 2.
[10] *Die stigmatisierte Therese Neumann von Konnersreuth*, München, p. 400.

the like. Moreover, is not the science of pedagogy based on the principle that man can, by his psychic powers, dominate to a certain degree the mechanical impulses of his organism? that he can check the spontaneous responses, which in a purely material being would be realized according to the maxim, the cause equals the effect? Are we not aware that at times we need only concentrate our attention on certain actions we are about to perform in order to inhibit them instantly? Do we not know some individuals who can carry out certain actions perfectly so long as they are alone, but who become absolutely incapable of them the moment they are observed by others? Excessive attention to certain parts of the body can induce hyperesthesia or anesthesia! Often the only purpose of massage is to concentrate the patient's attention on the paralyzed limb and this simple psychological expedient sometimes actually restores sensibility and power of movement!

All these facts — and we could enumerate many more — are well known to students of psychopathology. They are nothing but exaggerations of the normal influence exercised by the psychic on the material part of man: a feeling of shame causes blushing, fear causes us to grow pale, and so on.

Gerlich, though an excellent historian, had little knowledge of modern psychology. He was even less acquainted with the data of psychosomatic medicine, which today has become a specialized branch. It deals, as is well known, with illnesses caused by a combination of psychogenic and physiogenic factors. Doctors generally admit that at least 30 per cent of all patients who visit their offices are subject to strictly organic illnesses. The remainder are afflicted with ailments brought on by a combination of psychological and organic causes. Indigestion, for example, can sometimes be caused by strictly organic factors (e.g., poisoning), sometimes by neurosis, sometimes by a combination of organic and functional (emotional) disturbances. For these reasons, treatment of psychosomatic illness must be simultaneously medical and psychological. And in the psychological treatment, *suggestion* made to the patient either while he is awake or under hypnosis plays an important role. Almost all psychosomatic syndromes, write M. Brenman and M. Gill, can be treated successfully, especially various skin disorders (for example, psoriasis), asthma, muscular rheumatism, constipation, epilepsy, nausea, insomnia, menstrual irregularities, and so forth.[11]

For all these reasons we cannot accept Gerlich's method of approach to the Konnersreuth phenomena. If this method oversimplifies the problem of Konnersreuth, it likewise distorts it. Rejecting a naïve "psychologism," which would confer on our souls an almost unlimited power over our bodies, the "natural" method falls into the other extreme which is not less harmful from the scientific point of view; it degenerates into "physicalism."

A truly scientific approach to the phenomena of Konnersreuth must avoid both these extremes. It must accept, on the one hand, a real influence of the soul on the body, but, on the other hand, it must limit this influence in accord with the data of experience.

We are not concerned here with the nature of the attacks, spasms, and paralyses suffered by Theresa during the year preceding her loss of sight. We shall consider them later. Suffice to note that the general condition of her health, of which we have spoken previously, was not of such a nature as to exclude a priori the "psychological method."

This is not all. Certain symptoms of her blindness *positively* invite us to employ this method. We have already noted one circumstance: Theresa's eyes reacted normally to light stimuli. Consequently it is very probable that her ailment was purely functional, or, in other words, of psychogenic origin. Another point: her eyes, especially the left one, were so lacking in *sensitivity* that the cornea could be touched with the finger. The particular locality of this anesthesia is interesting; it was strictly "logical," that is, it corresponded to the preconceptions

---

[11] *Hypnotherapy*, publications of Joseph Macy Foundation, Review Series, Vol. II, No. 3, 1944, p. 39.

of the patient, not to the distribution of the nerves in the organ. Indeed, not only the eyeball, but the whole region of the eye (notably the eyelids), as Theresa herself tells us, was insensible. When Dr. Seidl applied an electric current to her eyes she felt the shock on both sides of her face, but not in her eyes nor in their immediate area. Such circumstances demand we make use of the "psychological method."

Some may offer the objection that Theresa's blindness did not happen suddenly. On the contrary, it was progressive. At first she experienced difficulty in reading; then she found it impossible to distinguish the features of her associates; some time later she could not perceive even silhouettes; finally total blindness ensued. Gerlich and his numerous followers explain the progressive loss of sight as the result, continually aggravated, of repeated hemorrhages.

The psychological method, however, is quite capable of accounting for the progressive development of the malady. When a psychoneurotic person suffers a sudden, severe emotional shock, his habitual asthenia is accentuated and often followed by pronounced abulia which leaves the patient incapable of any sustained attention, any prolonged intellectual effort. At first, he cannot read handwriting, then fine print, until finally any reading whatsoever becomes impossible. An initial difficulty in distinguishing features gradually develops into a general incapability to distinguish the outlines of objects; and this because autosuggestion and abulia increase with the progress of the disorder. All voluntary effort, all personal initiative becomes difficult. The sufferer finally lapses into a state of discouraged passivity; he believes that he can no longer see anything.

These stages of progressive blindness are well known to psychologists. M. Georges Dumas, for one, made a great study of them. It is not at all impossible that Theresa's blindness could have been explained in this way. Furthermore, this hypothesis is reinforced by Theresa's own statement that before losing her sight she seemed to see everything in a dense fog. Now it is a known fact that psychoneurotic blindness is often preceded by achromatic (or "twilight") vision. Theresa Neumann's blindness, therefore, appears to have resulted from progressive *retinal anesthesia.*

We admit that this type of blindness usually affects only one eye, and that if it should affect both eyes simultaneously it does not ordinarily last for such a long time; more than four years![12]

We need only consider the circumstances of Theresa's illness to obtain the solution to this difficulty: (1) Theresa's blindness was preceded and accompanied by continual neuropathic seizures. If these attacks were related to the blindness, it is not surprising that the latter lasted for such a long period. (2) By the time Theresa lost her sight, she had already been bedridden for some months, and was thus protected from the dangers ordinarily encountered by the blind; she knew that she would not fall or injure herself. In the main, her blindness did not make her too unhappy. She was almost indifferent to a cure. (3) Theresa herself stated that her blindness did not cause her very much suffering; on the contrary, it allowed her to give free play to pleasant daydreaming, to which she was very much inclined. Later she would even cherish happy memories of the period of her blindness. This is one reason why she was not too anxious to recover her sight and why a condition of psychoneurotic blindness might be prolonged indefinitely.

The circumstances of Theresa's *cure* harmonize perfectly with the etiology which we have just outlined, and afford further confirmation of our theory.

To cure psychoneurotic blindness it is very important to rouse the patient from the torpor which oppresses him, to stimulate his energy, to evoke some personal initiative, and thus bring about a real will to be cured. (We note in passing that

---

[12] "Always following an emotion, Jm . . . believed that she saw before her eyes what looked like red lightning. She closed her eyes; when she had opened them again, she was completely blind in the right eye as well as in the left. This blindness lasted 12 days and disappeared as suddenly as it had come. This serious incident happened again another time, but the blindness lasted only 7 days" (Pierre Janet, *L'état mental des hystériques* [Paris: Alcan, 1911], 2 ed., p. 462).

Herr Neumann often reproached his daughter for lack of energy and will power.) Now the events of that memorable April 29, 1923 — the day of Theresa's cure — were perfectly suited to provide her nerves with the all-important shock they needed. Here are the facts: (1) At six o'clock in the morning her father told Theresa that he was going to get the medicine prescribed by Dr. Seidl the day before, and which the doctor said would cure her ailment. The effect of such an assurance on many patients is very well known. But that is not all. (2) We must not forget that on April 29, 1923, St. Thérèse of Lisieux was beatified. Theresa Neumann had a very strong affection for the Little Flower and had ardently looked forward to this day. The coming of the great feast moved her profoundly and filled her heart with joy and confidence. (3) Then the climax. Herr Neumann had left for Waldsassen. Theresa fell asleep again. Suddenly, she heard a scratching noise near her pillow. She was seized with a horrible fear and awoke with a start. She opened her eyes — and then she saw her own hand, which very likely had been scratching the pillow while she slept. Her blindness was gone completely.

We cannot resist the temptation to cite similar sudden cures reported by Benedict XIV in his monumental work.[13] A paralytic, the Pope tells us, who was bedridden for several years (*complures annos*) saw a fire, and sudden fright restored the use of his limbs. Another man, paralyzed for six years, was completely cured when he raised his arm in anger to strike an awkward servant; a woman, incapacitated for thirty years, was cured when terrified by a clap of thunder. He also cites other examples, adding that fear and anger are most efficacious in healing illnesses of this kind. Modern psychology can add a long list of its own. Consequently we cannot rule out a priori all influence of fright in Theresa's cure.

In short, the conclusion must be that it is perfectly *possible* that Theresa Neumann's blindness was purely functional, and that its cure was due to the activity of psychological forces.

---

[13] *Op. cit.,* Book IV, Chap. XII, n. 2.

Such being the case, our duty is to follow the directives of the Church and reject a miraculous explanation: *de miraculo non constat*.

Before concluding, however, we must consider a possible objection to our theory, namely, that Theresa had no special *desire* to be cured of blindness on that occasion.

The objection is based on a misunderstanding. When we speak of Theresa's "desire" to be cured, we do not mean to say that her wish was clearly defined or even perfectly conscious. Coué, though not a psychologist by profession, observed that the best physiological results of autosuggestion are often obtained when we have expelled from the subject any conscious desire for these results. Autosuggestion succeeds best when the subject is entirely absorbed in the physiological effect to be obtained, without desiring it explicitly. On the contrary, when he begins to will the effect consciously, he breaks the efficacy of autosuggestion.

For this reason autosuggestion often obtains its best physiological results during sleep, when higher mental activity is suspended for the most part. So it happens that some people will awaken from a terrifying nightmare partially paralyzed, while others owe their cure to the salutary impressions of a dream. A hypnotist can sometimes at will call forth or suppress psychotic symptoms, such as catalepsy. In psychiatric cases, obsessions, compulsive reactions, phobias, manias, feelings of depersonalization generally appear most acute when they are treated on the level of reflective consciousness. When, on the contrary, the course of psychic life is allowed to follow a psychological automatism, the patient feels better.

All of which shows that no cogent argument can be advanced against the possibility of a purely psychological cure of Theresa Neumann's blindness.

We conclude with one more important fact. Theresa had trouble with her eyes in 1924 and again in 1926 when bloody serum flowed from them.[14] This fact shows that the healing of

---

[14] Fr. Gerlich, *op. cit.*, I, pp. 81–82.

1923 was not complete. For this reason it is difficult to attribute it to God whose "works are perfect."[15]

HEALING OF A FOOT WOUND

The second cure to be considered is that of the foot wound, which is described in Part I. Must we look upon it as miraculous, as some authors do?[16]

Again, let us examine the *circumstances* of the cure. Theresa's mother suffered much at the possibility that her daughter's foot might have to be amputated. Her suffering moved Theresa profoundly. She wished with all her heart to console her. Now, under the circumstances, the only way to eliminate this worry was to obtain the cure of her foot. Theresa, then, would desire with all her soul an immediate healing of the wound.

Full of confidence in the supernatural intervention of St. Thérèse of the Child Jesus, she ordered that three rose petals which had been touched to the tomb of the Saint be slipped between the bandage. In a few moments the pain in her foot ceased, and when the bandage was removed the next day the wound was healed.

We must admit that the rapidity of the cure is amazing. Certainly the *possibility* of a miraculous intervention must be taken into account.

But is a miracle the *only* possible explanation? This is the problem. In our opinion there are *insufficient* data to give an affirmative answer. First of all, there always remains a well-grounded fear that the sudden disappearance of *pain* with the application of the rose leaves might have been produced through suggestion and imagination, always powerful forces in neurotic individuals. We can say little about the *cicatrization* observed the following day, because we have no information about the con-

---

[15] We will develop this idea later.

[16] "Among the cures of Theresa Neumann's ailments, one possesses a supernatural character that stands without doubt; the cure of deep sores" (J. Teodorowicz, *Mystical Phenomena in the Life of Theresa Neumann* [St. Louis: Herder, 1940], p. 124). "Only the cure of the sores must be accepted as supernatural with mathematical certainty" (*ibid.*, p. 132).

dition of the wound when the rose leaves were placed in the bandage. And the recurrence of pain — could it not have been due possibly to the process of cicatrization? Moreover, was the malady really as serious as it appeared to Theresa's mother? Our doubts cannot be brushed aside because there was "a fear of eventual amputation of the foot," for we know, as Theresa tells us, that only her mother entertained such a fear. Finally, we do not know whether the cure took place at the time the pain disappeared, or whether the wound had slowly and gradually reached the condition discovered by the nursing sister when she changed the bandage.

The only fact known with certainty is that the cure was preceded by an ardent desire for a speedy recovery on the part of Theresa. What effects can such a desire produce in a neurotic person? Among others, it can accelerate the process of cicatrization to an amazing degree.[17] Delboef could even bring about the disappearance of the organic effects of a burn.[18]

Referring to miraculous cures, Benedict XIV laid down the following principle: Only those cures "for which no remedies have been used" or "for which we are *certain* that the remedy has brought no relief" can be considered as true miracles.[19] We have no such certainty here. "For in every case," adds the Pope, "where there is a probability that the cure has come about in a *natural* manner, we must put aside all thought of a miracle."[20]

Our uncertainty increases when we carefully study the *details* of the alleged cure. "My sister Zenzl," Theresa tells us, "had changed the bandage one evening. The following day, at about the same hour, we placed some rose leaves in the bandage. When, the following day, the bandage was changed, the foot was found to be healed."[21]

---

[17] P. Janet, *Névroses et Idées fixes,* II, pp. 506–512.
[18] Cf. W. James, *The Principles of Psychology,* Vol. II, p. 612.
[19] *Op. cit.,* Book IV, c. 8 (*ed. cit.,* p. 112).
[20] *Op. cit.,* Book IV, c. 8 (*ed. cit.,* p. 135).
[21] L. Witt, *Konnersreuth im Lichte der Religion und Wissenschaft,* I, p. 83. Cf. also Gerlich, *op. cit.,* I, pp. 83–84.

It is evident from Theresa's own account that about forty-eight hours elapsed between the time the bandage was applied and the cure discovered. Now, Benedict XIV insists that, for a cure to be considered miraculous, it must be sudden (*ut sanatio sit subita et momentanea*), at least where there is question, as in this instance, of a "third degree" miracle, that is, miraculous "as to manner" of occurrence (*quoad modum*). He warns us to be "cautious, prudent, and severe" (*cautos, prudentes et severos*) in pronouncing on the "instantaneousness" of the cure because "an illness can often be cleared up in a short time" (*saepe intra modicum tempus*).[22]

But is it possible for *deep* sores to be healed naturally in such a short time? We think not. Was Theresa's sore really deep? L. Witt, who describes this cure in Theresa's own words, does not say that the wound was *deep*. A writer like Witt, who stresses every scrap of evidence in favor of a supernatural intervention, would certainly not have neglected to mention such a significant detail. How could he have passed over such a critical, nay decisive, detail in silence? On the other hand, Gerlich states expressly that the ulcers which often infested Theresa Neumann (since the spring of 1919) disappeared when treated with chicken fat (*Hühnerfett*), and in place of the ulcers a "fine skin" appeared.[23] Gerlich, too, fails to say whether the wound on the foot was "deep."

Dr. Poray-Madeyski, in his excellent medical study of the cures of Theresa Neumann, comes to the conclusion that this wound "was not and could not have been deep . . . only the inferior epidermal layers were affected, not the dermis itself." He draws this conclusion from the nature of the secretion which was "serous and sanguinolent rather than purulent . . . which indicates the angioneurotic origin of the lesion."[24] Now Benedict XIV forbids us expressly to consider miraculous "*the cure of wounds which are not mortal*" (*vulnerum non laetalium*).

---

[22] *Op. cit.*, Book IV, c. 8, n. 17 (*ed. cit.*, pp. 112, 120, 123); n. 2 (p. 112).

[23] *Op. cit.*, t. 1, 1929, p. 70. See also pp. 69, 83, 84.

[24] B. de Poray-Madeyski, *Le cas de la visionnaire stigmatisée — Thérèse Neumann de Konnersreuth* (Paris: Lethielleux, 1940), p. 246.

After reading this section, one of our critics (J. Piwinski) concluded that we reject the miraculous character of *all* events which are not brought about "instantaneously." This amazing deduction is certainly not supported by anything we have written. The reason we doubt the miraculous character of the cure of the wound on Theresa's foot is that the healing took place, by all accounts, over a period of *forty-eight hours,* that is, over a period of time sufficient for a natural cure under the circumstances, which are: (1) the wound was not at all deep; (2) medication had been applied; (3) the healing was not noticed until forty-eight hours after the application of the bandages; (4) Theresa's constitution is very susceptible to psychological influences.

Moreover, the distinguished critic overlooked one circumstance of great importance, which was stressed repeatedly. If the alleged cure were really due to the supernatural intervention of God, it would be classified among miracles designated by Benedict XIV as *"miracula tertii generis — miracula in modo."* The healing of wounds as such is an everyday occurrence. In Theresa's case, however, the healing is supposed to have taken place in a different *manner.* It is precisely this last circumstance that would constitute the miraculous character of her cure: *miraculum quoad modum.*

Benedict XIV declares expressly that a cure *miraculum quoad modum* must take place "instantaneously" (*subita et instantanea*) in order to be accepted as miraculous. He quotes in favor of this doctrine several renowned theologians and physicians of his time. This opinion, he adds, "has been adopted and always followed by the Sacred Congregation of Rites" when miracles are offered in causes of beatification or canonization. The Sacred Congregation follows this method "so rigorously" (*tanto cum rigore*) that it has several times refused to accept as miraculous cures attributed to the intercession of a servant of God because the patient "at first experienced some improvement" (*coepisse melius se habere*) and only later recovered "perfect health."

Such a process "rules out an instantaneous cure" (*subitam excludit sanationem*).[25]

Some eminent theologians and physicians, notes Benedict XIV, require that *every* cure without exception be wrought instantaneously if it is to be considered miraculous. Other writers would *never* require instantaneousness as a criterion for a miracle. Benedict XIV unhesitatingly rejects both these extreme views, because the first errs by excess, the second, by defect. The true method follows a middle course. If a cure surpasses natural forces not merely as to *manner,* but also in *substance,* it can be accepted as a true miracle even though it did not occur instantaneously. Instantaneousness is a prerequisite only for miracles of the "third class" (*quoad modum*).[26]

The reader can readily observe that we have followed step by step the teachings of Benedict XIV and the Sacred Congregation of Rites in considering the cure of Theresa's foot wound.

CURE OF THE SPINE

Theresa's recovery from an illness of the vertebrae made a profound impression on her adherents, for not only were the symptoms so striking: repeated horrible spasms, contortions, convulsions, fainting spells which kept her confined to bed, but also because her malady was generally considered incurable. Theresa herself never completely lost hope of recovery; bedridden though she was she looked forward with pleasure to the time when she would be able to get up and learn to walk once more. But her friends and family had no illusions as to her future. They believed more and more firmly what a doctor is supposed to have told them: that only a miracle could cure her, that only death could end her sufferings.[27] For this reason

---

[25] *Op. cit.,* Book IV, Part I, Chap. VIII, n. 16.

[26] *Ibid.,* nn. 12–15.

[27] Theresa had recourse to quacks as well as to legitimate physicians. The former diagnosed her illness as fatal from an examination of her hair! Cf. Gerlich, *op. cit.,* p. 74.

her father, who at first reproached her for lacking energy rather than health, ceased to blame her and began to sympathize with her.

In these circumstances we can easily understand the sensation caused by the news that Theresa, after six and a half years in bed, got up and began to walk. And since her cure was accompanied by a "vision" of St. Thérèse of Lisieux, it was, of course, attributed to the supernatural intervention of this Saint.

We are not concerned here with the character of the alleged vision, which we shall consider in a later chapter. It is the cure which we wish to consider here.[28]

Whoever is thoroughly acquainted with the facts as stated in Part I will easily realize that Theresa, despite her preference for heavy manual labor, is endowed with an extremely sensitive temperament. This is evident in her weeping at the account of the passion of our Lord, in her moodiness with the change of weather, in her strong aversion to long-haired animals, in her dislike for the doctor who attended her at the hospital, in the irritability which made her unbearable to her friends, in the suffering caused by the touch of a stranger's hand (the physician's, for example), in the tears she sheds even today whenever she recalls the diagnosis of Dr. Burkhardt after examining her spine, in her anger when the doctor did not tell her: "You will soon be better," in the same tone of voice as he did the other members of the family, in planning to flee from the hospital, in her outburst of weeping when the vision of light disappeared (May 17, 1925), and so on. Such behavior is an indication that Theresa has a highly emotional temperament.

Psychologists are well aware what profound effects can be

---

[28] Considered historically, the vision forms one unit with the healing. Nevertheless, it is possible to discuss the problem of the latter independently of the alleged vision. In the ontological order the vision should occupy the first place as the supposed cause of the cure, but in the noetical order the healing is more important, for, in the circumstances, the cure is the principal criterion for the authenticity of the vision. For this reason L. Witt, who cannot claim to be "hypercritical," asserts: "If there were only a question of revelations and visions, I would not move a finger to write. I rely on external facts which can be verified (*kontrollierbar*)" (L. Witt, *op. cit.*, 2 ed., 1927, p. 125).

produced by emotional shock (a sudden terror, deception, or pain). These effects can also result from more hidden emotional states (emotion-sentiment).[29] Indeed, every powerful emotion breaks down the synthesis built up by the conscious effort of the superior psychical powers; it introduces loosely bound associations which develop autonomously and bring organic activities under their influence. Weaker individuals subjected to such shocks may lose their sense of sight or hearing, suffer gastric disturbances or various paralyses or anesthesias.[30] Not infrequently they lapse into amnesia.[31]

Of course the effects of violent emotions do not follow the same course in each individual. In some the result is a more or less generalized disturbance of the psychic mechanism ("an emotional state"); in others, the effects are organized into a definite pattern, that is, they take a strictly determined form. A terror experienced under certain circumstances, for example, will recur whenever the subject encounters an analogous situation. Therefore, a stereotypy, automatism, and astonishing periodicity will characterize the morbid symptoms. Sometimes the psychic syndrome, returning periodically, is exactly the same as the original emotion; at other times it is more or less disguised. It can readily be observed that when the emotion attains a high degree of intensity it takes on a strictly "personal" form; thus, when a child's life is in danger a mother may begin to fear for her own life.

---

[29] The "emotion-sentiment" is either a simple habitual reminder of the "emotion-shock," or a new system of pathological affective states developed under the influence of some traumatic ideas or feelings.

[30] A normal person, under the impact of a powerful emotional stimulus may feel his knees buckle. Very high-strung individuals in similar circumstances feel as though their legs were cut off, or as though their bodies were divided at the waist.

[31] Clinical studies have shown that highly emotional women are particularly susceptible to morbid symptoms if they are emotionally upset during the period of menstruation. It is impossible at this late date to determine Theresa Neumann's condition (with regard to her menstrual cycle) on the day of the fire (March 10, 1918). We know that, with the exception of July, 1918, menstruation has not occurred since then. In 1920 (or 1921) medical treatment caused her to menstruate, but this ceased when she discontinued using the medicine. Since then menstruation has ceased entirely.

It has also been observed that the effects of emotional trauma are all the more dangerous for an individual when his previous life presented a normal appearance.

When there is a problem of organizing a defense against the results of pathological emotional states, there is nothing more detrimental than to have the patient concentrate on the original cause of the disturbance. Such individuals feel a morbid desire to return to the original crisis. This is not, of course, an impulse of the conscious will, but the effect of a hypertrophy of the system of associations brought about by the shock.[32] The individual may even carry out certain actions which he is convinced do not proceed from him at all and which he ascribes to some external agency, good or evil, depending on the quality of the acts he is compelled to execute.[33] In fact, since he cannot recognize his own conscious ego as the source of these actions — for it was split into psychically loose systems of associations — the subject naturally looks for their explanation in an external source.[34]

How does all this apply to the problem of Theresa Neumann? As appears from the study of the history of her case, the point of departure for all the strange phenomena was the fateful March 10, 1918, a day of intense emotion for Theresa.

At sight of the fire, says Dr. Seidl in his official report, she began to "tremble from head to foot and stood petrified with fright."[35] She had hardly recovered from her first emotional upheaval when she was seized by it again on her return to the scene of the fire. She felt herself, as Gerlich says, "trembling

---

[32] If the individual is rather intelligent, a counselor may be able to turn his attention from the emotional crisis and persuade him to lead a useful and energetic life. If the individual is less intelligent, he may consider the counselor either ignorant or malevolent and find another who will accept him as a "sick" person and not a dreamer.

[33] Such an action executed "in spite of the will" may be brought about by "contrasting association." A man, fearing that the candle he holds in a dark room may be extinguished, may (unwittingly) blow it out himself.

[34] When we speak of a split ego or personality, we do not mean the *ontological* (metaphysical) personality, which is always one and indivisible, being the nature of man itself, but simply the psychological or phenomenological personality, the immediate object of our intuition.

[35] Cf. Dr. G. Ewald, *Die Stigmatisierte von Konnersreuth*, p. 13.

with fear." Her terror resembled, as she herself tells us, the panic experienced by children "when they meet St. Nicholas."[36]

This terror was all the more intense in that it assumed a very *personal* form. Theresa was afraid that the fire might reach the house in which she was living. We may remember the words her employer spoke to her: "We ourselves are in very great danger" (*in der grössten Gefahr*). And, in fact, she beheld her employer's hayloft burst into flame.

In addition to her terror, we must remember the despondency she suffered from being continually scolded by her employer for alleged "laziness" and lack of good will.

All this must have caused a severe shock to Theresa, already exhausted by hard work and fasting. As long as the work absorbed Theresa's attention to the extent that she could forget herself, all went well; "I did not feel at all fatigued," she said later to L. Witt. But as soon as she felt the painful twinge (*Kniks*) in her back, her attention was suddenly centered on herself; she became aware of her dreadful fatigue and at the same time felt incapable of doing any more work.[37]

This feeling of exhaustion and incapacity increased day by day.[38] In a short time even the lightest effort resulted in fainting

---

[36] Fr. Gerlich, *op. cit.*, I, p. 18.

[37] Some physicians believe that Theresa suffered from "*meningitis spinalis acuta*" (cf. Dr. Windolph's article in the *Deutsche Allgemeine Zeitung*, No. 449, Sept. 25, 1927, Supplement). He cites the instance of a soldier who, as a result of exhaustion and chill, experienced the same symptoms as Theresa, though not with the same intensity. (It was later diagnosed that the soldier's symptoms were of emotional origin.)

[38] It is not without reason that we enumerate many details concerning the illnesses of Theresa Neumann. In highly emotional persons it is not unusual to discover a tendency to celebrate "anniversaries." On a particular day or during a particular season of the year they will relive their original emotional crisis. This tendency is based on psychical attitudes and follows the laws of association of ideas. Such association can sometimes take on a very "elective" character. Theresa had special difficulty buttoning one of her dresses. It would be interesting to know if the dress in question was the same one she was wearing on the day of the fire.

As for the cough which troubled her so persistently, we lack the data necessary to determine its precise character. Psychologists are very familiar with the "hysterical cough." It is characterized by a rhythmic regularity (it conforms to the dactylic foot of Greek prosody: the first prolonged cough is followed by two

spells, or caused her to fall to the ground in painful contortions. These attacks increased in frequency and violence. The continual uncertainty of her situation, fear for the future, alteration between hope and despair, and passionate longing for immediate recovery caused progressive deterioration. At the same time, paralleling her physical breakdown, a radical transformation took place in her character. She became sad and irritable.

A person in such a condition is to be pitied. But how can he be helped? In the first place, it is necessary to attempt to alleviate such a one from his continual and exhausting interior struggles and fears. "A definitive misfortune is better than perpetual fear," says Janet.[39]

And, indeed, Theresa began to recoup her moral strength under the guidance of her spiritual director. She gained courage and resigned herself to her physical condition. She learned to overcome the egocentrism into which her first emotions had plunged her and resolved to live once more for others: for God and her neighbor.

When a sick person has arrived at this point, he is already on the way to health. In order to hasten recovery, a new emotion should be cultivated which would replace the other with its morbid association synthesis. We do not mean that a complete cure will ensue, but rather that new and milder symptoms will replace the former severe ones. A relative cure at least will result.

This desirable emotional replacement occurred for Theresa when she received the vision of the light and heard the voice of St. Thérèse on the day of the Saint's canonization. Here, then, is a "psychological" explanation of her cure.

We will not find it too surprising if we recall the wonderful

others, usually feebler) and by its dryness and noise. This cough disappears during sleep. It reacts especially after strong emotional stimulation. Was Theresa's cough of this kind? We do not know. But the description of the cough, given by Theresa herself, resembles that of the hysterical variety. The fact that she is said to have contracted it when perspiring and wet does not prove apodictically its organic nature. The hysterical cough may have an objective point of origin.

[39] *Névroses et Idées fixes,* II, Paris, 1924, p. 53.

effects which, according to Benedict XIV, can result from the emotions of "paralytics." We have mentioned them above. The back trouble, from which Theresa was cured May 17, 1925, bore a striking resemblance to functional paralysis. We mean to say that it was not organic, not caused by a luxation or fracture of the lumbar vertebrae. If it were, the symptoms would have been entirely different, as we are assured by that capable student and eminent Catholic, Dr. Lhermitte. The onset of paralysis would have been immediate; the lower limbs would not have been subject to spasms, but would have become flaccid. There would have been no loss of hearing, of speech, or of sight.[40]

Moreover, Dr. Poray-Madeyski notes that if there were severe organic injury Theresa would not have been able to travel about five miles to visit Dr. Burkhardt.[41] He considers the theory of luxation of the lumbar vertebrae "completely absurd."[42] Dr. Burkhardt, who was the first to examine Theresa, must have come to the same conclusion. Dr. Deutsch surmises as much from the treatment prescribed, for instead of immobilizing her back in a plaster cast, massaging and warm baths were ordered. It was not even considered necessary to take X rays.[43] If he

---

[40] Dr. Lhermitte, "L'énigme de Thérèse Neumann," *Étude Carmélitaines*, Apr., 1934.

[41] *Op. cit.*, p. 171.

[42] *Op. cit.*, p. 168.

[43] Dr. J. Deutsch, *Ärztliche Kritik an Konnersreuth! Wunder oder Hysteria?* (Lippstadt: Selbstverlag, 1938), p. 78. Cf. another study by the same author, *Où en est actuellement l'affaire de Konnersreuth* (Paris: Lethielleux, 1937), p. 24.
Some writers assert that Dr. Deutsch retracted his opinion on the phenomena of Konnersreuth in his publications shortly before his death. This assertion must have better proof before we can accept it. The statement is founded on the testimony of an *anonymous* individual who is said to have witnessed Deutsch's death and to have heard the statement (cf. Hans Fröhlich, *Konnersreuth Heute* [Wiesbaden: Credoverlag, 1950], p. 30).
In what mental state did he retract his opinions? In fever — in hallucinations? What exactly did he retract in his opinions? In what terms? Perhaps he regretted only his manner of defending his opinions, not the opinions themselves? But did he retract anything at all? Who is this anonymous witness (*jemand*)? Why does he so obstinately guard his anonymity? To make impossible for us the scientific verification of his testimony? All this history of the retraction by Deutsch seems to be but a *legend*.

had discovered a dislocation of the vertebrae, notes Poray-Madeyski, the doctor would certainly not have allowed his patient to walk.[44] After Dr. Burkhardt's death (in February, 1919) Dr. Seidl attended Theresa and mentioned expressly in his account of February 27, 1919, that there never was any luxation of the vertebrae but only some muscular strain.

To our mind, this is the most plausible hypothesis. The "twinge" Theresa felt in her back on March 10, 1918, was probably caused by muscular strain brought about by the continuous lifting of buckets of water to her employer. This slight injury developed out of all proportion to its cause and the contractures, spasms, convulsions, paralyses, anesthesias, and the like were brought on by Theresa's emotional temperament.

"It can be stated with certitude," declared Dr. Mansion to the Medical Society of St. Luke, "that Theresa Neumann suffered from none of the serious ailments ascribed to her by the Konnersreuth circle and broadcast throughout the world by popularizers: neither fracture, nor luxation of the vertebrae, nor cerebral hemorrhage. Theresa Neumann has suffered serious nervous attacks . . . as a consequence of emotional upset. . . . These cases are classical."[45] The same opinion is voiced by Drs. Deutsch,[46] Heermann,[47] and Franz L. Schleyer,[48] all of whom are Catholics.

Theresa's parents and Sister Regintrude (a Franciscan from the convent at Mallersdorf) discovered some abnormality in that Theresa had an especially painful locality on her back. Merely touching this point sufficed to bring on convulsions. This abnormality disappeared when her back was cured. We have no reason to question the presence of such an abnormality, but we feel that it could have been caused rather by muscular distension than by injury to the vertebrae.[49]

[44] *Op. cit.*, p. 171.

[45] Published by *Saint-Luc Médical* of Brussels, No. 5, 1933, p. 386 ff.

[46] *Où en est actuellement l'affaire de Konnersreuth?*, Paris, 1937, p. 11 ff.

[47] "Um Konnersreuth," reprint from *Theologie und Glaube*, Paderborn, 1932, No. 2.

[48] *Die Stigmatisation mit Blutmalen* (Hannover: Schmorl and Seefeld, 1948).

[49] What was the nature of this supposed injury to the vertebrae? The most

Theresa says that at the very moment she tried to sit up (after the vision of May 17, 1925) she felt a sharp pain in her back. Some authors conclude that this was the moment when the vertebrae were cured. But such a deduction is too hasty. We know that whenever a muscle which has been contracted for a long time returns to its normal position, there is a painful sensation.

The thesis which explains Theresa's cure on psychological grounds appears to find confirmation in the fact that recovery

---

fantastic explanations have been advanced: hematomyelitis, syringomyelia, myelitis, chronic inflammation of the spinal cord, multiple sclerosis, injury to the spinal cord, and finally Friedrich's ataxia.

Hematomyelitis is characterized by paralysis of the upper and lower limbs accompanied by sensory disturbances. It usually follows from rarefaction of the air caused by an explosion.

Syringomyelia occurs in young adults between the ages of ten and forty. It can be recognized by muscular atrophy which starts with the hands, by paralysis of the lower limbs, disturbance of sensory functions, and finally by various disorders of the vegetative apparatus.

Myelitis can result from syphilis, from a tumor, from a malformation of the organs or from a lesion of the vertebral column. It appears in two forms: acute and chronic. Acute myelitis is accompanied by pains along the vertebral column (especially in the lumbar region), by numbness in the limbs; depending on the situs of the lesion there may be paralysis of the bladder and the rectum (with resultant loss of sphincter control). Chronic myelitis has the same symptoms, but its development is slower and sometimes lasts for months or years. It frequently produces a transverse inflammation (*myelitis transversa*) and is centered in the waist area.

Multiple sclerosis is distributed at random on the spinal medulla, the cerebellum, etc. This disease is prevalent mostly among manual laborers, farmers, woodsmen, etc. The first symptom is spasmodic paralysis, especially of the lower limbs: the legs become stiff, the feet can be raised only with difficulty, the gait is stumbling, reflexes are exaggerated, but general sensibility remains intact. Sometimes paralysis of the eye muscles is noticed, together with trembling of the eyeballs when the patient is told to look to the side (nystagmus). The speech becomes slow, monotonous, and hesitant. The illness may last from five to ten years. There may be recurrence or the patient may recover entirely.

Lesion of the spinal cord may be produced by any piercing object, a bullet, for example. The victim has the impression of being "cut in two," falls to the ground, and is unable to arise unassisted. At the most he may be able to crawl for a few feet. Generally there is complete paraplegia, destruction of the reflexes, anesthesia of the paralyzed parts, loss of sphincter control, and muscular atrophy. Death may follow within a few days or a few months.

Friedrich's ataxia is a disease of the spinal medulla of children under fourteen; it is usually hereditary and its symptoms resemble those of hardening of the plaques.

was *slow* and *progressive*. In the light of Christian philosophy this detail is very important. *"Opera Dei sunt perfecta"*: the work which proceeds directly from the hand of God — and a miracle would be such — ought to possess all the perfection due to its nature. Any defect in a work of God could come only from secondary causes of which the principal cause makes use. When St. Peter said to the lame man: " 'In the name of Jesus Christ of Nazareth, arise and walk.'. . . Immediately his feet and ankles became strong. And leaping up, he stood and began to walk and went with them into the temple, walking and leaping and praising God" (Acts 3:6–8). When Christ said to the paralytic: " 'I say to thee, arise, take up thy pallet, and go to thy house.' . . . Immediately he arose and, taking up his pallet, went forth in the sight of all" (Mk. 2:11–12).

What a contrast between these miracles and the cure of Theresa's ailment! Hearing the voice of the vision: "You can now sit up and walk," she leaped up energetically crying: "In the name of God!" and stood up at the side of her bed. Theresa's father and a nun rushed to take her arms. With their help she was able to walk half the length of her room, limping painfully on her left foot. Then she went back to bed. When her family left the room she arose once more and attempted to walk; she took a few steps, but had to support herself by grasping the furniture. At nightfall she once more satisfied the desire to walk, but again from one article of furniture to another. After twenty-five days of such practice, her mother, yielding to her importunities, allowed her to leave the house for the Feast of Corpus Christi (June 11). Not feeling strong enough to walk by herself, she leaned on her father's arm and supported herself with a cane. In this manner she was able to go to the church. Her father had her seated comfortably, while he himself stood behind her. Suddenly she felt ill. No doubt the exertion was too much for her. He led her back to the house and she had to resign herself to staying in her room for another long period. She had to admit that her parents and the pastor were right when they opposed her leaving the house. Nevertheless, the following Sunday she insisted once more on going to church and taking part in the procession. Her parents consented, but as soon as she had left the house she felt ill, and regretfully had to return to bed.

Her convalescence dragged on until September 30, the anniversary of the death of St. Thérèse of the Child Jesus. During the night, while Theresa was reciting the litany in honor of her patroness, a soft light appeared and a voice spoke to her: "Now you will be able to walk without assistance." Theresa arose and, without any support, whatever, walked about in her room for fifteen minutes. Early the next morning, slowly and wearily but without any misadventure, she was able to walk alone to the church.

We may add that even today Theresa Neumann is not yet completely cured. A most zealous friend of Konnersreuth writes: "I once saw Theresa Neumann as she rose from the sofa with great exertion and with an expression of much pain in her face. To my query about what was wrong, she answered: 'Those are still the pains in my back which God has left me. . . .' "[50]

All these details point up the difficulty of accepting the theory of supernatural intervention in Theresa's cure of May 17, 1925. On the other hand, they do not prove the absolute impossibility of such intervention. It may be said that the healings we have cited from Holy Scripture imply two miracles: (1) the healing of sick limbs, and (2) their immediate use. Perhaps there is question here of only the first miracle in Theresa's case.

We agree that such a distinction is not without some foundation. A patient who has been bedridden for some months upon recovery always experiences great difficulty in his first attempts to walk. He must, so to speak, learn to walk again. We must also take into account the atrophy of her muscles and a general weakness resulting from insufficient nourishment. Are these facts

---

[50] Teodorowicz, *op. cit.*, pp. 115–116. The author adds the following observation: "If the ailment had had merely a nervous basis and cause, we would not speak of a remnant. Only in cases of organic suffering can such circumstances be explained." This remark shows how unfamiliar the author is with psychology.

not sufficient to account for the progressive nature of her cure?

Even these distinctions, however, do not entirely dissolve our doubts. Since an organic malady of the vertebrae has never been established, the only criterion of a miracle in her case would be the *suddenness* and *completeness* of the cure. This seems to be an absolute condition for any recognition of a miracle.

But there is another and more important consideration. The voice which she claims to have heard on May 17, 1925, did not say: "Your *legs* are now *healed*," but, "You can now *walk*." Yet this "walking" was very imperfect and hardly worthy of a supernatural intervention of God, of a "miracle."

Nor is this all. While Theresa was undergoing the observation ordered by the Bishop of Ratisbon, in 1927, she suffered "a nervous attack" (during the night of July 16) which lasted twelve minutes. While in a semiconscious state she thrashed about (*um sich geschlagen*) and cried out that she was being stabbed in the heart. Now if the nervous disorders suffered by Theresa up to the time of her "cure of the spine" were of the nature claimed by the advocates of Konnersreuth, that is, the result of a lesion or dislocation of a vertebra, how are we to account for the nervous attack of 1927?

Before closing this section we would like to anticipate an objection which might be raised against our psychological explanation of Theresa's illness and its cure. The theory, it may be said, contradicts the laws of psychology. Whenever a psychiatrist examines a patient he must investigate both the personal psychic background of the patient as well as that of the family. Now Theresa manifested no signs of abnormality prior to the day of the fire, and her family has a record of excellent physical and psychic health.

The reply to the above objection is that there is no guarantee that Theresa's health was perfectly normal before the day of the fire. The fact that an individual does not *betray* anything abnormal does not prove that there is no psychic abnormality present. Many persons of psychoneurotic disposition may go through life without any overt breakdowns as long as they are protected from emotional shock. There may be no demand made on their psychic energy strong enough to evoke abnormal behavior. On the other hand, a trifle may sometimes precipitate a conflict and breakdown which no one could have foreseen.[51] Moreover, we have already pointed out a number of incidents which lead us to believe that Theresa was always of a highly emotional temperament.

As for her family, the *Münchener Medizinische Wochenschrift*[52] states that Herr Neumann's sister Catherine was psychotic. Village reports claim that she set fire to her family's house and was seriously burned. While such reports do not constitute evidence, the fact that the woman was considered capable of such a deed gives us food for thought.

Even if it could be proved that all her near relations were normal, we could not rule out the possibility of psychic weakness in Theresa herself. Psychopathology knows too many case histories which cannot be explained by heredity.[53]

Of the five doctors who attended Theresa (Goebel, Hitzelsberger, Frank, Seidl, and Burkhardt), four diagnosed her trouble as "a severe case of hysteria accompanied by blindness and partial paralysis" (*schwerste Hysterie mit Blindheit und teilweiser Lähmung*). Some have claimed that the physicians pronounced such a verdict only to help the family claim compensation. But they could have accomplished this purpose much better by declaring organic injury of the vertebrae! For this reason even L. Witt is obliged to admit: "Theresa's recovery from so-called paralysis cannot be considered miraculous in the strict sense of

---

[51] The condition of Theresa's teeth, as she admits, was certainly not desirable. More precise information might provide some clues concerning childhood illnesses. We only know that she lost her teeth some time before the onset of her nervous attacks.

[52] No. 46, p. 1931.

[53] Cf. P. Janet, *Névroses et Idées fixes*, II, 3 ed. (Paris: Alcan, 1924), pp. 42, 117, 188–189, 232, 288, 312, 379, 498; D. K. Henderson and R. D. Gillespie, *A Textbook of Psychiatry for Students and Practitioners*, 6 ed., Oxford, 1947, pp. 32–50.

the word . . . there is not here a question of things which every-body that has eyes can see."[54] Dr. Hans Fröhlich, who main-tains "a miraculous revelation of God"[55] in the events of Kon-nersreuth, does not consider this healing as a certain miracle.[56]

In their efforts to prove, at all costs, that the cure of the spine was miraculous, some authors point to a fact which Theresa herself reported. About a year after her "cure" another illness confined her to her bed for thirteen weeks. When she attempted to walk for the first time after her illness she felt her knees buckle and strike against each other. This did not occur after the "miraculous" healing of May 17, 1925.

This argument has very questionable value. A difference in psychological attitude can explain her reactions to the separate instances. When Theresa arose from bed on May 17, 1925, she was so completely absorbed in the vision she had just experienced that it must have been almost impossible for her to notice whether or not her legs were trembling. We must remember, too, that after her visions Theresa enters a "childlike state" during which her attention is constantly narrowed.

Neither can we overlook the objection raised by certain critics (Teodorowicz, Piwinski, Philips) to our use of the principle, *"Opera Dei sunt perfecta."* We have employed the principle in a much too narrow sense, they tell us. A miracle, indeed, is a perceptible fact surpassing the powers of nature. Now there may be certain sensible facts which may be imperfect and in-complete in their physical reality, but which nonetheless are beyond the scope of nature. By way of example they cite the recovery of vision recorded in the gospel of St. Mark: the blind man, after the first imposition of the Saviour's hands, saw "men as though they were trees, but walking about" (8:24).

Benedict XIV was well acquainted with this gospel text. Nevertheless he affirms categorically that *only* a cure which is

---

[54] This opinion is shared by many eminent Catholic physicians, e.g., Poray-Madeyski, H. Heermann, Deutsch, to mention only a few.

[55] *Konnersreuth Heute. Schau eines Arztes* (Wiesbaden: Credoverlag, 1950), p. 5.

[56] *Ibid.,* p. 74. To him the supernatural intervention of God in this healing is only "more probable."

"perfect, not defective or incomplete" (*perfecta, non manca et concisa*),[57] can be recognized as a miracle. No doubt there may exist some occurrences which "in themselves and in the sight of God" (*in se et coram Deo*) are genuine miracles. They are not accepted, however, as evident miracles by the Church, for she must judge by external evidence (*judicat de externis*).[58] Only perfect and complete cures, in her eyes, deserve to be called miracles.

What, then, are we to think of the cure of the blind man narrated by St. Mark? Scholastic theology furnishes us with an appropriate term: *"Via ad miraculum,"* or a process which terminates in a miracle. The miracle itself is clearly expressed in the twenty-fifth verse of the same chapter: "He saw all things plainly." Actually we are not dealing here with two distinct miracles, but with one miracle attained in two stages. The "stages of the miracle" are not themselves "miracles," but, in scholastic terminology, *"motus ad esse,"* not pure and simple *"esse."*

CURE OF APPENDICITIS

It is not our intention to spend too much time discussing this alleged cure. Before attempting to explain any fact, we must first be sure of the *reality* of that fact. Briefly, we have no assurance that Theresa really had appendicitis. It could very well have been a transitory intestinal disorder. Every physician knows how easily certain painful spasms in the intestines can be mistakenly diagnosed as appendicitis. Prudence is all the more in order when these symptoms occur in highly nervous patients who are quite capable of exaggerating the least indisposition. How often have surgeons opened the abdomen only to find the organs perfectly healthy!

Dr. Deutsch made an interesting study of such cases from the files of the University of Bonn clinic. Of 1325 diagnoses of "acute inflammation of the caecum," 10.37 per cent were found

---

[57] *Op. cit.*, Book IV, Part I, Chap. VIII, n. 19.
[58] *Ibid.*, n. 34.

to be erroneous. In the 1112 cases subjected to surgery, the diagnostic error was 11.52 per cent. At the clinic of the University of Würzburg these figures were respectively 11 and 5 per cent; at the University of Zurich (from 1921 to 1925) 20 and 5 per cent.[59]

There was all the more likelihood of erroneous diagnosis in Theresa's case, for she suffered from chronic disorders of the stomach and intestines. Moreover, we must not overlook the ease with which neurosis can imitate organic symptoms with such accuracy as to deceive even the most experienced specialists. A review of the circumstances attending this attack of "appendicitis" makes the hypothesis of purely nervous etiology not only possible, but highly probable.

As we mentioned in Part I, Dr. Seidl made his diagnosis in Theresa's home without the aid of a blood count or any other means which would definitely substantiate his opinion. If specialists in hospitals can record such a high percentage of false diagnoses, it would be rash for us to accept Dr. Seidl's diagnosis without reservation.

But let us recall some other aspects of Theresa's illness. Father Naber tells us that Theresa "was writhing on her bed like a worm."[60] Is this possible? Those of us who have had the opportunity to observe a victim of acute appendicitis know that he lies motionless as a log; he avoids the least movement, for such would only intensify his sufferings. Dr. Poray-Madeyski stresses this point: "This fact in itself is perfectly sufficient to rule out definitely the hasty diagnosis of Dr. Seidl."[61] The whole trouble was probably one of gastric distress.[62]

The fact that Theresa observed, some hours after her cure, that she voided pus does not solve the problem in favor of a

---

[59] Deutsch, *Où en est actuellement l'affaire de Konnersreuth*, Paris, 1937, pp. 17–18. Cf. also his *Ärztliche Kritik an Konnersreuth! Wunder oder Hysteria?*, p. 75.

[60] Gerlich, *op. cit.*, I, pp. 97, 113.

[61] *Op. cit.*, p. 265.

[62] A. Abadir, "Sur quelques stigmatisés anciens et modernes," *Étude historique et médicale*, Paris, 1932, p. 52.

miracle. How did she know that this pus came from an infected appendix? In fact, how did she know whether it really was pus?

But let us assume that it really was pus, and that the pus came from an infected appendix. Would this fact prove a supernatural intervention in the ordinary course of nature? Not likely, for pus can be discharged in a purely natural manner and, when it does, the fever is lowered almost immediately. In such circumstances Theresa could go to church the same day.

One final argument in favor of the miraculous character of the cure, which L. Witt considers decisive, is that the mysterious *voice* which accompanied the cure told Theresa: "That men may realize that a superior power is working here, you will not now have to undergo an operation." This is an egregious sample of a logical fallacy known as the *petitio principii* — the assumption of the very point at issue. The supernatural character of the vision itself has never been proved. We cannot prove the authenticity of the vision from the cure, and that of the cure from the vision! As cited above, Witt himself had written previously: "If there were only a question of revelations and visions, I would not move a finger to write. I rely on external facts which can be verified."[63] But the vision, being strictly psychical, cannot be directly verified. We must prove its authenticity by some external criterion. In the case under consideration, the only possible criterion of the vision would be the cure.

The fallacy of this argument is so flagrant that it did not escape the writer, for he hastens to add that his argument "from the voice" is not based on its heavenly origin (*weil es eine himmlische Stimme war*) but on the fact that this voice had helped Theresa (*weil . . eben diese Stimme . . habe Therese geholfen*).[64] But this is no way out of the difficulty. What is questioned here is precisely the nature of this "help," or cure.

We get nowhere analyzing the contents of the message with Witt. "The voice," he writes, "confirms the accuracy of the

---

[63] See note 28.
[64] *Op. cit.*, p. 147.

medical diagnosis: you will not have to undergo an operation."
From this he concludes triumphantly that Theresa really suffered
from an inflamed appendix and required immediate surgery to
save her life! His triumph is premature. The authenticity of the
message depends on the authenticity of the voice itself. Moreover, even if we were to assume, with Theresa, that the voice
really came from heaven, we cannot be certain that she really
had appendicitis. The voice did not say so; it merely told her
that she would not have to undergo surgery, contrary to the
doctor's decision. The message tells us nothing about the objective value of the diagnosis.[65]

CURE OF PNEUMONIA

The last of Theresa's cures was that of pneumonia, which
occurred in November, 1926. Can this cure be attributed to the
supernatural intervention of God, as so many affirm?

We cannot agree with the adherents of a miraculous cure.
Pneumonia commonly follows a cyclic course. After maintaining
a fixed intensity for about a week, it can suddenly clear up. The
fever may drop from 40 degrees C. to normal overnight. Convalescence is usually of brief duration. Such a cure is common in
young persons with good resistance, and in about 75 per cent
of adult cases. In some cases the cure is preceded by a short
crisis during which the symptoms are aggravated.[66]

Theresa Neumann contracted a cough toward the end of October. A few days later (on a Friday) she began to show symptoms of pneumonia which soon became intense.[67] By November
19, according to the *natural* course of events, the disease had a
greater probability of terminating favorably than fatally.

Benedict XIV cautions us not to consider miraculous a cure
which takes place "in the final stages of a disease when a turn

---

[65] Teodorowicz commits the same error. He maintains that even though the
recoveries were natural, the fact "that they were a fulfillment of the prophecies
. . . must be a proof for the theologian of the supernatural character of these
cures" (*op. cit.*, p. 143). In another place he states that "the truth of Theresa's
visions is attested by the miracle of her cure" (*ibid.*, p. 152. Cf. also pp. 142–144).

[66] *Larousse Medical*, p. 1064.

[67] Gerlich, *op. cit.*, I, p. 118.

for the better may be expected" (*ut non sit in ultima parte status, ita ut non multo post declinare debeat*).[68] He quotes the authority of a learned Zacchias, who says that "in such a stage, as appears from the writings of Hippocrates . . . all the symptoms [of the illness] become stronger, so that the sick person passes through a dangerous crisis. But after having passed the crisis a sudden and unexpected change for the better takes place, which for this very reason seems miraculous to many people; for because of the dangerous symptoms they suppose that the patient will soon die; and just at that time he recovers his health. Now when the sick person is in such a state, they very quickly have recourse to supernatural aid, and make innumerable promises to God and the saints. For this reason, when the illness subsides, they look upon it as a miracle, especially when health returns unexpectedly in such a short time. In reality it was in the nature of things for the illness to slacken and disappear."[69] Later on Benedict XIV cites a certain Hoffmann to the effect that "in no other fever are the crises more frequent than in the disease called pneumonia (*febris pneumonica*)."[70]

For these reasons we cannot consider the healing of Theresa's pneumonia a demonstrated miracle.

CONCLUSION

From an examination of the evidence given above, we are forced to conclude that *none* of Theresa's cures can be proved miraculous; none of them compels us to assert: "The finger of God is here."

Some authors have not hesitated to compare the above-mentioned healings with the cures reported at Lourdes. This is a dangerous practice. Lourdes has witnessed complete cures, often instantaneous, of strictly organic, often fatal and incurable, diseases. They have been verified by the "*Bureau des Constatations*

---

[68] *Op. cit.*, Book IV, Chap. 8, n. 2.
[69] *Ibid.*, Book IV, Chap. 8, n. 6.
[70] *Ibid.*, n. 38.

Médicales" in which sit the most distinguished authorities of modern medical science, some of them non-Catholic. We know the desperate efforts made by enemies of the supernatural to discredit the miracles of Lourdes and put them on a level with a recovery "after the crisis in pneumonia," with a cure of blindness which cannot be verified, with recovery from hysterical paralysis.

No doubt some of the cures reported at Lourdes resemble those of Konnersreuth. But these are not officially accepted as authentic miracles. Let us cite one example of such a cure.

During the author's visit to Lourdes (August 19–22, 1930) a young lady was the center of a crowd of people gathered in front of the basilica. "She was cured by a miracle," I was told. I learned that on leaving the baths she had been suddenly cured of paralysis, from which she had suffered for fifteen years. I went to see the parish priest who had brought her to Lourdes to ask for details. He replied: "Do not believe it, please! (*Méfiez-vous!*) She has been sick a long time, but the *Bureau des Constatations Médicales* declared upon her arrival that even if she were cured they would not recognize her recovery as miraculous because there were some serious doubts as to the nature of her paralysis."

CHAPTER 6

Stigmatization

AMONG the extraordinary phenomena associated with Theresa Neumann, her stigmatization has attracted the widest attention. Some writers even say that the stigmata constitute the very focus of the enigma of Konnersreuth, "the principal fact around which all the rest centers."[1]

Is stigmatization always the effect of a supernatural intervention of God? Does it really surpass all the powers of nature? In short, is it miraculous? This is the question. Various solutions have been offered:

First solution: Stigmatization *must* be explained as a *natural effect,* for the modern critical spirit cannot accept a miraculous explanation. Such a ready-made solution is the logical effect of atheism (a denial of God's existence) or of pantheism (a denial of God's transcendence), and can be refuted by the same arguments which expose the errors of atheism and pantheism.[2]

Second solution: Stigmata which appear on the body of a person come from *God* if that person has the spirit of God, that is, if he is distinguished for his piety; otherwise we must attribute them to the intervention of the devil. This solution, as can be seen at a glance, poses a dilemma based on the conviction that stigmata must come either from God or from the devil. In either case they surpass the powers of nature. All investigation

---

[1] Dr. Van der Elst, *Études Carmélitaines,* Oct., 1932, p. 92.

[2] A miracle is a breach in the laws of nature. As such it can be produced only by a power capable of opposing nature, by a force which is neither subject to nature nor identical with it, consequently by a *super-natural* force. Whoever denies the existence of such a Force, or identifies it with nature, must exclude a priori any true miracle.

of a particular instance must therefore limit itself to discerning which of these two supernatural causes (God or the devil) is at work. Excluded a priori, and without a hearing, is the *third* hypothesis: Stigmata can be produced by natural causes.

Such an attitude might have had some excuse at the dawn of psychological science, but today such manifestation of anti-scientific spirit is inexcusable. This, then, is our first objection. Another objection to this solution is that our Catholic religion teaches us that there is no intrinsic connection between sanctity and stigmatization, just as holiness is possible without visions, the reading of hearts, levitation, and other extraordinary gifts. On the other hand, we know from history that stigmatization has often been found in individuals who were not very notable for virtue. An outstanding scientist, who is likewise an eminent Catholic, once visited me in Rome. He was engaged in preparing a study of the lives of stigmatics, and he was quite surprised, he said, to find among them a great number of persons of definitely inferior morality. This fact would not be shocking if we realize that stigmatization, according to the teaching of Catholic theology, along with visions, prophecies, and the like, even if divine gifts, belong in the category of "charisms," or what are called *"gratiae gratis datae."* These are merely gratuitous gifts which God grants to certain persons without regard to their merit, their piety, their sanctity, or their mystical life. God can grant them — and this is in accord with sound theology — to *any* person, even one in the state of mortal sin, or one outside the fold of the true Church (*Ethnici seu Gentiles*).[3] God grants charisms in order to reawaken religious life, to stimulate fervor, and the like. This is why *personal piety*, not having any intrinsic connection with stigmata, cannot serve as a norm to determine whether, in a given case, they come from God or not.

Third solution: We must attribute stigmatization to natural causes as long as the *contrary has not been proved.* This attitude is definitely in line with the spirit of the Church, which has never

---

[3] Benedict XIV, *De Servorum Dei Beatificatione et de Beatorum Canonizatione,* Book III, Chap. 45, n. 8; Chap. 42, nn. 1, 5; Chap. 44, nn. 8, 9.

wished to settle this problem categorically. In the official document treating of the heroicity of the virtues of St. Gemma Galgani, the Church refused most resolutely to pass judgment on the origin of the marvelous phenomena (visions, ecstasies, stigmatization) which abound in the life of this great saint. Here are the words of the document: *Nullo tamen iudicio lato per praesens decretum (quod quidem numquam fieri solet) de supernaturalitate charismatum Servae Dei.*[4] Thus the Church leaves us complete liberty to accept or reject a divine origin of the stigmata of St. Gemma Galgani, and of all other persons concerning whom she has not made any pronouncement, as she appears to have done (at least indirectly) with regard to the stigmata of St. Francis of Assisi.[5]

The Church's prudent reserve in the matter of stigmatization is simply an application in a particular field of a general and well-established principle of Christian philosophy: *Non est recurrendum ad causam primam ubi sufficiunt causae secundae* — we must not have recourse to causes which are not strictly necessary. When we have a job that can be done by ten workmen, common sense tells us not to send for a hundred. Now, prudence and common sense are of universal application. In the concrete case which concerns us here, we must first of all prove that natural forces are *incapable of* producing stigmatization before we are allowed to attribute it to a miracle. Then and only then will we have shown that the intervention of God in the production of stigmata is not only possible (which, of course, we admit), but absolutely *necessary*. Science does not consider mere possibilities; it endeavors to discover *necessary* connections. It is quite possible, for example, for a tile to fall from a roof and strike a pedestrian. But if a person, for fear of such a *possibility*, would resolve never to leave his house, he would be

---

[4] *Acta S. Sedis*, 1932, p. 57 — "However, there is no general judgment through the present decree (which indeed is never the case) concerning the supernatural charisms of the Servant of God."

[5] If the Church has — as some writers hold — actually recognized the stigmatization of St. Francis as "supernatural," she certainly did not intend by this to settle the general *possibility* of natural stigmata, i.e., she does not oblige us to believe that under *no* circumstances can it be brought about naturally.

considered abnormal, pathological. The positive sciences are not concerned with a simple possibility; they are concerned with the necessity inherent in the data. They search for law, and law implies necessity.

Consequently the statement of the problem concerning the origin of stigmatization takes the following form: "Is it *necessary* that God intervene in a miraculous manner in the development of stigmatization?"

Some outstanding modern theologians caution us not to be too hasty in affirming such a necessity. The psychological and physiological sciences, they say, do not appear to be sufficiently advanced to allow us to take a decisive stand as to the possibility of natural stigmata. The progress of the medical and psychophysiological sciences may one day raise serious objections to a theory which considers stigmatization as a miracle.[6]

Several modern theologians are not content with this *negative* attitude. They believe positively that stigmatization can be explained *without a direct* miraculous intervention on the part of God. Among them we find such names as Th. Coconnier, O.P.,[7] H. Thurston, S.J.,[8] J. Lindworsky, S.J.,[9] A. F. Ludwig,[10] G. Wunderle,[11] Zimmer,[12] W. Moock,[13] M. Waldmann,[14] L. Lenz,[15] and so on.

---

[6] A. Poulain, S.J., *Des grâces d'oraison*, Paris, 1909, Chap. 31, p. 582. Also Thomas Coconnier, O.P., *L'hypnotisme franc*, Paris, 1903 (3 ed.).

[7] *Op. cit.*

[8] "Some Physical Phenomena of Mysticism," *Month*, 1919, Vol. 134, pp. 39 ff., 144 ff., 243 ff., 289 ff.; "The Latest Stigmatica," *Month*, 1927, Vol. 149, p. 545 ff.; "The Problem of Stigmatization," *Studies*, 1933, Vol. 22, p. 221 ff.; "A Little Known Stigmatica," *Month*, 1933, Vol. 162, pp. 125 ff., 205 ff.

[9] "Gedankenkraft," *Stimmen der Zeit*, 1928, Vol. 115, p. 29.

[10] "Stigmatisation," in M. Buchberger's *Kirchl. Handlexikon*, Freiburg, 1912, Vol. 2.

[11] *Die Stigmatisierte von Konnersreuth*, Eichstätt, 1927; *Zur Psychologie der Stigmatisation*, Paderborn, 1928.

[12] "Über Stigmatisation und ihre Erklärung," *Pastor Bonus*, 1927, Vol. 38, p. 343.

[13] *Eine Studie zu den Stigmatisationserscheinungen*, Hochland, 1930, Vol. 27, p. 306.

[14] "Stigmatisation," *Lexikon für Theologie*, Vol. IX, Freiburg, 1937; "Zum Problem der Stigmatisation," *Theologisch-Praktische Quartalschrift*, 1939, pp. 558–574.

[15] "Die Stigmatisierte von Konnersreuth," *Pastor Bonus*, 1927, Vol. 38, p. 433 ff.

Having recalled the general principles which guide us in our *method* of research, we shall now consider the concrete case of Theresa Neumann. Many studies treating of the phenomena of Theresa make the following assertion: Theresa Neumann's stigmata cannot be healed by any remedy, they persist "in spite of every curative method."[16] The reader is thus led to believe that every possible treatment has been applied to her wounds. This implication is certainly misleading, for on only two occasions did a physician (Dr. Seidl) apply salve to Theresa's stigmata. And on each occasion the application was removed a few hours after the doctor had left the house.[17] All that can be said is that "some medicine applied to the stigmata, for some hours, did not remove them." To say that "no curative method" can efface them is to draw a conclusion not warranted by the premises.

It is also helpful to know the attitude of the stigmatized person with regard to his stigmata and how he conducts himself with respect to them. St. Francis of Assisi concealed his stigmata most carefully from others.[18] We can be certain that he did not make them deliberately in order to derive some advantage from them. Theresa Neumann, on the contrary, readily shows them to her visitors,[19] and — what is more serious — sometimes without even being asked to do so.[20] She speaks about them fre-

---

[16] Teodorowicz, *Mystical Phenomena in the Life of Theresa Neumann* (St. Louis: Herder, 1940), p. 297. The writer says this of Christian stigmatization in general, but his application to Theresa Neumann is obvious.

[17] We have mentioned this fact in Part I. Dr. Seidl complained: "Despite my instructions not to remove the bandages, Father Naber yielded to the wishes of Theresa Neumann and removed them" (Lehmke, *Die Stigmatisierte von Konnersreuth,* p. 98).

[18] Cf. S. Bonaventure, *Legenda S. Francisci,* Chap. XIII, nn. 5, 8, *Opera Omnia,* 1898, pp. 543, 544.

[19] If more recently Theresa has shown greater reserve in this matter, and exposes her stigmata only to those who are sympathetic to her, it is because of the positive prohibition imposed by her pastor. The motive for this prohibition was the scandal caused by Theresa's alacrity in showing her stigmata. History knows a great number of persons who fabricated their stigmata themselves. The most famous among them are two nuns of the sixteenth century, Magdalena de la Cruz and Maria de la Visitacion. They were both sentenced by the Inquisition to lifelong imprisonment and other extremely severe penalties.

[20] A friend of mine (Rev. J. S.) wrote to me recently that he had the privilege of speaking for two hours with Theresa Neumann (on January 10, 1946). After

quently and is clearly preoccupied with them. This attitude has scandalized many people and called forth severe criticism in some publications. And rightly so, for history records some frauds with self-inflicted stigmatization. Personally, we do not consider Theresa a fraud;[21] but she is so absorbed in her wounds that she looks at them continually and touches them frequently, which may — involuntarily and even unconsciously — contribute to their persistence and perhaps even to their development.[22] We all know individuals who constantly pick at their sores, to such an extent that even slight lesions heal with great difficulty. Their fingers, attracted like a magnet to the pole, are constantly drawn toward these spots, scratching and irritating them more or less unconsciously. For some emotional temperaments, the very resolution to avoid irritating the wounds only strengthens the tendency.[23]

To rule out definitely the possibility of Theresa irritating her stigmata (unconsciously), it would be advisable to conduct a series of careful observations, such as has been done in similar cases. Father Debreyne, O.Cist.Ref., tells us that in 1840 sealed bandages were placed on the hands of one such person in order to ascertain whether the stigmata were the effect of mechanical irritation.[24] For the same reason an ecclesiastical commission enclosed Louise Lateau's hands in gloves securely fastened and sealed. Later (1875), Dr. Warlomont, acting in behalf of the Belgian Academy of Medicine, enclosed her arm in a special

---

about a half hour, she *asked* him whether he would like to see her stigmata. When he answered in the affirmative, she immediately removed the mittens from her hands and showed him the wounds.

[21] Theresa's friends say her readiness to show her stigmata is due to her simplicity and kindness.

[22] When the bandages placed by Dr. Seidl were removed from her hands and feet, Theresa is said to have asked St. Thérèse, not indeed to take away her stigmata, but simply to advise her how to act in their regard. This detail is most interesting. The extraordinary pain she felt when her wounds were treated with "a perfectly nonirritating aluminum oxide" (Lehmke, *op. cit.*, p. 78) is also intriguing. A critic can hardly avoid wondering whether this exaggerated pain might not have been caused by *her fear of losing the stigmata.*

[23] Such a resolution merely accentuates the attention of these people on themselves.

[24] *Essai sur la Théologie morale*, Bruxelles, 1846.

glass apparatus. By means of such controls it was proved that her stigmata bled spontaneously. Three centuries earlier similar precautions were taken in examining the stigmata of St. Lucy of Narni. Would not some such procedure be called for at Konnersreuth, the more so since Theresa's skin has a tendency to erupt easily? A simple pressing of one foot against the other (as often occurs in insomniacs like Theresa) could produce a pathological condition of the skin.

These preliminary observations enable us better to examine some of the theories advanced to explain stigmatization *naturally*. First, there are those who claim that the efflux from the wounds is not true blood but a bloodlike *sweat*. This opinion might have had some plausibility in the days before chemical analysis, but today it is inadmissible. Chemical analysis has proved that at Konnersreuth real blood is shed, not merely reddish perspiration.[25] This theory can be refuted even without chemical analysis. Reddish sweat, no more than ordinary perspiration, does not flow from deep lesions of the epidermis. Its reddish color is due to the presence of *micrococcus prodigiosus*. In Theresa's case the skin first breaks out in little pustules; these rupture and expose the corium; blood then begins to flow.[26]

Another hypothesis admits that real blood flows from Theresa's wounds, but suggests that she herself causes the bleeding by *mechanical* means. In other words, she is a *fraud*. This theory cannot be accepted for the following reasons: (1) the bleeding starts *spontaneously*. This was observed by a number of physicians, some of whom observed it through a magnifying glass. (2) Artificial means could not easily produce such a quantity of blood without leaving telltale scars, for example, in the conjunctiva of the eyes. (3) Instead of blood, a reddish, serous liquid flows from the wound in her side. To produce this by artificial means would be a difficult task. (4) The wounds show no tendency to fester. Artificially induced bleeding would inevi-

---

[25] Cf. *Münchener medizinische Wochenschrift*, Nov. 18, 1927.

[26] Cf. F. L. Schleyer, *Die Stigmatisation mit Blutmalen*, Hannover, 1948, p. 110; Dr. Lefebvre, "Louise Lateau," *Étude médicale*, Part III, Art. 1.

tably become infected. (5) The transformation which the stigmata of the hands undergo toward the close of the ecstasy correspond perfectly to Theresa's somatic condition at this phase. (6) The two weeks' observation of Theresa by the nursing sisters (in 1927) ruled out "the hypothesis of deliberately induced bleeding."[27]

At this point, we would like to mention a fact which might tend to weaken the above arguments. Professor Martini, director of the medical clinic of the University of Bonn, observed Theresa Neumann from March 22–23, 1928, in the presence of Bishop Buchberger of Ratisbon and his suffragan, Bishop Kierl. He was assisted by Professors Killermann, Hilgenreiner, and Stoeckl. His main interest was to observe the *bleeding* which occurs during Theresa's ecstasy. Despite all efforts, he detected only "stagnant blood" on her wounds and face. "He could never see blood *flowing* from her eyes and hands." Theresa's repeated insistence, after 2:50 p.m., that he and his assistants should leave the room and return later "because nothing else would be happening until five o'clock" made him wonder. His suspicions were strongly aroused when, at 3:05 p.m., he was dismissed from the room at the very moment when, as he discovered later, a new layer of blood was to cover that which was already coagulated. He was forced to leave the room again between 8 and 8:25 p.m., and a third time at about 11:30 p.m.

Despite all protests of Professor Martini and the other members of the commission, all without exception had to leave Theresa's room during the intervals mentioned above. They were dismissed at times by Theresa herself, sometimes by her parents. The latter forced them to leave on the pretext that either the air was getting foul and that it was necessary to ventilate the room, which was untrue, or that "Theresa needed a complete hour of rest," which occurred at noon. From this Professor Martini concludes: "The fact that the observers had to

---

[27] Cf. *Münchener medizinische Wochenschrift*, Nov. 18, 1927; *Revue Générale de clinique et thérapeutique*, July 5, 1930, p. 11 ff.; Teodorowicz, *op. cit.*, pp. 284–285.

leave on two or three occasions just at the time when a new flow of blood was to cover the wounds aroused the suspicion that during that time something had to be done which must not be observed. No more was I pleased by Theresa's frequent manipulations under the bed clothing." Professor Martini saw Theresa "two or three times pull the bed clothes up over her so that only her head was more or less visible. Beneath the sheet she moved her arms, and sometimes raised her leg so high under the covers that her knee appeared at the left edge of the bed and her left foot was hanging out.[28] I was very much struck by such a strange series of occurrences. They have compelled me to adopt an attitude of the greatest reserve toward these phenomena."[29]

The publication of these observations aroused the keenest interest among all the experts who had been studying Theresa Neumann's stigmatization. How was this report to be reconciled with the statement published the previous year by the *Münchener medizinische Wochenschrift?* Some experts favored the hypothesis of a "pious fraud"; a hypothesis upheld explicitly by Professor Martini himself. According to his theory, the Konners-

---

[28] Dr. Seidl told Martini that he had observed the commencement of the bleeding from the wound in the side. Martini pointed out that he was in error, for Dr. Seidl did not see the skin "in its normal state." By the time they began their observation there was already present a streak about one inch in length, whose origin had not been observed.

Dr. Fröhlich states that he had seen a continuous bleeding from the wounds of Theresa during a five-hour period (April 15, 1943), but he does not affirm to have seen the *commencement* of this bleeding (cf. *Konnersreuth Heute. Schau eines Arztes*, p. 35). He asserts also that Professor Martini and his collaborators were ordered by Theresa's parents to leave her room on account of her "severe urinary trouble" (*durch starken Harndrang*) on that day (*ibid.*, p. 35). Unfortunately, Theresa's parents tried to justify their behavior in quite a different way, as we have just seen. Moreover, it remains to be explained why "the observers had to leave . . . just at the time when a new flow was to cover the wounds" of Theresa.

[29] The complete report of Professor Martini's observations at Konnersreuth may be read in Deutsch, *Ärztliche Kritik an Konnersreuth! Wunder oder Hysteria?*, pp. 13–31; Dr. Poray-Madeyski, *Le cas de la visionnaire stigmatisée — Thérèse Neumann de Konnersreuth*, pp. 117–131; Hilda Graef, *The Case of Therese Neumann*, pp. 53–64. Dr. Peter Radlo tried to refute Martini's conclusions (cf. *Trug oder Wahrheit* [Karlsruhe: Badenia, 1938]). We do not think he was successful, nor do we believe that the conclusions of Martini are contrary to morals.

reuth phenomena had been advertised too hastily. But once set in motion it was too late to retract, since not only Theresa's reputation and that of her family would be in jeopardy, but also, as they thought, the honor of the Church herself. Then, too, an admission of deceit might be the cause of great scandal to so many people to whom these portents had been of spiritual value. Thus she could quite easily convince herself that she was not obliged to make such an avowal, and the same might be said of her parents if they had countenanced such an irregularity at the outset.

But how could Father Naber be an accomplice to a pious fraud? To this Professor Martini replies: "This objection is not conclusive. For we cannot tell to what extent Theresa considers herself free from blame, provided she feels that all her activities are pleasing to God and useful to Jesus Christ and His Church, even if she must help events in one way or the other. Here we must never lose sight of Theresa's definitely hysterical constitution, about which I cannot entertain the least doubt, especially after my conversation with Dr. Seidl."[30]

Relying on Professor Martini's report, Father M. Waldmann, professor of moral and mystical theology at Ratisbon, believes that "it was only later that someone at Konnersreuth began to 'help the miracle,' because people would not be satisfied with dried-up stigmata. They wanted to see them bleed."[31] This is an attempt to reconcile the observations of Professor Martini with those cited in the medical journal, and advances the following arguments: In the course of Martini's observation, Professor Killermann was permitted to take a sample of Theresa's bleeding with a wad of cotton.[32] An analysis of this blood showed that it was *menstrual blood,* and not ordinary blood.[33] We must admit that the theory is impressive, but it is far from settling the problem definitely, for it concedes that at least *in the beginning*

---

[30] Cf. Deutsch, *op. cit.,* pp. 29–30; also Poray-Madeyski, *op. cit.,* pp. 129–130.
[31] He expressed this opinion in a letter to the author in 1951.
[32] Cf. Deutsch, *op. cit.,* p. 20.
[33] Cf. Hilda Graef, *op. cit.,* p. 60 *n.*

Theresa's stigmata bled "spontaneously," and with that concession the whole problem returns.[34]

A third group of scholars would ascribe the onset of the stigmata either to scurvy or to complementary menstruation. What can we say to this? Scurvy is an organic disease and therefore subject to organic determinism, governed by physical causes. The course of this ailment is lacking in the plasticity which characterizes Theresa's stigmata, which bleed or fail to bleed according to a schedule based on purely moral considerations. Thus she will bleed on no other day but Friday, but not on the Fridays of the joyful liturgical seasons (Christmas and Easter).

As to the theory of "complementary menstruation," we must confess we face an enigma. Among the hundreds of individuals who have been stigmatized there are only two definite instances of men bearing the perfect external marks of the five wounds;[35] all the others were women.

A still more significant fact is that the stigmata bleed copiously and *periodically* on successive Fridays only in women. What is the reason for this astonishing selectivity? An investigation of Theresa's stigmatization brings out the following interesting circumstances: The appearance of the stigmata was preceded for some years (1918–1926) by a definite halt in menstruation. Was the blocking of the menstrual flow a mere coincidence, or was it perhaps the real *cause* of the stigmatic bleeding? This is the question,[36] and the question becomes all the more involved

---

[34] The learned professor agrees with us on this point.

[35] They are St. Francis of Assisi and Padre Pio of Foggia. Cf. H. Thurston, S.J., "The Problem of Stigmatization," *Studies*, June, 1933, p. 225. Dr. Imbert-Goubeyre, in his celebrated book on stigmatization, mentions forty-one men. But, as Fr. Thurston says, this book "is irritating both from its entire lack of historical criticism and from its pretension to constitute a complete record" (*ibid.*, p. 223 *n.*). Moreover, Dr. Imbert-Goubeyre includes among his stigmatics even those who are said to have felt the pain of the wounds but had no external marks or only imperfect ones. Cf. also Maurice Apte, *Les stigmatisés*, Paris, 1903, p. 12; Le Gac, *Sur un cas de lésion figurative*, Bordeaux, 1932, p. 13; P. Debognie, *Études Carmélitaines*, Oct., 1936.

[36] As was stated above, Theresa Neumann has not had a menstrual flow since April, 1918, i.e., since the fire, with the exception of the month of July, 1918.

when we remember that two years before the apparition of the stigmata (in 1924) Theresa Neumann was subject to some sort of hemorrhaging from her eyes.[37]

In seeking to solve this problem, it would be interesting to determine whether the stigmata continue to bleed in a woman who has reached the menopause, or who, through medical treatment, has recovered normal menstruation. The question, which we stressed emphatically in our first study on Theresa Neumann (1931),[38] took on new interest when Father Naber told 10,000 visitors at Konnersreuth on Good Friday, 1951: "Until midnight of Holy Thursday everything was as it has been these past twenty-five years. She had the vision of Jesus on the Mount of Olives, which brought sweat to her body and caused blood to drip from her eyes. Then, all of a sudden, just before midnight, her eyes stopped bleeding. She endured further tortures in her visions of the Saviour's passion, and experienced mental and physical pains as she had done before. But the bleeding had stopped completely."[39]

Now this fact, while of great interest, is far from being decisive:[40] first, because we do not know whether Theresa's

In 1920 (or 1921) menstruation was produced under the influence of a "very strong medicine" which she obtained from a charlatan, Frederick Heinzl of Neustadt. But this treatment caused another malady and had to be abandoned. Since then menstruation has ceased entirely.

[37] Cf. Gerlich, *Die stigmatisierte Therese Neumann von Konnersreuth,* t. I, pp. 81–82. Did this bleeding occur at other periods of her life? Theresa does not know. Professor Franz L. Schleyer, in his study of stigmatics, notes that they are often subject, from childhood, to hemorrhage from the nose, gums, ears, stomach, intestines, and bladder (*op. cit.,* pp. 22, 24, 27–28, 33, 35, 42, 104, 113).

[38] *Konnersreuth . . .* , Kraków, 1931, p. 168. Cf. also our lecture at the Academy of Medicine, Rio de Janeiro (1940).

[39] Cf. *Time,* Apr. 9, 1951, p. 56; *The Register,* Apr. 1, 1951. We are told that on Good Friday, 1952, the bleeding recurred.

[40] The normal menstrual flow varies in quantity from five to seven ounces. Women in a weakened condition generally lose more blood than those who are healthy and strong. Abundant food, physical exercise, and warm weather increase the flow. The regular menstrual cycle averages about four weeks. Theresa, who bleeds from her stigmata every Friday, would experience a higher loss of blood than the average woman. However, we must not forget the very important fact that Theresa suffers no passion ecstasies during Advent, the Christmas and Easter seasons (the latter extending to Trinity Sunday), nor on Fridays on which joyful feasts occur. Consequently she is spared stigmatic bleeding for about five months of the year.

stigmata have ceased bleeding forever; second, because, as Carl Schroeder notes in his remarkable study on complementary menstruation, "It is impossible to attribute every periodic bleeding to menstruation, for such can take place in males also."[41]

Bleeding, however, is not the most important element in stigmatization, for the latter can exist without any loss of blood. The most important character of the stigmata is the *meaning* they express and the *idea* which they incarnate. The stigmata are obviously formed with the intention of imitating the wounds of Christ. This meaning appears from their location, dimension, and shape. Any theory which fails to explain this meaning leaves out the principal or, to use Aristotelian terminology, the "formal element" of stigmatization and is therefore inadequate. The true problem of stigmatization is that of determining the idea, or intention, underlying the stigmata.

A priori we might offer two possible answers to the problem: first, that God, by a special divine intervention, that is, by a miracle, produces the stigmata in the human body; second, that the human person himself, by means of natural powers, channelizes certain physiological processes which result in the wounds called stigmata. Which of these two hypotheses is the more acceptable? Following the principles expressed previously, we will choose the first solution only when the *second* is proved conclusively *insufficient*.

St. Francis de Sales, in his *Treatise on the Love of God*, endeavors to solve the problem of the origin of the stigmatization of St. Francis of Assisi. He writes: "This seraphic mortal, seeing the lively representation of the Crucified on a seraph, who appeared to him on Mount Alverno . . . was strongly affected

---

For this reason the attempt of certain authors to refute the theory of complementary menstruation by appealing to the "extraordinary quantity of blood lost in ecstasy" is of doubtful value. The quantity does not seem to surpass the normal amount to any great degree. Let us note in passing that the organs of complementary menstruation are usually the stomach, lungs, nose, eyelids, bladder, and sometimes the ears and membranes of the mouth.

[41] *Handbuch der Krankheiten der weiblichen Geschlechtsorgane*, 12 ed., Leipzig, 1898, p. 124. According to F. L. Schleyer, Angela della Pace received the bleeding stigmata in her hands, feet, and side at the age of nine! (*Op. cit.*, p. 35.)

with the sight, penetrated with the sweetest consolation, and at the same time, pierced with profound compassion. . . . He felt himself suddenly transfixed by the sword which had pierced the heart of the spotless Virgin. . . . He interiorly endured almost the same pain as he would have suffered had he been crucified with his Saviour. . . . This vision made on St. Francis an inconceivable impression of mingled love and grief. . . . Thus was the soul of St. Francis transformed, as it were, into Jesus and nailed to the cross; and then, exercising the influence of his seraphic soul over his body, he occasioned it to feel all the agony of the wounds inflicted on it, suffering in the very same places which had been the theater of the torments of Jesus Christ. . . . The effects produced by the imagination when it is inflamed with ardent love are most wonderful. . . . The imagination of women during their pregnancy . . . is capable of imprinting on the bodies of their children the representation of any object they desire with ardor.[42] An ardent imagination for but the space of one night can cause the revolution of the humors, turn the hair gray, and considerably injure the health.

"Divine love produced a similar effect on St. Francis; it caused his sufferings to pass from the interior to the exterior; the same arrow which had pierced his heart transfixed his body also. It is true that love which only exists in the heart was not sufficient to imprint the stigmata on the flesh and to effect the opening of the wounds; but the seraph supplied this defect by darting on the saint rays so bright and piercing, that they performed on the body what love had only been able to accomplish on the soul; that is, they engraved on the hands, the feet, and the side of St. Francis the wounds of his crucified Saviour, the marks and pains of which he retained during the remainder of his life.

"Rays of light were the instruments employed in making this incision, not the sword, to prove that the wounds of this seraphic

---

[42] St. Thomas Aquinas had expressed the same idea centuries before: "Imaginatio est vis quaedam in organo corporali: unde ad speciem imaginativam mutatur spiritus corporeus, in quo fundatur vis formativa, quae operatur in semine; et ideo interdum aliqua mutatio fit in prole ex imaginatione parentis in ipso coitu si sit fortis" (*De Malo*, q. IV, art. 8, ad 13).

man had been inflicted by divine love! How ardent his love! How intense the pain which diluted in bitterness the sweets of love."[43]

We consider this passage very important, because it not only shows us the mind of St. Francis de Sales, but also that the stigmata of St. Francis of Assisi were the effect of love, the love of compassion, a love most tender, a love which St. Bonaventure called *"caritas nimia, compassiva dulcedo, compassivus dolor."*[44] According to St. Francis de Sales, the role of the Seraph is limited to helping nature open exteriorly the wounds already organized in the body by the soul, the substantial form of the body. The Saint does not state clearly whether he considers such intervention absolutely necessary, because it is not clear from the text whether he is speaking of the intrinsic causes of the phenomenon or of the historical reasons which the earlier biographers of St. Francis have handed down to us. At any rate, the holy doctor explains the other phenomena accompanying the stigmata, for example, the physical pain, the alterations produced by the wounds, in accordance with natural laws as they were understood in his day. In the manuscript of the first edition of the *Treatise* he wrote that the stigmatization of St. Francis of Assisi was a "miracle," but in his final draft he omitted this word. This omission we consider highly significant.[45]

The theory of St. Francis de Sales (abstracting from the particular examples he alleges) conforms remarkably with modern psychology which is constantly learning more about the tremendous effects of the emotions on the human organism. These effects are the more striking when the organism has acquired greater plasticity as a result of a neurotic condition, or of heightened suggestibility to which it is subject either temporarily

---

[43] *Traité de l'amour de Dieu,* Book VI, Chap. XV.

[44] *Legenda S. Francisci,* Chap. XIII, n. 3 (S. Bonaventure, *Opera Omnia,* Ad Claras Aquas, 1898, t. VIII, p. 542; n. 10, p. 545).

[45] The same explanation of stigmata, at least in general outlines, is found in some fourteenth-century writers, for example, Francesco Petrarca (in a letter to the physician Thomas de Garbo, Lib. VIII, ep. sen. in 3a) and Jan van Ruysbroek (*Zierde der geistlichen Hochzeit,* Lib. II, cap. 48). The same explanation of the stigmata was also given by Peter Pomponatius (1462–1524).

or habitually, whether induced artificially or spontaneously.

Parrot relates of a woman who shed tears of blood under the stress of great grief. Then she would experience painful hemorrhaging of the breast, the lower eyelids, the knees, the hands, and sometimes of the forehead.[46] Dr. Apte witnessed hysterical persons break out in skin eruptions and reddish blisters after any emotional shock. Burot and Bouru were able to produce a bloody sweat by suggesting it to a hysteric. One of these investigators traced his name on the shoulder of the same patient with a blunt stylus and told him: "This afternoon at four o'clock, you will fall asleep, and immediately afterwards blood will ooze from the lines I have traced on your body." At the hour indicated the lines began to redden and some drops of blood oozed from them.

By means of suggestion made during hypnosis or even during the waking state, it is possible to produce fever, accelerate or retard the rate of heart beat, relax or contract the muscles of the body, destroy hunger sensations, modify the circulation of the blood and basal metabolism, and, finally, to bring about such organic effects as redness, pimples, and blisters.

The experiments which have been conducted to produce this last phenomenon are of particular interest to us. In 1886 Focachon succeeded in producing blisters on the body of a hysterical woman. In 1888 Jendrassik, in a rigorously controlled experiment, produced a blister on a certain Ilma S. five hours after the suggestion had been given. In 1890 Rybalkin told a sixteen-year-old girl that on awakening from her hypnotic trance she would burn herself by accidentally touching a liquid (which, in fact, was cold), and that soon afterward a burn would appear on her arm. Three hours later a reddish swelling and erythemic papules appeared on the spot indicated; the following day two blisters developed. In 1906 Doswald and Kreibich hypnotized Dr. U., one of their assistants, touched his forearm with the tip of a match, and told him that a

---

[46] Parrot, *Études sur la sueur sanglante et les hémorragies névropathiques*, Paris, 1859.

blister would form on the spot. Three minutes after he awoke the spot began to redden; six minutes later a blister formed; in four hours the area was covered with dead tissue resembling gangrenous skin. The subject was not a hysteric. In 1909 Heller and Schultz, by means of hypnotic suggestion, produced erythema on the back of the hand. Six hours later (in the posthypnotic state) the spot had blistered and was covered with dead tissue. In the same year Podiapolski induced two erythemas on the body of a healthy, though easily hypnotized, peasant woman. The following day she complained of pain, which came from an open blister. Smirnoff (in 1912), Westerstrand (in 1915), Hadfield (in 1917), Schindler, and several other experimenters have employed suggestion to bring on similar phenomena in subjects, some of whom were certainly healthy.[47]

The experiments conducted by Dr. Adolph Lechler on a young woman patient, a certain Elizabeth ———, are also instructive. She presented a wide variety of symptoms: gastric disturbances, skin lesions, tremors, spitting of blood, smallpox, and the like. Dr. Lechler, succeeding in causing all these symptoms to disappear by suggestion, concluded that they were of hysterical origin. The patient's health, however, was not completely restored, for as soon as one syndrome disappeared it would be replaced by others: depression, paralysis, anorexia, visual and auditory hallucinations. He finally had recourse to hypnosis and discovered that the patient was capable of manifesting the symptoms of practically any illness of which she had heard or read. Sometimes she contracted an illness after having visited a sick person. On Good Friday, 1932, her hands and feet experienced pain after she beheld a crucifix.

Acting on this clue, Lechler decided to find out whether he could induce his patient to imitate some of the phenomena which made Theresa Neumann famous. Once while the patient was under hypnosis, he suggested that she tell herself during the night: "In the very same places in which I now feel pain,

[47] Frank A. Pattie, *The Production of Blisters by Hypnotic Suggestion,* pp. 279–291.

wounds will appear." Next morning she showed Lechler the moist wounds which had appeared during the night. He then told her that her wounds would soon become deeper, and endeavored to have her concentrate on her wounds. By noon the wounds actually were deeper. Next he told her to think continually about the tears of blood shed by Theresa Neumann, suggesting that she too would experience them. Two hours later she came to him shedding tears of blood similar to those of Theresa Neumann. Finally, he assured her that the tears of blood would disappear. They vanished forty-eight hours later.[48]

This was not the end of the experiment. Through suggestion he was able to produce on her head the stigmata of a crown of thorns, which caused her intense suffering. Later he made them bleed. He ordered her to think, during the night, of Christ carrying His cross. As a result her shoulder became painfully inflamed and her body assumed a leaning position. All the phenomena disappeared under the influence of a new suggestion.[49]

Lechler observed that the effectiveness of his suggestion was generally in proportion to the degree of concentration attained by the patient. He attended the young woman for four years and, together with his nurses, kept a close observation.[50]

---

[48] There are some differences between the stigmata of Elizabeth and those of Theresa Neumann. The former were superficial; the latter are deep. The former disappeared in a short time; the latter last for many years and do not show any tendency to disappear. But these differences are rather *accidental*. The stigmata of Elizabeth were superficial because they had no time to develop. Indeed, they were checked in their evolution by the contrary suggestion given by Lechler.

In October, 1949, a meeting of the *Freie Forschungsgesellschaft für Psychologie und Grenzgebiete des Wissens* was held, and many different theories on the above experiment were presented.

[49] *Das Rätsel von Konnersreuth im Lichte eines neuen Falles von Stigmatisation*, Elberfeld, 1933.

[50] It is true that Lechler's experiments, limited as they were, are not conclusive proof that stigmatization is purely *natural*. Nevertheless, they are of some value, and we cannot agree with the opinion (as, for example, Piwinski) that "Lechler was a victim of mystification and fraud." According to Father Waldmann, "This opinion is but a fable (*ein Märchen*) invented . . . to eliminate an important fact of a stigmatisation produced by means of hypnosis" (a letter to the author, July 9, 1952). This opinion seems to him "ridiculous" (*lächerlich*), and maintains that Lechler discontinued his experiments only because of the health of his patient. Wunderle, a remarkable scholar, was "quite satisfied" with Lechler's experiments

The stigmata of Arthur Otto Moock, a timber merchant in Hamburg, is an interesting case. After an automobile accident in May, 1928, he experienced strange phenomena, and seven years later (1935) the wounds of the crown of thorns appeared on his head. Some time afterward the other stigmata also appeared on his hands, feet, and side. They seem to be genuine stigmata and not *artefacta*. However, they lack a religious meaning, for Moock is a Protestant, and his wounds are not a result of an intense religious experience or of an active participation in the suffering of the Saviour. He does not have any particular devotion to Christ, and he considers his suffering an annoyance from which he eagerly desires to be freed. Besides the stigmata, Moock also has a bad heart condition and a defect of the spine. For this reason he was never called into military service.

The bleeding of Moock's stigmata is preceded by a violent headache and a strong pressure on both sides of the head; this is followed by the vision of Christ approaching him from a distance, speaking to him some consoling words, and slowly disappearing into space.[51] His senses, particularly those of sight and hearing, are occasionally impaired: he often sees himself beside or opposite himself, and objects, such as chairs and tables, sometimes appear double, sometimes transparent. He has also the gift of clairvoyance, often foretelling visits of friends, letters which are to arrive, and the like. He goes without sleep, and has lost half his normal weight.

All the above-mentioned incidents and experiments weaken to some extent the argument against the possibility of natural stigmatization. This is not all. If the stigmata are natural, we are asked, why is it not always possible to produce them voluntarily?

---

and method which he studied in Lechler's hospital. This "fable" appeared for the first time in Dr. Witry's book *Die Resl* (Saarbrücken, 1934, p. 16). It was repeated by W. Schamoni (*Stigmata, Hysterie oder Gnade* [Wiesbaden: Credoverlag, 1951], p. 50), F. A. Höcht (*Grösse, Erhabenheit und Beurteilung der Stigmatisation,* Waldsassen, 1938, p. 75), Dr. Peter Radlo (*op. cit.*), and others. Dr. Witry founded his unfavorable opinion of Lechler on the testimony of a "materialist physician." The value of this anonymous witness should be carefully examined.

[51] Professor Georg Anschütz, *Nord-West Illustrierte,* July 23, 1949.

Such an argument violates the fundamental laws of logic, because it draws a conclusion more extensive than the premises allow. Actually there are many perfectly *natural* phenomena which lie beyond the possibility of voluntary effort. For the will to produce any effect, all necessary *conditions* must be present. Can we, by a mere act of the will, produce in another person such a compassionate love for Christ, a love so intense, that his soul, so to say, will melt with love? Can we inspire him with an ecstatic desire to share in the Saviour's torments? Can we excite his imagination to such a degree that he has an immediate intuition of the sacred wounds? Are we able to have our subject focus his entire attention on some subject "chosen at will" and maintain it at a high degree of psychological tension? We cannot even do this with a hypnotized subject, for the hypnotized person does not suffer complete loss of liberty, nor does he accept every suggestion or believe everything he is told. "Often enough," Pierre Janet tells us, "the somnabulist carries out orders merely to be obliging; first of all he generally wishes to please the hypnotizer and not to contradict him; then again he is generally in such a state of indolence that he does not desire to offer unnecessary resistance; finally he finds some amusement in his experiences and is often anxious to make a success of them. . . ."[52]

Wolff and Rosenthal maintain that "The hypnotized person is always able to break the trance." He is always aware that he is "participating in an experiment and that the experimenter wishes to get certain results."[53] Professor Erickson, after numerous experiments in hypnotic suggestion, forms the following conclusion: "Instead of blind, submissive, automatic, unthinking obedience and acquiescence to the hypnotist and the acceptance of carefully given suggestions and commands, the subjects demonstrated a full capacity and ability for self-protection, ready and complete understanding, with a critical judgment,

---

[52] *L'automatisme psychologique,* 9 ed. (Paris: Alcan, 1921), p. 177.

[53] B. Wolff and R. Rosenthal, *Hypnotism Comes of Age* (New York: The Bobbs-Merrill Co., 1948), pp. 95, 98.

avoidance, evasion, or complete rejection of commands."[54] Some authors believe that the subject can be made to do whatever the hypnotist wishes to the extent that even criminal acts can be easily obtained through hypnosis. Even W. R. Wells defends this opinion. But the more rigorously controlled experiments prove that this assumption is wrong. If the subjects appear willing to attempt certain criminal actions, they are really not in earnest. They are well aware that the hypnotist, whom they trust absolutely, will not actually demand them.

Thus we see the difficulty of inducing stigmata in a psychological laboratory, for the sublime religious symbolism of the stigmata is beyond the understanding of most practitioners. Incapable as they are of producing in their subjects the powerful emotions of which St. Francis de Sales speaks, the psychologists are not able to bring about the psychological conditions necessary for the appearance of the stigmata.

Let us now consider some *positive* reasons in favor of the theory which would explain the appearance of stigmata by means of the emotions.

1. Stigmata are strictly connected with *ecstasy* which, considered psychologically, is an *emotional* state. There is no instance where stigmatization has occurred independently of ecstasy. All scholars agree on this point. Some go so far as to say that "ecstasy forms the touchstone of stigmatization. Only that stigmatization is genuine which is born of ecstasy and is nourished by it, whose wounds open while in an ecstatic state. . . . The stigmatic wounds are explained by and through the ecstasy. . . . The stigmatization and ecstasy form a harmonious unity. . . . Stigmata that are not born of ecstasy are to be looked upon as suspect."[55]

---

[54] Em. H. Erickson, "An Experimental Investigation of the Possible Antisocial Use of Hypnosis," *Modern Hypnosis*, ed. by L. Kuhn and S. Russo (New York: Psychological Library Publishers, 1947), pp. 277–278.

[55] Teodorowicz, *op. cit.*, p. 304. My argumentation here moves on *historical* ground. History does not know any case of genuine (that is, not fabricated by the individual himself) stigmatization that appeared independently of the ecstatic state.

Theresa Neumann is no exception to the rule. All her stigmata appeared for the first time in an ecstasy during which she witnessed the passion of Christ. Those of her stigmata which still bleed do so only during ecstasy, and the others are inflamed only on the days of her ecstasies.

Then, too, the stigmata do not make their appearance at the very beginning of the ecstasy, but only after it has lasted for a notable time. This fact is also demonstrated in Theresa's case. The opening of her stigmata does not coincide with the beginning of her ecstasies, nor do her tears of blood appear at her first sight of the suffering Christ, but much later.

This being the case, the question arises: If it is really God who produces the stigmata by a "miraculous" intervention, why should He have imposed the state of ecstasy as, so to speak, an indispensable condition? Ecstasy, in itself, as we shall see, does not possess any supernatural character. Why should God *never* grant the stigmata to *pie meditantibus* — to persons who contemplate the passion of Christ with all the intensity of mystical love but without ecstasy? Why did He not grant such a favor to saintly men like SS. John of the Cross, Philip Neri, John Vianney, Francis de Sales, Vincent de Paul, or Francis Xavier? They had a great devotion to Christ crucified and ardently desired to suffer much for Him! On the other hand, how many women of inferior piety nevertheless possessed the stigmata![56] Could it not be because the saints mentioned possessed a robust psychological constitution, while the stigmatized women were highly emotional?

Again, why should God *never* grant the stigmata at the very moment the ecstasy begins, but only after a notable lapse of time? And a more important question: Why should He not produce them *at once,* in their perfection, rather than *by degrees?* Several weeks before Theresa Neumann's stigmata appeared, the doctor stated that there was pronounced sensibility in the places where the wounds later developed. Theresa tells us that a few hours before the apparition of the stigmata on the back of her

---

[56] Cf. H. Thurston, S.J., *op. cit.*, pp. 225–226.

left hand (March 26, 1926) she observed a slight *reddening* there. At the time she dismissed it, thinking she had inadvertently struck her hand on something.[57] The wound on the back of her right hand developed only eight days later (April 2, 1926), and those on the palms of her hands the following year (Good Friday, 1927).[58]

These facts are difficult to reconcile with the theory which would explain the stigmata as the result of miraculous intervention. On the other hand, they are quite *understandable* in our hypothesis, for the organic functions, like all natural processes, must operate for some time in order to produce such an overt symptom as a wound. Sometimes they result in incomplete stigmata.[59]

2. Our theory is the only one able to furnish a satisfactory explanation of the fact, that *all* stigmatized persons whose life we know in some detail gave evidence of *hysteria* or related *nervous disorders* some time before the appearance of the stigmata.[60] Those who write about the stigmatization of Theresa Neumann, observes Father Thurston, pass over in silence such stigmatics as Marie Julie Jahenny, Palma Doria, Mother Constance, Juliana Weiskircher, George Marasco, and others who were victims of conversion hysteria.[61] He adds that a hysterical condition, without forming an integral part of stigmatization, constitutes its "atmosphere." He concludes: Must we really admit that God has chosen precisely such persons to manifest His miracles? The ecstasies experienced by some of them, par-

---

[57] L. Witt, *Konnersreuth im Lichte der Religion und Wissenschaft*, I, p. 304.

[58] *Ibid.*, p. 19. These facts are admitted by the Konnersreuth apologists. Cf. Teodorowicz, *op. cit.*, p. 283. The same progression has been observed in many other stigmatics. Cf. F. L. Schleyer, *op. cit.*, *passim*.

[59] Many persons have had only this kind of stigmatization, among them: Mary Beatrice Schumann, of Pfarrkirchen (✝ 1887), Pirona Hergods, of Mechlin (✝ 1472), Mary Agnes Steiner, of Nocera (✝ 1909). Cf. H. Thurston, *op. cit.*, p. 224 *n*. Many of the "stigmatized persons" named in Imbert-Goubeyre's study lacked external stigmata, at least in their complete development. Such "interior stigmata" can easily be accounted for by natural causes.

[60] Cf. also W. Jacobi, *Die Stigmatisation. Beiträge zur Psychologie der Mystik*, München, 1923.

[61] *Op. cit.*, p. 223. Cf. also Jacobi, *op. cit.*

ticularly by Elisabeth de Herkenrode and Dominica Lazzari, were simply bizarre.[62]

If stigmata really are the effects of a miracle, why is it that a nervous weakness or even hysteria seems to be a necessary condition for their appearance, if we are to believe history? Some may reply (with Father Kneller): It is because God, before allowing a person to participate in the terrible sufferings of the crucifixion, prepares them for it by lesser pains! But again the question: Why should God prepare them precisely by *nervous disorders,* above all by *hysteria?* Why would it not suffice for God to send them purely organic pains or moral sufferings?

3. Among the more eminent stigmatics, some, for example, St. Catherine of Siena, St. Catherine of Ricci, St. Joanna of Jesus and Mary, St. Veronica Juliani, Louise Lateau, had the body wound on the *left* side, just as in the case of Theresa Neumann, while many others had it on the *right* side. How can this undeniable fact be explained? We find it difficult to explain this inconsistency by a theory of miraculous intervention. God would not intervene to modify history, for Christ had the wound on one side and not on two. Our theory explains this inconsistency quite well.

Many experiments have been conducted with persons in cataleptic states, both those which have been induced artificially (by hypnotic suggestion) and those which have come about naturally (through somnabulism or some other pathological cause). In each case, when the one conducting the experiment asked the patient to repeat his movements, the movements were repeated by the patient mirror-wise. That is, when the left arm was extended, the patient invariably extended his *right* arm. Since the higher mental powers are retarded in the patient, he will react to the stimulus just as presented by the senses. Now such a retardation of the higher mental powers has been observed at times in Theresa Neumann, as was stated elsewhere.[63]

It is to be expected, therefore, that a person in this state,

---

[62] *Ibid.,* pp. 228–229.
[63] See Part I, Chap. 3.

beholding the wound of our Lord on His right side, would automatically reproduce the wound on his own left side. The result will be the same if the person in question happens to be convinced that our Saviour was actually pierced on the left side.

Has it been determined which side of our Lord was pierced with a lance? The Evangelist does not tell us. He simply writes: *Et latus ejus aperuit,* "he opened his side" (Jn. 19:34). But which side? The Church offers us no further information. The Fathers of the Church generally considered it to have been the right, and see therein a certain religious symbolism: the right side represents the Church, whence proceed the sacraments; the left side represents the rejected synagogue. In modern times the trend has been in favor of the left side, the side of the heart. Any stigmatic who accepts this viewpoint, and Theresa Neumann is one, will instinctively reproduce the wound of the left side.

Here, then, is an extremely simple solution to an enigma well-nigh insoluble by the "miracle" theory. One of our distinguished critics (G. Philips), however, argues against our position, claiming that God's purpose in granting a grace of this kind is not to provide us with historical information, but to promote piety. Whether the wound was on the right or left side has nothing to do with such a goal.

We agree that the purpose of charisms (and of Divine Revelation in general) is not to teach history or science, but to promote our salvation and increase our devotion. We have insisted on this very point elsewhere.[64] We merely inquire whether, in granting stigmata, God could not achieve His purpose just as well by conferring them on the same locality in which they were inflicted on Christ. Why should God have recourse to a kind of *illusion?* The stigmata are a living *participation* in the wounds of the Saviour and, consequently, a person who receives the wound on his right side is led to believe that Christ bore His wound on that same side. But, on the other hand, by observing that other stigmatized person bore the wound on the left side,

---

[64] *Au coeur du Spinozisme* (Paris: Desclée de Brouwer, 1952), p. 190.

he is left a prey to doubt concerning the divine origin of his stigmata. The "consolation" to which our critics attach so much importance is put to a severe test.

What we have said does not constitute any definitive proof against the divine origin of stigmatization, nor have we any intention of basing our theory on it. We merely wish to indicate a problem which has not been solved and which, together with other considerations developed here, may encourage the unprejudiced reader to give serious attention to another theory of stigmatization, one which lays great stress on the *subjective* element.

4. The theory we have chosen also explains the following fact which has confused many students of stigmatization: In some stigmatics the wounds *correspond* exactly to those depicted on the crucifix before which they are accustomed to pray. Thus the stigma of the cross on the body of Catherine Emmerich corresponded to the Y-shaped crucifix at Coesfeld before which she prayed since her childhood.[65] Moreover the shape of the stigmata varies and does not *remain* constantly the same for the same person. In Theresa Neumann, for example, the wounds are sometimes square, sometimes round.[66] According to our theory, the stigmata are the effect of a powerful *emotion* (compassionate love); they are governed, therefore, by the *idea* which evokes the emotion, and their form is determined by this idea or image.

We can go even further. We can ask whether suggestion or

---

[65] Cf. Schmoeger, *Life of Ann Catherine Emmerich* (Eng. trans.), I, p. 4. The stigmata of St. Gemma Galgani corresponded in position and shape to the wounds depicted on a crucifix before which she prayed (cf. Father Germanus, *The Life of Gemma Galgani* [Eng. trans.], p. 69).

[66] Cf. Bruno, "Notes prises à Konnersreuth," *Études Carmélitaines*, Oct., 1933, p. 166. Father Naber told Gerlich that the wounds he had seen on the back of Theresa's hands and feet (soon after their appearance) were round (cf. Gerlich, *op. cit.*, I, p. 105). Professor Ewald stated that Theresa's stigmata (on the hands) resembled a ten pfennig coin as to their shape and size. However, in the pamphlet written by Dr. Louis de Versailles (*La Semaine Sainte de 1930*), we read: "On the back of the left hand I see the head of a nail of rectangular form." Dr. van der Elst, Dr. Poray-Madeyski (*op. cit.*, pp. 65–66), and Dr. Hans Fröhlich (*op. cit.*, p. 28), confirmed the same shape of the stigmata.

autosuggestion brought on under hypnosis or an analogous mental state could perhaps bring about the same organic effects as "compassionate love." St. Francis de Sales did not take this hypothesis into consideration, for hypnosis was not known in his time. Today, however, we must face this problem.

If we consider the *effects* obtained by means of *hypnotic* suggestion, we will find them not inferior to those produced by the genuine *emotion* such as love. We have indicated some of these effects previously. Consequently we see no legitimate reason for denying that a subject under *hypnosis* might produce the same wounds as those resulting from the emotion of love.

Must we call such stigmatization "pathological"? That depends on our concept of hypnosis itself. If we agree with Charcot and his school that only hysterical persons can be hypnotized, then hypnotic stigmata would, of course, be pathological. Today, however, the value of Charcot's theory is being questioned. Many modern experimenters claim "that every normal individual can be hypnotized,"[67] provided appropriate methods are employed. E. H. Erickson says that "any really co-operative subject" can be hypnotized, "regardless of whether he is a normal person, a hysterical, neurotic, or a psychotic patient." Schiller and Wolberg hold the same view.[68] If we accept this opinion we can speak of "natural stigmata" which would not be "pathological."

How does all this apply to Theresa Neumann? To answer this question we would first have to study her "ecstatic emotion," a subject we will discuss in the following chapter. For the present we will endeavor to solve certain objections which undoubtedly will be raised. First of all, we would like to cite and answer a remark made by Theresa Neumann to a physician who suggested that her stigmata might be due to her meditation

---

[67] Samuel Kahn, *Suggestion and Hypnosis Made Practical* (Boston: Meador, 1945), p. 77; M. Bramwell, *Hypnotism: Its History, Practice and Therapy*, rev. ed., Philadelphia, 1928; Margaret Brenman and Merton M. Gill, *Hypnotherapy*, Joseph Macy Foundation, Vol. II, No. 3, 1944, pp. 30–36.

[68] B. Wolff and R. Rosenthal, *op. cit.*, p. 71. Only normal individuals are considered here.

on the passion of Christ: "Oh, according to your explanation, a poor sinner who thinks about the devil (because of his bad conscience) should grow horns on his head!" This statement is found in many accounts of Konnersreuth, and several writers consider it the best answer to our theory. We agree that it is a witty rejoinder, but it is hardly an argument against our position. We do not affirm that *thinking itself* can ever produce stigmatization. We insist that the *emotional* factor (or a particular kind of suggestion) is indispensable. And this emotion must be sufficiently *persistent* and *intense*.

In order to comprehend how a powerful emotion can induce the wounds of the Saviour in the body of one who contemplates a crucifix, it is sufficient to note that one of the most outstanding traits of strong emotions is their tendency to lose their "objective" character and become "personal." A mother, for example, who has passed through an emotional crisis of fear for her child's life often experiences a similar dread with regard to her *own* life. This fact is not too difficult to understand. In an emotional crisis which deadens our synthetical and critical powers this moral identity easily passes over to what we might call *physical* identity.

We have pointed out that the emotion experienced by Theresa Neumann during her vision of the sacred passion overwhelms her completely. She becomes insensible to all external stimuli. She pays no heed to things not connected with the subject of her contemplation. Oblivious of her surroundings, she seems to be present no longer at Konnersreuth, but in Jerusalem. She sees Jesus, she hears His voice, she weeps over His sufferings, she extends her arms to shield Him from the blows which threaten Him. She is completely absorbed in His presence.

The *idea*, of itself, does not produce its effects directly, but through the *emotions*. Always associated with the material functioning of the organism, the emotion affects some nerves in the peripheral members. For this reason ideas are capable of producing only those bodily effects for which there exists a specialized mechanism. They cannot directly hasten physical growth; they cannot cause horns to appear on our head! But we can see no a priori impossibility in an emotionally charged idea organizing stigmatization.

Another objection to our view stems from the genesis of the wound in Theresa's side. This wound appeared for the first time during her vision of Jesus in the Garden of Olives. Now in that particular phase of the passion, Theresa could not *see* any wound in the side of Christ. How, then, could she induce it in her own body? Where are we going to find the corresponding causal "idea" of which we spoke above?

It is a historical fact that the wounds on Theresa's hands and feet appeared while she was contemplating the crucifixion, Good Friday, 1926.[69] While it is true that Theresa could not see the wound in the side of Christ during her vision of the agony in the garden, nevertheless, she *did* see *blood* flowing from His body. Thus she had the idea of bleeding. The only difficulty lies in accurately determining the *place* from which the blood was to flow. The difficulty, however, is not insuperable. Stigmatization always implies the intervention of the *imagination*. It is common knowledge with what ease this faculty glides from one object to another, with what agility it can co-ordinate the most disparate images by means of the laws of association. A person contemplating Jesus Christ shedding His blood in the garden for the love of mankind can easily associate the blood with the heart, the symbol of love. Theresa especially could make such an association, because she has a special devotion to the Sacred Heart of Jesus.

We are now able to answer the objection raised by Father Spirago: "If compassion for Jesus Christ could produce Theresa's wounds, they should appear principally on her *back* (as a result of carrying the cross), and on her whole body (as a result of the scourging)."[70] In order to uphold this assertion it would first have to be proved that Theresa had the type of image of which we spoke previously, while she contemplated the flagellation.

---

[69] Fr. Spirago, *Klarheit über Konnersreuth*, Lingen, 1929, p. 26.
[70] *Ibid.*, p. 60.

Another apparent difficulty is in the argument: "Several stigmatized persons (and Theresa among them) never had any *desire* for stigmatization. How then could they induce them?" This is merely the old argument of the occasionalists: *Quod nescis quomodo fiat, hoc non facis* — "If you are ignorant of the manner in which you have done something, it is not you who have done it!" This argument is not tenable. To produce a bodily effect it is not necessary to *will* it, especially not with a *clear* and *conscious* desire. This is evidenced by the presence of reflexes which are caused by the simple presence of danger, or, more accurately, by the awareness of danger accompanied by a subconscious or semiconscious impulse. Further proof is offered by the strange phenomena of *Cumberlandism,* which are the result of the motor force of imagery. When we are thinking of some movement, we "involuntarily" execute more or less overt motions. Such slight cues serve to explain a number of the marvels attributed to telepathy and clairvoyance, to the divining rod and the rotating tables of the Spiritualists. Finally the fact of the unconscious suggestion is demonstrated by the effects of *posthypnotic suggestion* which do not imply the intervention of the conscious will and which, as Cuénot observed, are the more efficacious the more the suggestion is applied to the automatic mechanisms of the unconscious.

Another objection against our theory: The stigmata of Theresa Neumann have persisted for a *very long time;* how can the effect of an *emotion* be so durable? There is nothing strange about the durability of the stigmata, provided the emotion which causes them is repeated at sufficiently regular intervals. Theresa Neumann experiences these intense emotions *every Friday* in her ecstasy of the passion.

Again, "The stigmata cause Theresa suffering!" We answer: What is surprising in this? Is not the very purpose of the stigmata to "participate in the sufferings" of Christ? But how is it possible to "participate in His sufferings" without enduring pain?

Before concluding this chapter we must say a word about the objection known as the "Five-Wound Illness" (*Fünf-*

Wunden-Krankheit). If stigmatization were really the symptom of some illness, we would have to admit that it affects only those who profess the Catholic faith, because in almost every case those who have had the stigmata were Catholics. In other words, we would have to acknowledge that there is something about the Catholic faith which predisposes a person to this illness, which is tantamount to admitting a "Catholic illness." Unless we are willing to accept such an absurd conclusion, we must accept the stigmata as a supernatural fact of which faith is the root.

Now it is true that almost all the persons in whom the wounds of Christ have been observed belonged (or were thought to belong) to the Catholic Church.[71] But it would be very arbitrary to conclude from this fact that the stigmata, considered in their *essence*, necessarily surpass natural forces and are therefore supernatural occurrences. Our only concern here is whether they are of natural or supernatural origin. Perhaps stigmatization occurs only among Catholics because their faith alone provides the conditions essential to the production of stigmatization. Tender, compassionate devotion to the passion of Christ (the *affectus compassiva teneritudo* of St. Bonaventure), the idea of an "active participation" in the sufferings of Christ in order to "complete" them and to "make them fruitful" for the salvation of souls are definitely characteristic of the Catholic religion.[72]

Certain writers affirm that even if stigmatization "in general" cannot be shown to surpass natural forces, yet Theresa Neumann's stigmata must be ascribed to a supernatural intervention

[71] A. Abadir writes: "Dr. von Arnhard speaks of the frequent stigmata observed among the Moslem ascetics who immerse themselves in contemplation of the life of Mohammet. These stigmata correspond to the wounds received by the Prophet during his battles for the spread of the faith. Yogis and Brahmin ascetics are able to produce similar phenomena" (*Sur quelques stigmatisés anciens et modernes,* Paris, 1932). The fact here reported may be extremely valuable, but it requires further study. The occurrence of stigmatization among the Jansenists has also been reported.

[72] Father Thurston speaks of the "crucifixion complex" which was occasioned by the stigmatization of St. Francis of Assisi. Contemplative souls, he says, became accustomed to the idea of a "physical union" with Christ crucified by means of the visible marks of His passion. The result was a "pious obsession" in some emotional persons which caused them to realize the stigmata in their bodies (*op. cit.,* pp. 223–224).

of God because of certain *circumstances* which characterize them. They are therefore at least miracles of "the third degree" (*quoad modum*). Archbishop Teodorowicz[73] gives us a complete list of these circumstances, which we repeat here, and offer the following refutations:

1. "They are prophetically predicted wounds." We *deny* this assertion. St. Thérèse of Lisieux never foretold that Theresa would have the "stigmata," but that she would have "to suffer much."

2. "The wounds are permanent . . . they do not fester or heal," nor can they be cured by any medication. Wounds produced by mechanical means, such as scratching, cutting, and the like, fester, it is true. But does it follow that wounds of *emotional* (or hypnotic) origin must also fester? As to the assertion that no medication can cure the stigmatic wounds of Theresa, this has never been proved, for she would not permit medication to remain on them.

3. "They are protected wounds . . . over her stigmata there is this transparent skin, so tender that, for example, the bumping of the hand at the place of the stigma would suffice to burst it and let the blood pour out." Where has it been proved that this kind of wound surpasses the natural powers of the human organism? To assume it is to beg the question.

4. "They are marked wounds," as if they had been made with a compass. This proves only that stigmatization cannot be brought about without the intervention of an idea, as we have insisted above. But is this idea divine or human in the sense we explained before? This problem has not been solved by our adversaries.

5. The stigmata are "intelligent, eloquent wounds," because they bleed only at appropriate times. The problem, again, is whether the "intelligence" which guides their activity is divine or human. To know when it is Friday, or Christmas, or Easter is certainly not beyond the power of human intelligence!

---

[73] *Op. cit.*, pp. 295–305.

6. The stigmata are "power producing wounds" in so far as they maintain Theresa's weight at the same level notwithstanding her bleeding. How can one prove that Theresa's prolonged *fasting* is the effect of her stigmata? We fail to see any causal relation between her stigmata and her alleged inedia. Moreover, can we be absolutely certain of the fact of her fasting? We shall turn to this problem in a later chapter.

7. The stigmata "are ecstatic wounds," that is, they owe their origin to ecstasy. This is a fact, as we have emphasized above. The real problem is, however, whether the *ecstasies* themselves are supernatural. We shall consider this question in our next chapter.

One final objection raised in regard to stigmatization is that no one can explain *by what mechanism* an emotion could produce the phenomenon. To this we reply: first, by the same token we would have to deny the production of certain material alterations of the skin under the influence of suggestion, for example, blisters, erythema, and the like, for no one can explain the mechanism by which these are produced. Second, we may not deny the existence of certain facts simply because we are not able to explain them scientifically. Third, some attempts have been made to explain the mechanism, and they merit our attention, for they have been offered by such eminent physicians as: Charbonnier,[74] M. Apte,[75] W. Jacobi,[76] G. E. Browne,[77] E. Juergensen,[78] P. Mansion,[79] H. Bon,[80] P. van Gehuchten,[81] J. Tinel,[82]

---

[74] *Maladies et facultés diverses des mystiques,* Brussels, 1875.

[75] "Les Stigmatisés," *Études historique et critique sur les troubles vasomoteurs chez les mystiques,* Diss., Paris, 1903.

[76] *Op. cit.* (*Grenzfragen des Nerven und Seelenlebens,* No. 114).

[77] *Brit. J. Physical Res.,* 1927, VII–IX.

[78] "Der Mechanismus blutig verfärbter Hautabscheidungen," *Deutsch. Arch. Klin. Med.,* 161, 1928, p. 271 ff.

[79] *A propos de Thérèse Neumann et autres Stigmatisés,* Louvain, 1934.

[80] *Précis de Médecine Catholique,* Paris, 1935.

[81] "Étude médicale des stigmates de Louise Lateau," *Études Carm.,* T. 20, 1936, II.

[82] "Essai d'interprétation psychologique des stigmates," *Études Carm.,* T. 20, 1936, II.

A. Abadir,[83] Bourneville,[84] W. Kroener,[85] Le Gac,[86] F. L. Schleyer,[87] and others.[88]

The final conclusion to our study, then, must be that there are no convincing reasons to hold that stigmatization, considered *in itself,* necessarily surpasses all the powers of nature, that it requires a special intervention of God, that it is strictly *miraculous.* As for the stigmata of Theresa Neumann, the "circumstances" accompanying them are not such as to prove their "divine origin."

Must we say, then, that stigmatization in general, and that of Theresa Neumann in particular, is a *purely natural* phenomenon? We are not yet in a position to answer this positively. As we remarked before, the stigmata are an *effect of ecstasy.* It will follow that, *if the ecstasy* is a supernatural state, then the stigmata, without being themselves *essentially* supernatural, would be supernatural *in cause* (*supernaturalia causaliter*).

Whether or not ecstasy is supernatural is the substance of the following chapter.

---

[83] "Sur quelques stigmatisés anciens et modernes," *Étude historique et médicale* (thèse), Paris, 1932.

[84] *Louise Lateau ou la stigmatisée belge,* Paris, 1875.

[85] *Das Rätsel von Konnersreuth und Wege zu seiner Lösung. Studie eines Parapsychologen. Geleitwort von H. Driesch,* Leipzig-München, 1927.

[86] *Op. cit.*

[87] *Op. cit.,* p. 114.

[88] A clear and concise summary of the various medical theories can be found in Schleyer, *op. cit.*

CHAPTER 7

Ecstasy

"A FIVE minutes' visit with Theresa," writes Teodoro-wicz, "would be sufficient to prove that her ecstasies are not natural."[1] Indeed, "almost all of them bear the stamp of the so-called mystical rapture," for "they set in suddenly, unexpectedly, in the midst of her daily occupations, during a conversation, a walk, or recreation." They are not preceded by prayer or any other intense mental work.[2]

Contrary to ecstasy, which can be the result of "an intense concentration of the soul in prayer," and therefore "may be regarded as an entirely natural phenomenon," rapture is "brought about directly through the power of God; it is a supernatural operation," a true miracle. And this is because "no one could of himself bring about such a sudden change, such a sudden transfer from the world of sense to the world of the super-sensible."[3] Moreover, the spiritual powers of Theresa Neumann in her raptures, far from being diminished, are heightened "to a great extent."[4] This is true not only during her "state of exalted quiet," in which "the gifts of prophecy and wisdom, the workings of the Holy Ghost, reveal themselves," but also in her so-called "childlike state."[5] Indeed, "she who, for example, is not able to express the name 'Pilate,' describes this man whom she cannot name in the following manner: 'The man

---

[1] *Mystical Phenomena in the Life of Theresa Neumann* (St. Louis: Herder, 1940), p. 252.

[2] *Ibid.,* pp. 169, 178, 179, 189.

[3] *Ibid.,* pp. 177, 178–179.

[4] *Ibid.,* pp. 204, 231.

[5] *Ibid.,* p. 231.

to whom I would not like to trust myself.' The complete personality of Pilate, his disposition, his attitude at the condemnation of Jesus, all are here correctly grasped." In like manner, she cannot mention St. Paul's name, but "substitutes for it an expression that is a complete description of him . . . she calls him 'the little stamper.' " The word *bishop* conveys no meaning to her while in this condition, but "she grasps the high mission of the bishop correctly from the viewpoint of faith." This mission is, according to her, "to draw all to the love of the Saviour." She cannot say the word *pope,* but her description of him is correct: she calls him the *greatest pastor.*[6]

The same author stresses two characteristics of Theresa's ecstasies. First, her *personality* remains unchanged in them. When contemplating the passion of Christ, she never imagines herself to be living in the time of Christ, to be a native of Jerusalem, to be younger or older than she really is. She always remains Theresa Neumann, and her visit to Jerusalem is only a pilgrimage.[7] Once when Father Naber asked her whether she would like to take her mother to Jerusalem, she answered: "My mother has cares enough at home; she should stay at home."[8]

The other characteristic of Theresa's ecstasy is that "she *remembers* what she beholds during the visions as well as she remembers anything else."[9] Not even the slightest details are forgotten.[10] While she is in her Friday ecstasy, however, she is not conscious of having witnessed the passion of Christ a week previous.[11]

"Because of all these premises," some authors conclude, "these states of Theresa Neumann are to be declared an effect of the grace of the Holy Ghost."[12] Those who try to explain them

---

[6] *Ibid.,* p. 228. The author adds: "She calls the souls in purgatory begging kittens. These souls with their ardent request for prayer are like little kittens crying for milk and bread" (pp. 228–229).

[7] *Ibid.,* p. 222.

[8] *Ibid.,* p. 231.

[9] *Ibid.,* p. 212. Cf. also pp. 213, 215, 223.

[10] *Ibid.,* p. 207. Cf. also p. 206.

[11] *Ibid.,* p. 209.

[12] *Ibid.,* p. 243.

naturally must have recourse to some theory of somnambulism or hypnotism. Now these two pathological states, it is claimed, differ completely from Theresa's ecstasy, since they are generally accompanied by "a lessening of the spiritual powers"[13] and the phenomenon of dual personality.[14] Moreover, the hypnotized subject remembers very well what he has experienced in a previous hypnotic state, but in his normal state suffers amnesia of what transpired under hypnosis.

It is true, these authors add, that Theresa also forgets what she said in her state of "exalted rest," but only because her words were "intended for others. What was intended for herself she retains in her heart and mind."[15] This remarkable "selectivity" of Theresa's memory affords new confirmation for the supernatural origin of her ecstasies, for "such a phenomenon could not be explained in a natural manner."[16]

Can these assertions stand the test of critical study? To begin with, it is important for us to determine whether there is an *essential* distinction between "ecstasy" and "rapture," for this constitutes the point of departure for many writers on Konnersreuth. Following the teaching of St. Thomas Aquinas[17] and of many other theologians (Arauxus, Scacchus, Consalvus Durantus, Castellinus, Antonius ab Annuntiatione, Cardinal Bona),[18] Benedict XIV states that rapture differs from ecstasy by a certain "violence" (*violentia, vis*).[19] He notes that, according to Cardinal Lauraea and Consalvus Durantus, the terms "ecstasy" and "rapture" are generally considered synonymous. Neither does Baldellus make any essential distinction between the two. Both ecstasy and rapture may be supernatural or natural in origin. The Church has never declared that rapture is necessarily supernatural.[20]

---

[13] *Ibid.*, pp. 229, 233.   [15] *Ibid.*, p. 243.
[14] *Ibid.*, p. 223.   [16] *Ibid.*, p. 217.
[17] II–II, q. 175, a. 2, ad 1: *"Raptus Super Hoc Addit Violentiam Quandam."*
[18] *De Discretione Spirituum*, cap. 14, n. 2.
[19] *De Servorum Dei Beatificatione et de Beatorum Canonizatione*, Book III, Chap. 49, n. 3.
[20] *Ibid.*, nn. 14–15.

The doctrine of St. Francis de Sales is basically the same as that of Benedict XIV: "Ecstasy is called rapture (*ravissement*) in so far as by its means God attracts us and lifts us to Himself; and rapture is called ecstasy in so far as by it we go out of ourselves and are lifted above ourselves in order to be united with God."[21] When discussing the nature of ecstasy and rapture, he continually employs either term synonymously.[22] Ecstasy as well as rapture may be divine, diabolical, or natural.[23] In the last-mentioned category he mentions particularly "sensuous ecstasy" (*l'extase sensuelle*) which consists in vehement voluptuous enjoyment.[24]

Dom Schram[25] and many other theologians follow the same doctrine. The *Dictionnaire des connaissances religieuses* does not mention any essential distinction between ecstasy and rapture. The *Dictionnaire de théologie catholique* distinguishes three kinds of ecstasy: a "simple ecstasy," "rapture" (*ravissement*), and "flight of spirit" (*vol d'esprit*), but adds that they differ only in degree; essentially they are the same. "Ecstasy, properly so called, rapture, and flight of spirit often signify one and the same reality," says Msgr. Albert Farges.[26]

Consequently we cannot prove that Theresa Neumann's ecstatic states are supernatural simply by calling them "raptures." We must show that *her* rapture really surpasses all the powers of nature.

According to Benedict XIV, the supernatural character of rapture can be demonstrated best by proving that it was not "preceded by any infirmity or other cause which might account for it in a natural way." Such causes would be "catalepsy, a vivid imagination, a melancholy disposition," some "affection of the uterus," or any cause that would make the "animal

---

[21] *Traité de l'amour de Dieu,* Book VII, Chap. IV (*Oeuvres Complètes,* t. II, 3 ed., Paris, 1866, p. 158).
[22] *Ibid.,* Chaps. IV–VI.
[23] *Ibid.,* Chaps. VI–VII (pp. 163–164).
[24] *Ibid.,* Chap. IV, p. 158.
[25] *Institut. Theol. Myst.,* II, Dt. XXV.
[26] *Mystical Phenomena,* London, 1926, p. 168.

spirits" flow in great volume to the brain, for when this happens the functions of the external senses are necessarily impeded.[27]

St. Teresa of Avila warns us that natural or morbid ecstasies are to be feared "particularly in women." "On account of their penances, prayers, and vigils, or even because of debility of health," they easily fall into a "trance" which they think is supernatural. In reality, "it is nothing but nonsense."[28] St. Teresa stresses this point. In another place she writes: "I am speaking of genuine raptures, not fancies that come from woman's weakness, which so often occur nowadays, making them imagine everything to be a [supernatural] rapture or ecstasy."[29] She mentions several striking cases to confirm her assertion. She knew some persons whose ecstasies lasted eight to nine hours.[30] They were cured of their ecstasies "by being made to eat and sleep well and to leave off some of their penances."[31] The prioresses "must apply themselves with all diligence possible to the banishing of these protracted fits of dreaminess" in their subjects by forbidding them "fasting and mortification," by "assigning them duties in the house for the purpose of taking their attention away from themselves," by preventing them "from spending more than a very few hours in prayer," and, finally, "by making them eat and sleep well until their usual strength is restored. . . . If the nun's constitution is so delicate that this does not suffice, let her believe me when I tell her that God only calls her to the active life. . . . Employ her in the various offices and be careful that she is never left alone very long."[32] Likewise, the confessor "should forbid her the fast and discipline and provide some distractions for her."[33]

---

[27] *Op. cit.*, Book III, Chap. 49, nn. 3–6, 13.

[28] *The Interior Castle*, Fourth Mansions, Chap. III, n. 11, trans. by the Benedictines of Stanbrook (London: Th. Baker, 1921), p. 116.

[29] *Ibid.*, Sixth Mansions, Chap. IV, n. 1 (p. 188).

[30] *Ibid.*, Fourth Mansions, Chap. III, n. 12 (p. 116). In *The Book of Foundations*, St. Teresa maintains that ecstasy is of very short duration. Cf. *The Interior Castle*, Fourth Mansions, Chap. III, n. 12 (p. 117); Sixth Mansions, Chap. VII, n. 16.

[31] *The Interior Castle*, Fourth Mansions, Chap. III, n. 13 (p. 118).

[32] *The Book of Foundations*, Chap. VI, nn. 6, 15–16.

[33] *The Interior Castle*, Fourth Mansions, Chap. III, n. 12 (p. 117).

The symptoms of natural ecstasy, writes Benedict XIV, are identical with those of the illness which provokes it, especially as regards the "determined time" (*determinatum tempus*) in which it takes place, "the darkening of the mind" (*mentis et intellectus objuscatio*), "forgetfulness of things passed" (*rerum praeteritarum oblivio*), particularly "forgetfulness of what one has said in ecstasy,"[34] and "mental confusion" following ecstasy.[35] If a person in ecstasy speaks in the name of Christ or of some saint as if he were possessed by them, he either deceives or is deceived (*aut seduci aut seducere*). The learned Silvius and Cardinal Cajetan de Vio are of the same opinion. The latter writes, not without indignation: *Et tamen mundus stultus miratur, stupet, adorat huiusmodi verba, huiusmodi actus, huiusmodi personas* — "Not withstanding this, stupid people admire, celebrate and adore such messages, such acts, such persons."[36]

In applying these principles to the ecstasies of Theresa Neumann, we discover first of all that they originated *during an illness* which, in Benedict XIV's time, would have been called "affection of the uterus." In fact, her various paralyses, anesthesias, convulsions, blindness, and the like, cannot be explained except by this illness, as we determined in a previous chapter.

Second, Theresa's ecstasies have a "determined time" in making their appearance. I remember with what enthusiasm Father Naber spoke to me (in 1929) of this very characteristic of Theresa. Very often in her ecstasy, he said, she will predict the precise moment of the next seizure. When the predicted time arrives, she undergoes a sudden change, her words come to a halt, and she falls into her ecstasy.[37] The regularity of her Friday ecstasies is well known. This circumstance, which is often quoted as an argument for the supernatural character of Theresa's

---

[34] Benedict XIV, *op. cit.*, Book III, Chap. 49, nn. 5, 6, 12.

[35] The Pope notes here that the mental confusion which sometimes follows supernatural ecstasy is neither profound nor long lasting (n. 6).

[36] *In II–II Thomae de Aquino*, Venice, p. 1096.

[37] Cf. Teodorowicz, *op. cit.*, pp. 233–234.

ecstasies,[38] has very doubtful value when compared to the principles laid down by Benedict XIV and other authorities on mysticism. Of course, God is free in the distribution of His supernatural gifts; He is under no obligation to follow set rules in granting ecstasies. Nevertheless, He has deigned to regulate His activity in the supernatural order as well as the natural order by certain "laws," so that we might recognize His special intervention. These laws form the subject matter of theology. Now, theology tells us that prediction of future ecstasies does not take place in persons who have really supernatural ecstasies. On the other hand, they are frequently found among hypnotized persons, somnambulists, and neurotics. Their predictions are fulfilled to the letter, for they are the result of suggestion or, rather, of autosuggestion. We will return to this point later.

Against this argument some writers appeal to the case of St. Gemma Galgani. She, too, predicted her ecstasies.[39] These writers mistakenly suppose that the Church has officially recognized the supernatural character of St. Gemma's ecstasies. She has never done so.[40]

Let us apply the *third* criterion mentioned by Benedict XIV. In the ecstatic condition called the "childlike state," Theresa Neumann's intellectual functions are retarded to the point that "the most simple concepts, such as brother, sister, parents, etc., become completely unintelligible to her."[41] She is incapable of solving the simplest arithmetic problems.[42] She cannot form a single sentence correctly or even pronounce words, and she does not recognize people, not even her own mother.[43]

Some writers would have us identify such a mental condition with the "spiritual childhood" so highly recommended by the

---

[38] *Ibid.*, pp. 262–263, 434–435.
[39] *Ibid.*, p. 267.
[40] Cf. *Acta Apostolicae Sedis*, 1932, p. 57.
[41] F. von Lama, *Theresa Neumann von Konnersreuth*, Karlsruhe, 1929, p. 60.
[42] Teodorowicz, *op. cit.*, p. 227; Fahsel, *Konnersreuth: Tatsachen und Gedanken*, p. 49.
[43] L. Witt, *Konnersreuth im Lichte der Religion und Wissenschaft*, I, pp. 191–195.

saints, especially by St. Thérèse of Lisieux. We feel that we cannot follow their line of thought. "Spiritual childhood," which St. Thérèse calls the shortest, simplest, and easiest way to heaven, does not consist in a physical or mental resemblance to little children, but in a moral and spiritual one. It does not imply a degradation of our mental powers, but a childlike confidence in our heavenly Father. In this sense the Church has always understood the command of Christ: "Amen, I say to you, unless you . . . become as little children, you will not enter into the kingdom of heaven" (Mt. 18:3. Cf. S. Bedae Presbyteri, *Commentarium in Marcum,* c. x, 13–21).

The problem becomes even more complicated when defenders of Konnersreuth tell us that "not only details, but entire scenes are puzzling to Theresa." Thus "she saw the angel's annunciation to Mary without understanding what this scene meant." She had not the least idea of having seen the Mother of God.[44] When she witnessed the gospel scene of the cure of the lunatic boy she could not comprehend "why our Lord spoke so sharply to the Apostles and the rest who were there." In another vision she was present at a court trial. She saw a young man standing before a judge; the latter bore a strong resemblance to one of the judges who had presided over the trial of Jesus. But who were these two men? She did not know and had to obtain the answer from Father Naber: "The young man is St. Stephen and the judge is undoubtedly the high priest Caiphas." Father Naber also had to tell her that another young man whom she saw suffer martyrdom was St. Lawrence. In her Friday visions she regularly witnesses the betrayal of Judas, the most monstrous piece of treachery the world has ever known. She hears, it is said, the Aramaic word for "traitor." Despite all this, she insists that Judas "loves" Christ sincerely. She refuses to recognize him as a traitor. She likewise manifests much sympathy for Pilate, for he attempts to save Jesus from the hands of the Jews. On the other hand, she has a marked dislike for St. Peter, because he shed the first blood when he cut off the ear of one of the

---

[44] Teodorowicz, *op. cit.,* pp. 435–436.

servants of the chief priest. She labels him disdainfully "the ear cutter."

It must be confessed that she has a poor understanding of the various scenes of the passion. She reacts to them like a four-year-old child. Why, indeed, does she show such sympathy for Judas? "Because he loves our Lord," she tells us. She arrives at this conclusion from the fact that he kissed Jesus in the Garden of Olives! Like a child, Theresa is incapable of making any mental abstraction, of dissociating the physical gesture of "kissing" from the "love" of which it is a natural sign. She cannot see the perfidy hiding beneath the gesture of friendship.

Her sympathy for Pilate and her aversion for St. Peter can be explained in the same way. Pilate "loves" Jesus because he tries to rescue Him from His persecutors. Peter is blameworthy because he shed human blood. Peter's noble intentions and his generous devotion to his Master's cause escape her completely.

Theresa reacts to the scenes of the passion merely as a chance passerby, just as a conscientious and tenderhearted Jew or pagan might have reacted nineteen centuries earlier. Actually, she seems ignorant of the gospel narrative. Or is it that she forgets it as the Konnersreuth apologists assert? "The thorough investigation of Theresa's visions has shown conclusively that in her visions her memory is completely paralyzed. . . . The faculty of memory ceases to function entirely during her ecstasy. Her memory is like a *tabula rasa.*" It "is entirely excluded and so not participating and inactive. . . . In the moment of her vision she forgets all knowledge of her catechism."[45]

However, if this is true, from what source does she receive all the details of the passion which she witnesses before her eyes? Her defenders maintain that she receives these details from the Holy Spirit, from God who illumines her in a supernatural manner.[46] These "details" which the Holy Spirit purportedly places before her eyes include such things as: The trees, the rocks, the people who lived in Palestine at the time of Christ,

---

[45] *Ibid.,* pp. 440–441.
[46] *Ibid.,* pp. 462–464.

their costumes, their manner of living, plans, and ranks, every corner in Jerusalem, the road which leads to Golgotha with all its turns and deviations, and the temple. She sees the Apostles, one of whom seems "very stupid" (*bloed*). Finally she sees Jesus, His hair, His beard, His eyes, and so forth. She sees Him in frightful suffering.[47]

Does she *understand* the drama of the passion? Does she realize *why* He is suffering? Has she any idea of the *meaning* of the tragedy of Golgotha? To answer these questions we need only pay close attention to her *reactions*.

When she saw a vicious youth kick aside Christ's garments (after the scourging) in order to steal them, she cried out: "That wretch has taken a fancy to the garments! I would like to give him a crack on the head." Another time, seeing the "wretched villains mocking Christ," she exclaimed irritably: "The rogues have not had anything to drink and yet they seem to be drunk." When she heard the thief insult Christ she cried out indignantly: "You should not shout like that when you are near the Saviour," meanwhile making every effort to "slap his face." Seeing Herod make mockery of Christ, she wanted to scream, "Down with him!"

Such is Theresa's amazing reaction to the great drama of the passion. Never does she direct her righteous anger toward *herself* and her own *sins*. Never does she think of asking Christ for *forgiveness*. Neither does she ever join the Saviour in His prayer for poor sinners: "Father, forgive them, for they know not what they do." Moreover, she is not even aware of His compassion for them. When Father Wutz, after witnessing her reaction toward the insulting thief, attempted to arouse in her some pity for the poor wretch who was suffering such agonies on his cross, she toned down her vindictiveness somewhat and said: "I would not have hurt him; just the same I would have given him a good slap."

It is interesting to contrast Theresa's attitude with that of our Blessed Lady. Mary did not give way to feelings of anger,

---

[47] Cf. F. von Lama, *op. cit.*, p. 47; Teodorowicz, *op. cit.*, pp. 172, 193.

revenge, or agitation. She meditated, prayed, pardoned,[48] because
she had a deep understanding of the *meaning* of the sacred
passion. She looked beyond the crimes of evil men and saw the
will of the heavenly Father and the salvation of sinners. She
knew that her divine Son had freely accepted His sufferings for
the salvation of mankind, and she associated herself in His
expiatory sacrifice.

Does Theresa have any idea at all *why* Christ is suffering?
There is no evidence that she does, and certain aspects of her
behavior lead us to believe that she has no understanding whatever of the meaning of the passion. Throughout the whole course
of her vision she is obsessed with one idea: to *rescue* Christ from
His sufferings. She attempts to put a stop to the proceedings
at all cost, thus preventing His death; to avert His gaze from
the odious cross; to "hinder the tragedy of Golgotha if possible.
. . . to lead Christ home. . . . She has formed a plan to save her
Master through flight . . . she has also brought in assistants
for the accomplishment of her plan of saving Him," which is
evidenced by her words: "I know a shorter way. . . . Her decided
tones reveal that she wants to enter into the minutest details of
carrying out her plan."[49] When Christ arrives on Mount Calvary,
Theresa trembles with joy and tells Father Wutz (who she believes is at the scene): "Run, now, to the Saviour's mother and
tell her that they have set Him free." When he hesitated to carry
out her order, she urged him: "Go and tell her that Resl says
that they have set Him free . . . they only made Him carry
the wood for building."[50]

All these quotations — and they are taken from unimpeach-
able sources — confirm what we have already said: Theresa has
no more idea of the *meaning* of the passion than she has of the
respective roles of Judas, St. Peter, and Pilate. She has a won-
derfully clear view of the scenery, the pageantry, the beautiful
costumes of the actors, but she understands nothing of the drama

---

[48] We have developed these ideas in two previous publications (1931 and 1933).
[49] Teodorowicz, *op. cit.*, pp. 192, 193.
[50] F. von Lama, *op. cit.*, pp. 60–61.

itself or of its *fundamental idea*. And the role she assumes for herself in this majestic tragedy is nothing short of startling. She is to Christ, we are told, what Joan of Arc was to the King of France. She has been sent by God to "save" Christ, who is so grateful to her: "With deathly tired, but thankful and acknowledging eyes, [He] looks upon her, and she smiles with exuberant joy of soul."[51]

It is said that Theresa Neumann "hears" the words spoken by Christ during His passion. Perhaps she does, but certainly does not "comprehend" them. Jesus said to St. Peter in the Garden of Olives: "Dost thou suppose that I cannot entreat my Father, and he will even now furnish me with more than twelve legions of angels? How then are the Scriptures to be fulfilled, that thus it must happen?" (Mt. 26:53–54); "Put up thy sword into the scabbard. Shall I not drink the cup that the Father has given me?" (Jn. 18:11.) If Theresa really grasped the meaning of these and similar passages of the Gospel, she would surely know that her plan "to lead Him home" by means of "flight" could hardly be acceptable to Christ, much less be "supernaturally inspired" by Him. We must conclude that this mental state is the result of the confusion referred to by Benedict XIV (*mentis et intellectus obfuscatio*). This conclusion is fatal for any supernatural theory of her visions, for the Pope tells us that *mentis obfuscatio* is a sign of a purely natural, even pathological, ecstasy.

Another criterion of natural ecstasy cited by Benedict XIV is, as we have seen, *forgetfulness* of what one has said while in the ecstatic state. All agree that Theresa cannot recall what she has said in her ecstatic state of "exalted rest."[52] Father Richstätter, S.J., maintains that such a phenomenon is unknown in mystical theology. Amnesia, which has always been considered evidence against the supernatural authenticity of an ecstasy, is allied rather to the abnormal conditions which constitute the object of parapsychology.[53] Father Westermayr, professor of

---

[51] Teodorowicz, *op. cit.*, p. 196.

[52] *Ibid.*, pp. 435–436.

[53] "Der Kirchenlehrer der Mystik," *Stimmen der Zeit,* 1930, pp. 206–207.

mystical theology at the seminary of Freising,[54] Dom Mager, O.S.B., professor of religious psychology and apologetics at the University of Würzburg, Father Leiber, S.J., of the Gregorian University (Rome), and the distinguished psychologist Father H. Thurston, S.J., are of the same opinion. They affirm that the ecstasies (raptures) of Theresa Neumann are notably *inferior* to those of authentic Catholic mystics.

"Of this I am certain," writes Father Bruno of Jesus and Mary, O.C., an editor of the *Études Carmélitaines,* "that Theresa Neumann's experiences, as they are generally reported, do not show any agreement with the classical psychology of St. Teresa and St. John of the Cross. From the medical point of view, her case calls for extreme caution. . . . We have not only a right, but a duty, to be skeptical. . . . We do not ask the faithful to rule out the possibility of the miraculous, but we ask them to realize how important it is, before crying 'miracle,' to be certain that there is question of the truly miraculous and not rather of an illusion."[55]

We are not surprised, then, that some eminent Catholic priests who at first accepted the supernatural character of the Konnersreuth phenomena later changed their view when they had examined them carefully in the light of Catholic theology. "I am not ashamed," confesses Father Westermayr, "that I have changed my first favorable attitude toward Konnersreuth . . . because of the criteria of mystical theology."[56] Father de Guibert, S.J., professor of mystical theology at the Gregorian University, considered subsequent amnesia a formidable argument against the supernatural character of Theresa's ecstasies. He believed that it would be contrary to the divine dignity for God to make use of the human person after the manner of an automaton, to

[54] "Liter," a reprint from the *Augsburg. Postzeit,* Feb. 19, 1930, p. 30.

[55] Cf. B. de Poray-Madeyski, *Le cas de la visionnaire stigmatisée — Thérèse Neumann de Konnersreuth,* p. 131.

[56] "Konnersreuth in der theologischen Kritik," *Augsburg. Postzeitung,* Sunday Supplement, July 12, 1930, p. 12. Cf. also *Augsburger Postzeitung,* Literary Supplement, Feb. 19, 1930; Wunderle, "Wie steht es heute um Konnersreuth?" *Fränkisches Volksblatt,* Würzburg, Nov. 24, 1932.

force the human mind to utter words of which it has not the least remembrance in its normal state.[57] The supposition that her words are for the benefit of others, not for herself, does not solve the difficulty. Moreover, Theresa forgets also the messages which she receives from Christ in her "state of exalted repose" for her own spiritual and material benefit. It is for this reason that she orders, then, Rev. Naber to remind her when she will be in her normal, natural condition.

The mental confusion which follows an ecstatic trance, is, according to Benedict XIV, another important circumstance to keep in mind when there is question of judging the nature of such phenomena. Mental confusion is clear proof that the ecstasy had a natural origin. What is Theresa Neumann's condition after her ecstasies? Her mother tells us: "After the apparition [of the light] she does not listen to us. When we speak to her, she at first, it seems, does not understand us. She must ask us several times: What did you say?"[58]

The last criterion laid down by Benedict XIV is fatal to a supernatural explanation of Theresa's ecstasies, for it shows that they have a pathological cause: "Any person who speaks in the name of Christ or of the saints as if he were possessed by them is either the victim of illusion (*seduci*) or is a deceiver (*seducere*)." Now, some writers maintain that in the state of "exalted rest" it is not Theresa herself who speaks, but Christ speaking through her. She is merely His instrument. The famous controversy between Gerlich and Dom Mager is very enlightening. Gerlich writes in his book that Dom Mager had no right to discuss Theresa Neumann, for "he spoke with her only once, and had very little to say (*fast nichts*)."[59] Dom Mager refuted

---

[57] Even the "confused and general remembrance" of which St. Teresa speaks would be unworthy of the human person. Cf. Benedict XIV, *op. cit.*, Book III, Chap. 49, n. 12. As is well known, Theresa Neumann refuses to answer questions about what she said in her state of exalted rest, admitting that she does not remember anything. She refers her questioners to those who were present when she spoke.

[58] Cf. L. Witt, *op. cit.*, p. 122.

[59] Gerlich, *Der Kampf um die Glaubwürdigkeit der Theresa Neumann*, München, 1931, p. 39.

this charge, quoting eyewitnesses and giving the exact time of his visits to Konnersreuth. He had conversed with her on two occasions, once for an hour in the company of Father Staudinger and, a second time alone, for a much longer period. Gerlich replied: "You have really spoken with Theresa only during your first visit. The second time you went to Konnersreuth you did not speak with Theresa, but with Christ, because it is He who speaks through Theresa in her state of exalted rest."[60] Some theologians, among them Father Fahsel, agree with Gerlich. On one occasion this good priest besought Christ to answer him through the mouth of Theresa. Having received His answer in the manner requested, he concluded that it was indeed Christ who was speaking through Theresa, for otherwise the one who gave him his information would have refused to answer the question![61]

Such writers are convinced that it is Christ Himself who answers the questions put to Theresa. He predicts future events, gives advice to people who visit Konnersreuth, foretells the exact date and hour of her next ecstasy and vision, and so on.

If we take the statements of Gerlich, Father Fahsel, Father Naber, and others literally, the case of Theresa Neumann would present no difficulties for Benedict XIV and Cardinal Cajetan. She must be either the victim of an illusion or an impostor (*aut seduci . . . aut seducere*). Several eminent theologians draw the same conclusion, among them Westermayr,[62] Wunderle,[63] Dom Mager,[64] and others.

The only possible escape for the supernatural theory lies in a forthright denial of the assertions made by Gerlich and Fahsel. Some writers have taken this way out. But even these apologists confess that "some instances of Theresa Neumann could be cited that might not be altogether free from doubt in this regard."[65]

---

[60] Cf. letter of Gerlich quoted by Dom Mager in *Études Carmélitaines,* Apr., 1933.

[61] Kaplan Fahsel, *op. cit.,* pp. 71–72.

[62] *Op. cit.*

[63] *Op. cit.,* June 2, 1930.

[64] *Katholische Kirchenzeitung,* May 5, 1932.

[65] Teodorowicz, *op. cit.,* pp. 246–247.

Theresa related to Dom Mager, O.S.B., details of his own life, adding "It is not I who tell you this. It is the Saviour. Afterward I shall know nothing of what I have just told you."[66]

We are of the opinion that the phenomenon can be explained without accusing Theresa of conscious imposture or ascribing her locutions to an evil spirit. The voice speaking through her lips during the state of "exalted rest" and replying to questions could very well come from a dissociated personality of Theresa herself.[67] Modern psychology can list any number of analogous cases. Indeed the state of "exalted rest" bears a striking resemblance to the "second state" which plays such an important role in psychopathology, parapsychology, and spiritism.

Father Naber unquestionably plays an outstanding role in this "second state" of Theresa Neumann. A number of distinguished scholars, notably Father Lucien Roure, S.J.,[68] Father H. Thurston, S.J.,[69] have recognized this point. They compare the relationship existing between Father Naber and Theresa to "the relationship of the hypnotizer to the hypnotized subject."[70]

There still remain some *positive* arguments advanced by cer-

---

[66] *The Physical Phenomena of Mysticism* (Chicago: H. Regnery, 1952), p. 128.

[67] Father Thurston, S.J., is of the same opinion, cf. "The Problem of Stigmatization," *Studies*, June, 1933, p. 231. When in the "state of exalted repose," she speaks of herself in the *third* person; for example, "Thou (*du*) canst not speak to Resl. *She* is asleep." Her words are authoritative in tone and seem to come from another personality.

[68] Cf. *Études*, Jan. 5, 1929, p. 91. He affirms that Father Naber plays an important role in the mental attitude which characterizes Theresa's ecstatic states. He notes, for example, that in her childlike state Theresa always calls the pope "the highest pastor." Was not this strange name suggested to Theresa by Father Naber? Some visitors once asked Theresa whether the pope would do something for the beatification of Ann Catherine Emmerich. Theresa could not understand the word *pope*. Thereupon Father Naber spoke to her: "Resl, you know me, don't you? I am the *Pfarrer* (pastor)." "Yes," replied Theresa. "Now above me there is a higher *Pfarrer*, the bishop." "Yes." "And above him there is one who is higher still, the *pope*." "Yes." "And now, Resl, what do you think that this *Pfarrer*, who is the highest of all, is going to say about this girl?" "He will say something, but not much."

[69] "The Stigmatica of Konnersreuth," *Studies*, 1929, p. 105.

[70] During Theresa's passion ecstasy Father Naber explains, for the benefit of the visitors, the meaning of the different gestures which she executes unconsciously with her hands and head. Father Thurston likens this role of Father Naber with that of "a master of ceremonies" (*ibid.*, p. 157).

tain apologists to establish the supernatural character of Theresa's ecstasies. Although we have mentioned these arguments above, we wish to consider them here in greater detail.

First, we are told that Theresa Neumann's *personality* undergoes no change whatsoever during her ecstasies. Thus, during her Friday raptures she does not imagine that she is a resident of Palestine in the time of Christ; she is there only on a visit.

This reasoning is very weak. Transformation of personality can assume different forms and have different degrees. The transformation of personality mentioned by Teodorowicz, far from being the general rule in abnormal psychological states, is of rare occurrence. It generally presupposes certain specific psychic conditions, especially suggestion (or autosuggestion). A hypnotized subject will behave like a soldier only in so far as the hypnotist has *suggested* to him that he is a soldier.

Another argument is based on some peculiarities of Theresa's *memory*. In her normal state she remembers perfectly what she has seen and heard in ecstasy, but she has not the least idea of what was revealed to her for the benefit of others. What possible natural explanation can be given for this "selectivity" of her memory? Conversely, in her normal state, she does not know when she is going to experience the future ecstasy which she herself had predicted in a previous trance.[71] Furthermore, in her Friday ecstasies Theresa is not conscious of previously having witnessed the passion of Christ. It is always new for her. Now, a subject in hypnosis remembers the details seen and heard in previous trances.

We may answer, in a general way, by pointing out that the facts enumerated above do not surpass the natural laws; they do not require a supernatural intervention of God. Theresa, it is said, remembers what she has seen and heard in her ecstasy, but she has no recollection of the messages she has communicated to others during the same ecstasy. This fact corresponds to what psychologists call the "selectivity of the memory" and can be ascribed to Theresa's peculiar mental state during her

---

[71] Cf. Teodorowicz, *op. cit.*, pp. 209, 216–217.

ecstasies. "Retroactive amnesia" (a loss of recollection for what has been experienced in the past) does not necessarily affect *all* the data of memory. It may obliterate only some of them, such as a certain period of one's past life (a determined day, month, or year) or certain systems of ideas (a particular person, one's own profession or trade). The former type is called "localized amnesia," the latter a "systematized amnesia." To account for this curious selectivity in any given case would demand a thorough psychological analysis of the person concerned, which is beyond our present scope. We simply observe the following facts: Items which are of little interest for the individual are more readily forgotten, while those of personal interest will be retained; second, a person awakening from a mental condition wherein his higher mental powers were hindered will be inclined to forget intellectual synthesis and judgments, whereas merely sensory data will be more easily retained. These two facts offer sufficient reasons why Theresa will remember, in her normal state, what she has seen or heard in her ecstasy, and not what she has said to others.

Then, too, the condition known as "exalted repose" has all the earmarks of deep hypnosis or somnambulism. In the case of Theresa Neumann, this state "quite regularly follows every ecstatic vision," being generally preceded by the ecstatic condition known as the state of absorption or the "childlike state." The same author continues: "Theresa lies there motionless, unconscious, with an expression of excruciating pain on her countenance. . . . No trace of any kind of meditation or of any disturbance of the will. Suddenly, at the stroke of eleven,[72] . . . an unseen interior light flashes over Theresa's face and changes the expression of great pain into transformed holy joy. She is changed completely. . . . She no longer feels the pain, Father Naber tells us. She enjoys physical refreshment that makes her vanished powers live again. This condition which appears when her physical lassitude has reached its height, she generally pre-

---

[72] Theresa had told Father Naber during her ecstasy that she would enter the state of exalted rest at eleven o'clock.

dicts in a previous ecstasy, although she does not know that she has done so."[73] In this condition her eyes are usually closed, as Gerlich testifies.[74] Sometimes, however, says Von Lama, they are open. The ecstatic state lasts as a rule for twenty minutes or a half hour and terminates like ordinary sleep. Theresa opens her eyes and rubs them, yawns, and stretches. Gerlich reports that on Christmas Day, 1927, Theresa suddenly collapsed in her room, fainted, and passed directly into the ecstatic state of exalted repose which restored her energy.[75] On April 14, 1938, she slipped from her armchair in the church and swooned. A few moments later she entered the state of exalted repose, and again recovered her strength.[76] On a certain Friday Theresa "had a fainting spell and lost consciousness. This did not interfere with her ecstasies, however." The three ecstasies she experienced that day developed according to the usual pattern.[77] In Professor Martini's report of Konnersreuth (March 22–23, 1928) we read: "At 2:05 a.m. Father Naber told us that Theresa was asleep. Dr. Killermann disagreed, as I did too, for I did not consider her condition that of sleep. Theresa smiled, turned to Killermann, and said: 'You too will believe some day.' Killermann answered: 'You only imagine that.' She smiled again. Killermann, raising his voice deliberately, asked whether this might not be called somnambulism. Theresa answered him immediately: 'No, it is not that.' "

Theresa has no memory for what she sees or says in this condition. Therefore, if Christ should communicate something which concerns her personally, she asks Father Naber to tell her about it later: "You must tell me afterwards, because I will know nothing at all later on of what I am saying now." At other times she will order him "not to tell her."[78] These instances, we believe, are sufficient to prove that the state of exalted rest does

---

[73] Teodorowicz, *op. cit.*, pp. 233, 234.
[74] *Die stigmatisierte Therese Neumann von Konnersreuth,* I, p. 175.
[75] *Ibid.,* I, p. 193.
[76] *Ibid.,* I, p. 243.
[77] L. Witt, *op. cit.,* II, p. 25.
[78] Gerlich, *op. cit.,* I, p. 172.

not differ essentially from deep hypnotism or somnambulism.

Having proved that the condition of "exalted repose" is essentially hypnotic, and since it is a well-established fact that the subject often "forgets" what has occurred during the hypnotic trance, it is not too difficult to explain the fact that Theresa Neumann, in her normal state, is completely ignorant of the precise moment of her next ecstasy which she had predicted in her ecstatic state. This "forgetfulness" is more apparent than real, for by using appropriate techniques, it is possible to have the subject recall the events which took place during hypnosis. The amnesia is therefore *artificial,* a form of *distraction* which. prevents the subject from making use of his knowledge. If, for example, I should say to a hypnotized subject: "At 5 o'clock you will see a bird fly through your room," he will not recall the suggestion I made during his trance. However, at the time indicated he will "see" the bird flying through his room.

If a hypnotist wishes to make sure that his subject will *not* recall certain details of his trance, he will make an appropriate suggestion, telling him, for example, that when he awakens he will not recall a certain event. As we have seen, Therese Neumann *gives herself* this suggestion. She tells Father Naber that when she will awaken from her state of exalted rest she will forget everything.

But if this conception of the state of exalted rest is true, must we not admit that Theresa's ecstasies are likewise *hypnotic* states, since they too are "foretold" by Theresa. "One thing that was striking to me . . . in Theresa Neumann," writes Teodorowicz, "was the prediction of the ecstasies during the state of exalted rest. The hour and the moment or general facts which exactly and punctually took place at the time specified were foretold." He cites several instances, for example: "She predicted in the morning that she would have an evening vision ecstasy of the transfiguration of Christ on Mount Thabor, and actually at the stroke of nine this same began."[79]

The fact is undeniable. What about its explanation? We are

[79] *Op. cit.,* pp. 265–266.

willing to concede that Theresa's ecstasies are best explained as the effects of suggestion or, more exactly, of *autosuggestion*.

The real crux of the problem of Theresa Neumann's ecstasies, with which we are more concerned, is her *nonchalant* manner of speech during the very ecstatic state about the vision which has just caused her to shed "tears of blood." "Anyone who has witnessed Theresa's deep, excruciating pain during her ecstasy, can hardly understand how fire stirred up in her soul can seem to be suddenly extinguished. During a pause that ended a series of scenes from the passion of Christ just before the crucifixion, the pastor asked Theresa what she saw. And she, who but a few moments before was almost overcome with the pain of soul, speaks of her experiences in a manner that is astonishing to the beholder. No glowing spark seems any longer to warm her words. Her speech, which during the ecstatic condition expressed pain, now that it is over, is calm, almost cold, without any enthusiasm, without an 'Oh' or an 'Ah.' . . . I am still under the impression of that antithesis. . . . I am entirely overcome by the violence of the expression of pain and then the almost frigid answers that she gives to the pastor when he asks her: 'Resl, what happened to the Saviour?' 'He died,' she answers in an ordinary tone of voice as if it were something indifferent."[80]

The only possible solution that recommends itself to Teodorowicz is that "during the ecstatic visions" Theresa's "imagination . . . is possessed by a higher power that makes use of it to cause a supernatural, sympathetic love in her heart. . . . This power ceases to act after the ecstasy, and she is once more herself left to her own reflections."[81]

Such a solution does not seem to us to be in accord with good method. We maintain that, before having recourse to a miracle, an investigation should be made to see whether the fact could be explained naturally. According to our theory, the phenomenon can be explained naturally. The emotion experienced by Theresa

---

[80] *Ibid.,* p. 465.
[81] *Ibid.,* p. 466.

in her ecstasies is of a *hypnotic* order. Consequently it subsides the moment she emerges from her ecstasy, as we might expect. By means of appropriate suggestions we can cause a hypnotized subject to pass from weeping to exuberant happiness, or to a state of *indifference*. Another interesting observation is that during her paroxisms of emotion, while Theresa is shedding tears of blood, her *pulse is normal!* What sort of emotion is this that has no effect on the pulse? Only what we should expect if the emotion is of hypnotic origin, for such affective states follow a psychic rather than a physical course.

As we have stated above, Theresa contemplates the passion of Christ in each ecstasy as if for the *first* time. This according to some writers, cannot be explained naturally. Modern psychology, however, knows many analogous phenomena. Some hallucinations recur regularly. The essence of any hallucination is that the patient always believes it to be a "new" experience. Memory is a very complex mental activity.[82] It is a *synthesis* of a high order, for it implies the use of the abstract concept of *time,* as we have shown in a previous study.[83] Theresa is incapable of such a synthesis and, consequently, is an easy prey to hallucination. We must remember, too, that in her Friday ecstasies Theresa is convinced that she is assisting at, or rather, taking part in, the "actual" passion of Christ; that is to say, in the passion as it took place nineteen centuries ago. Now, how is it possible to take part repeatedly in an event which of its very nature is unique! This is the psychological reason why each Friday she must experience the passion as a "new" event.

Why does Theresa in her "childlike state," forget the *names* of St. Paul, St. Peter, Pilate, and other persons, and why does she not know the *meaning* of such common words as *pope,*

---

[82] For this reason amnesia is usually found in patients whose higher nervous centers are partially degenerated. Where such degeneration is lacking, the amnesia is more apparent than real, since it is possible, by means of hypnosis, for example, to restore the forgotten data. Theresa Neumann's amnesia seems to be of the latter nature, i.e., merely apparent, depending as it does on the emotions experienced in her Friday visions. It is an "emotional amnesia," well known to psychology.

[83] *Psicologia Experimental,* Univers. Catolica de Rio de Janeiro, 1949, pp. 194–210.

brother, sister, and the like? This fact, too, can be explained naturally. Words are "arbitrary signs" (*signa ad arbitrium*) and, as such, imply an abstract relation to the individuals signified by them. Since such abstractions are most difficult for persons whose higher mental activities are impeded, we can understand why they find difficulty in understanding words.[84]

Some will not agree with our conclusion. They claim that Theresa, while she does not know the names of the persons mentioned, nevertheless describes them in an "absolutely superior manner." From this they argue that her ecstatic states must be supernatural. But are her descriptions superior? If they are, then why does she call St. Paul "a little stamper," the pope, "the greatest pastor," the souls in purgatory "begging kittens," and so on? Such characterizations do not surpass natural powers. Moreover, some of them, for example, that of the pope, she received from Father Naber. We have seen this before.

One final argument in favor of the supernatural origin of Theresa's ecstasies, drawn from her "memory," is that she remembers perfectly the contents of her visions. Pathological trances, it is claimed, especially those induced by hypnosis, are characterized by complete amnesia for what took place in them.

The argument is not very weighty. Not *all* hypnotic trances are followed by amnesia; sometimes this will not even occur after deep hypnosis. Suppose the hypnotized person is told to add the numbers 2, 3, 6, and 9 and is revived before he can answer; if, some hours later, he is asked to think of some number or other, he will answer "20," a number which represents the sum of these numbers. Posthypnotic memory can also be produced by a suggestion given in the trance state. Then, too, after hypnosis the subject may encounter an object similar to that seen under hypnosis which may be sufficient to stimulate recall. It is simply not true that hypnotic trances leave absolutely no traces in the normal state.

---

[84] If the reader will excuse a personal reference, it is our experience that the first symptom of cerebral fatigue is usually difficulty in speech. A brisk walk furnishes the necessary relief and interruption from intellectual work to rectify the defect.

Some authors attempt to prove the supernatural character of Theresa's ecstasies from the fact that during her trances she obeys *only* the orders of her spiritual director, Father Naber. No conclusions can be drawn from this supposition. The famous Madeleine, in her "ecstasies" at the Salpêtrière, was obedient only to the commands of Pierre Janet. Others were unable to elicit the slightest reaction even if they shook her, threw water in her face, or applied mustard to her feet.[85] We find the same phenomenon in hypnosis. The subject will only follow the directions of the hypnotist. Sometimes the hypnotist need express them only mentally. If we remember the role played by Father Naber in the Konnersreuth phenomena, especially his absolute and exclusive authority over the stigmatic, we are not surprised that Theresa obeys his orders during ecstasy.

We have been supposing that the alleged fact (of her obedience) has been established historically. It is not. Theresa herself tells us: "The pastor tried to speak to me during my vision. But he told me that he did not succeed. I made no response at all *(nicht im geringsten)*. During my visions I am not conscious of my surroundings."[86]

This last statement is not entirely true. Sometimes external stimuli can arouse Theresa from her ecstasies. On one occasion two persons who had previously been denied admittance to her room came to witness her vision. Theresa immediately ordered the two undesirables to leave the room and reprimanded the pastor sharply for having disobeyed her orders. When the visitors left, her vision resumed its course.[87]

It is sometimes said that the posture maintained by Theresa during her ecstasies defies the laws of gravitation.[88] Theresa says: "I could not possibly reproduce these positions outside my ecstasy." We believe her. But a cataleptic patient can also

---

[85] P. Janet, *De l'angoisse à l'extase* (Paris: Alcan, 1926), p. 51.

[86] L. Witt, *op. cit.*, p. 151.

[87] Gerlich, *op. cit.*, t. I, p. 152; Von Lama, *Konnersreuth in 1928*, trans., Mulhouse, 1930, p. 31. The object of this vision was the stigmatization of St. Francis of Assisi (cf. also Teodorowicz, *op. cit.*, p. 269).

[88] Von Lama, *op. cit.*, p. 58.

achieve physical postures which would be utterly impossible in his normal state.[89] No one has ever proved that Theresa's achievements in this regard are beyond natural powers. Accurate observers report only that her postures are very difficult to maintain, that only a trained athlete could reproduce them, and then only for a short time.

Then there is the argument that Theresa's ecstasies must be supernatural because they are accompanied by the charismatic gift of visions. The problem of her visions deserves more consideration and, therefore, we will discuss it in the next chapter. Here we shall note merely that if Theresa's visions are really supernatural, then her ecstasies occasioned by them must be considered supernatural. They would be supernatural, however, only "causally" (*supernaturales causaliter*). In their essential nature they are still natural phenomena. In this sense we used the term "supernatural" in connection with the ecstasies of authentic Catholic mystics and seers.

Ecstasy must be considered as a reaction to some idea or feeling. If the idea or feeling is purely natural, the ecstasy which results from it must also be adjudged natural.[90] If in a given case the mental state is really supernatural, then the ecstasy which results from it must be called supernatural — not in its formal reality — but in its "cause" (*quoad modum*). This is the nature of ecstasies experienced by those men and women who are in a genuine mystical state, or who receive revelations directly from God.

Our explanation is in perfect harmony with the best theological doctrine. "Ecstasy," we read in the *Dictionnaire de théologie catholique*, "is a kind of weakness, an imperfection (*faiblesse, imperfection*) of human nature, which is incapable of supporting the divine invasion in mystical contemplation. This imperfection of our nature does not appear to be morbid. It is not a proof of illness when the knees sag under the weight of

---

[89] Cf. Pierre Janet, *L'automatisme psychologique,* Paris, 1921, 9 ed., pp. 14–19.

[90] Richard of St. Victor had already taught that divine ecstasy "can be occasioned by wonder" (*admiratio*), by "intense love, or by great joy" (Benedict XIV, Book III, Chap. 49, n. 8).

100 kilos."[91] Dom Williamson, O.S.B., compares ecstasy with the blindness we experience when we gaze directly at the sun.[92] We find similar ideas in the works of J. de Guibert, S.J.,[93] J. Maréchal, S.J.,[94] Ag. Gemelli, O.F.M.,[95] Dom Baker, O.S.B.,[96] Aug. Saudreau,[97] to mention but a few.

This concept of ecstasy is in accord with the following facts: First, ecstasy is to be found only in persons who have not arrived at the summit of the mystical life. When the soul has undergone a complete purification, notes St. John of the Cross, "ecstasies no longer take place; the soul enjoys the liberty of the spirit without losing the liberty of the senses."[98] St. Teresa of Avila writes: "The person who lives in the seventh mansion does not go into ecstasies except perhaps on rare occasions."[99]

Second, according to Catholic theologians, the Blessed Virgin and our Lord never experienced ecstasy. Father Lallemant, S.J., says: "Without rapture a soul will sometimes have a more sublime light, a clearer knowledge, a more excellent operation of God than another with extraordinary raptures and ecstasies. The Blessed Virgin was raised to a higher state of contemplation than all the angels and all the saints put together, and yet she never had raptures. Our Lord enjoyed the beatific vision without ecstasy. The blessed in heaven will enjoy the perfect use of their senses."[100] These facts clearly show that ecstasy is "symptomatic" of a particular weakness (congenital or even morbid) of individuals. Indeed, if ecstasy, as Father Van der Veldt emphatically asserts, "is inherent in our very human make-up," we do not understand very well why our Lord, the Blessed

---

[91] Art. *"Mystique,"* A. Fonck, col. 1653.

[92] *Supernatural Mysticism,* London, 1921, Chap. 15, p. 42.

[93] *Étude de théologie mystique,* Toulouse, 1930, pp. 17–18.

[94] *Études sur la psychologie des mystiques,* Paris, 1924, *passim.*

[95] *L'origine subcosciente dei fatti mistici,* Firenze, 1939, pp. 6, 17, 65 ff.

[96] *Contemplative Prayer — Ven. Father A. Baker's teaching thereon from Sancta Sophia,* p. 39.

[97] A. Saudreau admits that the theory here proposed is "quite possible" (cf. *The Mystical State* [New York: Benziger, 1924], p. 99).

[98] *Dark Night of the Soul,* Book II, Chap. I, p. 53; cf. Saudreau, *op. cit.,* p. 98.

[99] *The Interior Castle,* Seventh Mansions, Chap. 10, p. 283.

[100] *Seventh Principle,* Chap. IV, a 7; cf. Saudreau, *op. cit.,* pp. 97–98.

Virgin, and the persons who have undergone a complete purification could enjoy the mystical life (even in its highest degree!) without any ecstasy. They had certainly a "very human make-up."[101]

On the other hand, "Pastida of Siena was subject to ecstasy almost from the cradle; Mary Frances of the Five Wounds, when she was four years old; St. Catherine of Ricci, Joanna of Cuba, Magdalen Rémuzat, and Catherine Emmerich from early youth (*dès le bas âge*); St. Catherine of Siena, at five years; Lucy of Narni, at eight years; St. Peter of Alcantara, Blessed Osana, St. Angela of Brescia, and Mother Agnes of Jesus at six years. . . ."[102]

Benedict XIV notes expressly that ecstasies have never been recognized as miracles by the Church.[103]

---

[101] "An Evaluation of the Konnersreuth Controversy," *The American Ecclesiastical Review,* June, 1953, p. 410.

[102] *Dictionnaire de théologie catholique,* art. "Extase," A. Hamon, col. 1895.

[103] *Op. cit.,* Book III, Chap. 49, n. 14. Cardinal Lauraea asserts the same.

CHAPTER 8

Visions

ARE Theresa Neumann's visions of divine origin, or are they too the product of natural forces? A decisive proof of the supernatural character of Theresa's visions would be a *miracle* worked by God in order to confirm them. "When a miracle is performed, and this intention (to confirm a vision or revelation) is expressly stated, or when circumstances show that this is the purpose, we cannot doubt the divine origin of the said revelation."[1] In this manner, we may note, Christ Himself and the Prophets of Israel proved their divine mission.[2]

Theresa Neumann seems to understand this very well and has attempted to offer such proof. "That you may know that everything I am telling you is true," she once said to Father Naber, "I now tell you there is a man coming here to Konnersreuth who is bringing several hundred marks in an envelope."[3]

Unfortunately, the fact of clairvoyance which Theresa offers as evidence can by no means be compared with the proofs which Christ offered to prove His divine mission. No one has ever proved that knowledge of hidden or distant events requires supernatural intervention. We shall understand this better in

---

[1] Poulain, S.J., *The Grace of Interior Prayer* (St. Louis: Herder), pp. 349–350.

[2] Discernment of true from false visions may also be the result of a special charism. Some holy persons are said to have possessed a certain infused gift of discernment. St. Paul alludes to this charism when he writes: "There are varieties of gifts, but the same Spirit. . . . To one through the Spirit is given the utterance of wisdom . . . to another, prophecy; to another, the distinguishing of spirits" (1 Cor. 12:4–10). Cf. Poulain, *op. cit.*

[3] Cf. Teodorowicz, *Mystical Phenomena in the Life of Theresa Neumann* (St. Louis: Herder, 1940), p. 402.

the following chapter when we shall discuss clairvoyance *ex professo*.

Some authors think that the supernatural origin of Theresa's visions is adequately guaranteed by "the *miracle of her cures*."[4] Since her cures, they say, were generally predicted in her visions, these latter must be of the same order as the cures themselves, that is to say, supernatural.

The weakness of this argument is quite obvious. As we have already seen, not a single one of Theresa's cures can be unequivocally attributed to a supernatural intervention; not one of them can be accepted as a true "miracle." We might add that other writers reverse the chain of argument, deducing the supernatural character of the cures from the fact of her visions.[5]

Still another group of observers contend that Theresa's visions are best authenticated by *"their inseparable connection with ecstasies."* Since the ecstasies are supernatural, we can be sure that the visions are in the same category: "Once established that the ecstasies or raptures are genuine, then the supernatural character of them [the visions] is also determined. Further proof is unnecessary."[6] This reasoning supposes the illogical method which we refuted previously. Ecstasy, far from proving the supernatural character of the visions, must itself be shown to be supernatural.

But let us suppose for the moment that Theresa's ecstasies are really supernatural. Would this be a guarantee of the supernatural character of the visions experienced during such ecstasies? Amort, a noted authority in the field of mysticism, answers in the negative.[7]

A really sound judgment on Theresa's visions demands thorough *study*. We must weigh carefully and individually each of the arguments advanced in favor of or against their supernatural

---

[4] *Ibid.*, p. 152.

[5] *Ibid.*, pp. 132, 142–144.

[6] *Ibid.*, pp. 430–431.

[7] "Non est certum signum revelationem esse a Deo, etiamsi fiat in extasi supernaturali" ("De Revelationibus, Visionibus, Apparitionibus, Privatis Regulae," *Regularum Summarium*, § 1, reg. 32, Augustae Vindelicorum, 1744, p. 268. *Ibid.*, reg. 5).

character. In practice, observes Father Poulain, such an examination affords only more or less *probability*. We need not fear to acknowledge this. Authors frequently remain undecided in the face of such problems.[8] Even if in a given case an investigator concludes, with certainty, that a vision is supernatural, such certainty is strictly *human,* since it is based on the testimony of the seer, who, of course, is not infallible.[9]

Because the value of private revelations must be judged from the testimony of the *person* who bears witness to them, it is extremely important to have a thorough knowledge of the person before accepting his revelations. In particular, we must investigate carefully (*sedulo examinandum est*) whether his visions "were not preceded by some *natural cause* which might produce them. In fact, persons suffering from some physical or mental illness, as well as those who are disturbed by their thoughts and emotions, easily believe that they see things which do not really exist." Visions reported by women must be examined with special care (*accuratior indago*), because females are more subject to emotional disturbances.[10] Cardinal Bona insists very much on this point.[11]

We should remember, says St. Teresa of Avila, "that natural weakness is very great, especially in women, and that it shows itself the more in this [mystical] way of prayer. It therefore becomes necessary that we should not immediately take it for

---

[8] *Op. cit.,* 8 ed., 1909, p. 367.

[9] Benedict XIV, *De Servorum Dei Beatificatione et de Beatorum Canonizatione,* Book III, Chap. 53, n. 15. Cf. also Book II, Chap. 32, n. 11; Amort, *op. cit.,* reg. 24 and 9; § 2, reg. 10. John Baptist Cardinal Pitra, *Analecta Sanctae Hildegardis opera,* Typis Sacri Montis Casinensis, 1882, p. XV: "Caeterum quisque novit privatis revelationibus etiam fide dignissimis liberum esse prorsus credere vel non credere. Etiam quando ab ecclesia approbantur non accipiuntur ut citra dubium credendae, sed tanquam probabiles."

[10] Benedict XIV, *op. cit.,* Book III, Chap. 51, n. 1.

[11] "Maior cautio erga feminas adhibenda, quarum sexus eo suspectior est, quo imbecillior. Naturae sunt humidioris, ut ex vehementia cogitationum et affectuum putant se videre quae cupiunt, et quod ab animi perturbationibus nascitur, quae in ipsis acerrimae sunt, a veritate oriri credunt. Cumque ratione minus polleant, non est difficile diabolo earum nativa imbecillitate uti, ut eas primum variis illusionibus decipiat, et per easdem alios in errores inducat" (Card. Bona, *De Discretione Spirituum,* Chap. XX, 3).

granted that every little fancy we may have is a vision."[12] "I know from experience," she writes elsewhere, "that there are souls which, whether because they possess vivid imaginations or active minds, or for other reasons of which I am ignorant, are so absorbed in their own ideas as to feel certain they see whatever their fancy imagines. . . . They themselves fabricate, piece by piece, what they fancy they see."[13] Many visions have their origin in *melancholia*,[14] by which word St. Teresa designated a variety of mental disturbances which were not well understood in her time. Excessive penance and fasting also occasion many visions.[15] Persons affected with visions must engage in some "distractions," eat and sleep well, and "keep from too much prayer."[16] We must try "to persuade them, as far as possible, to take no notice of their fancies."[17] This wholesome advice is difficult to carry out in practice. If we tell them that their visions have a natural explanation, for example, that they come from "melancholia," "there will be no end to the matter, for they will persist in maintaining they have seen and heard these things." In this case, it is better "to listen to them as if they were sick."[18]

This is the practical conclusion which St. Teresa draws for her spiritual daughters: "Do you, my daughters, go always for direction to *learned* men, for thereby shall you find the way of perfection, in discretion and truth. It is very necessary for prioresses, if they would execute their office well, to have learned men for their confessors; if not, they will do many foolish things

---

[12] St. Teresa, *The Book of the Foundations*, Chap. VIII, n. 7 (p. 74 of the translated edition).

[13] *The Interior Castle*, Sixth Mansions, Chap. IX, n. 6, p. 240.

[14] *Ibid.*, Sixth Mansions, Chap. III, n. 2.

[15] *The Book of the Foundations*, Chap. VI, n. 7, p. 52. This remark of St. Teresa agrees perfectly with modern psychology. Prolonged fasting brings on "autophagy" and produces toxic substances which, in turn, occasion hallucinations.

[16] *Ibid.*, Chap. VI, nn. 6, 7, 8, 14, 15, 16, p. 175.

[17] "If words be not enough" she tells the religious superiors, "have recourse to penances and let them be heavy, if light penances will not do. If one month's imprisonment is not enough, let them be shut up for four" (*ibid.*, Chap. VII, n. 5, pp. 65–66).

[18] *The Interior Castle*, Sixth Mansions, Chap. III, n. 2, p. 175.

thinking them to be saintly; and, moreover, they must contrive that their nuns go to confession to learned men."[19] How much easier the Konnersreuth problem would have been had these principles of St. Teresa been followed.

Many a person, says St. John of the Cross, when in the state of mental recollection, has such vivid images and such easy associations as to give himself the illusion of a divine revelation. He writes down, or has others take down, what in reality is of no value.[20]

Father Poulain points to a "special disease of the memory" as another important cause of so-called "visions." There are, he notes, certain individuals who sincerely believe that they are remembering things which actually never existed. Their stories, however, are so well constructed and accompanied by so many minute details of place and time that the listener is of the opinion that "there must be something to it." Let us suppose, the same author continues, that these individuals lead a secluded life. Then they will not speak of imaginary marvels seen on their journeys, but rather of their conversations with heavenly beings.[21] Modern psychologists list many other causes of illusions and hallucinations.[22]

If in a given case visions admit of no natural explanation, we must ask ourselves the question: Given a *supernatural* cause, is this cause God or the devil? In determining this, we must first of all give careful consideration to the moral character of the seer, especially to his humility,[23] his obedience, and his other virtues; then to the manner in which the visions take place

---

[19] *The Book of the Foundations,* Chap. XIX, n. 1, p. 162.

[20] St. John of the Cross, *The Ascent of Mount Carmel,* Book II, Chap. XXIX, n. 7 (London: Thomas Baker, 1928), pp. 225–226.

[21] *Op. cit.,* 1 éd., 1909, p. 359.

[22] We have treated of this matter in *Psicologia Experimental,* Chap. XXV, § 10, pp. 430–434.

[23] If the person who has visions is truly humble, we have the assurance that he does not intend to deceive. Moreover, "generally speaking, God does not reveal extraordinary things to a person who is not well grounded in humility" (*Prudentia Ven. P. Ludovici de Ponte,* c. 9, Prague, 1698, p. 75). Cf. also Gerson, *De Distinctione Verae Visionis Signorum,* 4.

(*modus quo contingunt*); and, finally, to their effects (*ab effectibus, qui ex eis sequuntur*).[24]

Even then we must avoid all rash conclusions, for the devil sometimes urges men to the performance of good works in order to lead them more easily to lamentable falls (*ad horribiles lapsus*).[25] For these reasons Amort and other writers on mysticism are determined to abstain from passing any judgment on the visions of persons who are still living.

But let us examine the case which concerns us here: the visions of Theresa Neumann. Were they not perhaps "preceded" by certain causes capable of producing them *naturally?* The physicians who attended Theresa for several years would answer this question affirmatively without the slightest hesitation. In their opinion her visions were definitely preceded by hysteria (*hysteria traumatica*).

The use of the word *hysteria* has been the cause of much debate. Those who support the supernatural character of the Konnersreuth phenomena consider it not merely a scientific error, but a slur on Theresa's moral character, for they accept the opinion of Father Spirago that "hysteria and Christian perfection cannot exist together; the hysterical person acts against the prescriptions of religion."[26] According to this view, the victim of hysteria is a liar, an egoist, or a sexual pervert, and so on.

This supposition is entirely false; Theresa is none of these. Hysteria, far from being a moral defect, is an illness, as we have shown elsewhere.[27] "The essence of hysteria," says A. Lechler, "does not consist, as often believed, in mental deficiency, weakness of will, or moral defect. . . . There are hysterical individuals who are distinguished for a high moral life and strength

---

[24] Benedict XIV, *op. cit.,* Book 3, Chap. 51, nn. 3, 4; Chap. 52, n. 1; final chapter, n. 9.

[25] *Ibid.,* Book 3, Chap. 51, n. 3. St. Catherine of Bologna is said to have been deceived during five years by the devil through "visions" of Christ and the Blessed Virgin (*Acta Sanctorum,* March 9, pp. 49–59).

[26] *Klarheit über Konnersreuth,* 2 ed., Lingen, 1929, p. 57.

[27] *Psicologia Experimental,* Chap. XXV, § 7.

of will."[28] J. Lhermitte notes: "One of the greatest of contemporary statesmen was afflicted, during World War I, with hysterical attacks, which did not result in any loss of will power or ability to carry out co-ordinated actions." He cites this to prove that not all the reactions of a hysterical person are marked with "the seal of hysteria."[29] "Practically all neurologists are now unanimous in affirming the great truth that hysteria is before everything else a mental disease consisting chiefly in an exaggeration of suggestibility. . . . There is at present an almost equally general agreement in the view that this suggestibility, manifesting itself on occasion through such disorders as aphasia, nervous anaesthesias, palsies, inhibitions of hearing and vision, etc., frequently occur in subjects who are in no way unbalanced. . . ."[30]

"We find hysteria even among the finest specimens of humanity, among persons who are eminent in the field of science, art, and morals," writes W. Kroener. For Professor A. Hoche, hysteria consists in a peculiar capacity of the bodily organism to react to psychic influences; as a result mental images will suffice to produce anesthesias, paralyses, spasms, and the like.[31]

Regard for scientific accuracy obliges us to recognize the fact that many symptoms of Theresa's long series of illnesses (starting from the day of the fire) were of a definitely hysterical pattern. We have in mind the spasms, convulsions, contortions, paralyses, anesthesias, and hyperesthesias which have been described in the first part of this book. We find the same opinion clearly stated in the medical report of February, 1920, where Theresa's ailment is diagnosed as *"hysteria traumatica."* Many eminent Catholic physicians, for example, Deutsch, H. Heermann, P. Mansion, Lhermitte, Martini, Poray-Madeyski, and so on,

---

[28] *Das Rätzel von Konnersreuth im Lichte eines neuen Falles von Stigmatisation,* p. 27.

[29] "Konnersreuth, L'énigme de Thérèse Neumann d'après les publications récentes," *Études Carmélitaines,* Apr., 1924, p. 222.

[30] H. Thurston, *The Physical Phenomena of Mysticism* (Chicago: Regnery, 1952), p. 102.

[31] *Die Wunder der Theresa Neumann von Konnersreuth,* 2 ed., München, 1939, p. 14.

agree with this opinion.[32] Even some supporters of the supernatural theory seem to agree with us, but they hasten to add
that "all these hysterical appearances were only in passing."[33]

It seems, however, that her morbid symptoms were not transitory. The nuns who observed Theresa Neumann in 1927 noted
that she suffered a nervous spell which lasted twelve minutes
during the night of July 17. In a condition of semiconsciousness
she cried out that she was being stabbed in the heart. The account
of this attack is conclusive evidence for Dr. H. Heermann that
it was an hysterical seizure.[34] Gerlich tries to weaken this contention by asserting that the attack was occasioned by the nuns
themselves. Such an explanation is valueless, because hysterical
seizures are generally occasioned by some external stimuli.

Let us suppose, nevertheless, that Theresa is now immune
to paralyses, spasms, convulsions, and the like. Can we conclude
with certainty that she is completely cured? It is common knowledge that external manifestations of hysteria can change frequently. It would be contrary to scientific method to rule out, a
priori, such a substitution of morbid symptoms in Theresa's case.
We must consider the possibility that the strange phenomena
which developed in Theresa immediately subsequent to the disappearance of her "hysteria" are perhaps different symptoms of
the same illness.

The visions of Theresa Neumann manifest a striking resemblance to the hallucinations typical of the "second state"

---

[32] Dr. P. Mansion considers the diagnosis of "grave hysteria" as "absolutely
certain and undeniable" ("Thérèse Neumann et autres stigmatisés," *Saint-Luc
Médical,* 1933, No. 5, pp. 387, 403). Dr. J. Lhermitte, together with other doctors
mentioned above, affirms that only hysteria can offer a clear explanation of the
enigma of Konnersreuth (*op. cit.*). Father Piwinski, on the other hand, distrusts
this opinion, because Witry, a psychiatrist, did not find any trace of hysteria in
Theresa Neumann. The confidence which he places in Witry's diagnosis appears
excessive. Moreover, Father Piwinski seems to be ignorant that there exist numerous
theories of hysteria. For this reason Theresa Neumann could be judged not at all
hysterical in the light of one theory, whereas according to another theory, this
would be the case. This is why we avoid as much as possible the word "hysteria";
we prefer to use other expressions which imply no particular theory.

[33] Teodorowicz, *op. cit.,* p. 257.

[34] "Um Konnersreuth," *Theologie und Glaube,* 1932, No. 2.

induced by suggestion or autosuggestion. This may seem an arbitrary statement, but can it be proved false? The best way to refute it would be to prove that certain characteristics of Theresa's visions *surpass* the powers of nature. If this is possible, they would then constitute so many criteria for the supernatural origin of the visions.[35] It behooves us, then, to examine the alleged criteria one by one.

The *transcendency* of the visions is offered as the first argument. In her visions Theresa does not simply "meditate" on the passion of Christ. She actually "sees" it as a real occurrence which unfolds before her gaze. How can a theory which attributes the visions to Theresa's own imagination explain this fact? A tremendous effort, says Teodorowicz, would be required to elicit such a vision and would necessarily leave Theresa in a state of "complete physical exhaustion." There is no evidence of such a state of exhaustion. Moreover, Theresa's visions strike her suddenly, like a clap of thunder. "There is genuine rapture. . . . She does not seek the object for her contemplation. . . . She takes no part in the composition of the pictures that she sees and comports herself like a museum visitor." She remains entirely passive, "incapable of thinking that she would particularly like to see this or that. . . . She does not possess the ability to follow her own desires or wishes in any way at all," her will being "entirely excluded." For this reason she "always repeats the same details about the appearance, form, color of hair, movements of persons, the number and names of the persons that come in this or that scene. . . . She never changes or reverses anything in her scenes of the passion even after they have reached their climax. . . . The expression of her eyes and her exact post-ecstatic memory are proofs that her visions are not dreams."[36]

The above objections cannot be ignored, for they are the classical arguments advanced by practically all Konnersreuth apologists. In order to refute these objectives, it is necessary for

---

[35] They would have to surpass natural forces at least as to the manner in which they are produced (*quoad modum*).

[36] Cf. Teodorowicz, *op. cit.*, pp. 431–443.

us first to examine the general characteristics of sensation and imagery, before we can determine the character of hallucinations.

While sensation makes us aware of the actual presence of an object, the imagination brings into consciousness the representation of an absent object. Hence the object itself is called an "image" or "phantasm."[37] But how can the imagination grasp the "absent object" so as to "represent" it? This is achieved by means of *sensation* of which imagery may be considered a prolongation. Experience teaches us that it is necessary first to have had a sensation before it is possible to elicit an image — persons born blind have no images of color, those born deaf lack auditory images, and the like. Thus it is the *same object* which is grasped both in the sensation and in the image. The latter is a kind of "revival" of sensation. Hence it is often called the "second state" or the "weak state" of sensation.

Sensation and imagery attain the same object, as we said, but they do not attain it in the same manner. The external senses are united with their object through an action which they receive from it, whereas imagery attains it by means of modifications left in the organism by sensations. Consequently, sensation can last only so long as the object stimulates the sense organ. Imagery, on the contrary, can continue for a long time after the stimulus has ceased to exist. This explains, too, why we feel rather passive during sensation, whereas in producing images we are conscious of a more active role.

Since images are a kind of prolongation of sensations, there cannot be an essential distinction between the two, but only a question of *degree*. For this reason we are likely to confound an image with a sensation. If there were an essential distinction between an image and a sensation, it would be impossible to confuse them, just as it is impossible to mistake a color for a sound.

There are, of course, "accidental" differences between sensations and images. Imagery is always poorer in content than

---

[37] Philosophy shows that imagination is, in fact, really distinct from particular images.

sensation. Let anyone attempt to draw from memory some familiar object, his own hand, for example. He will find it impossible to reproduce a number of details, such as the exact disposition of parts, their particular coloration, precise dimensions, and the like, all of which are easily observed in sensation.

This difference is so striking that when a person affected with psychasthenia wishes to express the feeling of unreality he suffers with regard to external objects, he will say: "I see everything as in a dream; I see everything in images." Likewise, when we wish a hypnotized subject to mistake an image for a sensation (in other words, when we wish to produce a hallucination), we may say: "Here comes your friend. Look at his beard, notice his smile, and so forth." In a word, we enrich the content of the image he has of his friend.

We must note, however, that certain images may be of remarkably rich content. Some artists (e.g., Thaddeus Styka, Muncaksy) had such clear visual imagery that they felt as though they were copying from memory, and their pictures are of remarkable exactness from an anatomical viewpoint.

"Afterimages" are sometimes endowed with extraordinary sharpness and clarity. Afterimages occur immediately after sensation and last from five to ten seconds, constituting a curious transition between sensation and imagery properly so called. Strictly speaking, they are not hallucinations, because the subject does not confuse them with sensations. The afterimage is usually negative, that is, it represents the object in a color complementary to that of the real object. Positive afterimages sometimes occur also.

So-called eidetic imagery is particularly rich and detailed. "Eidetikeas" can look at an object and then, much later, project the image against a suitable background, for example, a gray screen, and enumerate the precise details experienced in sensation. This type of imagery bears a close resemblance to certain "psychic hallucinations," that is, hallucinations imperfectly objectivated and externalized, found quite frequently not only in hypnosis but also in some of the less serious neurotic states otherwise compatible with apparently normal adjustment.[38]

The second difference between imagery and sensation is that the image is "less fixed" and "less durable" than the sensation. As long as we fix our eyes upon an object, we experience constancy of sensation. If we should turn away our gaze, that particular sensation ceases to exist. On the other hand, we find that we can exercise control over our imagery, altering details, clearness, outlines, and the like. Nor is this difference surprising. Sensation is the result of a present object over which we have no control. The image, on the contrary, is the result of our activity, and therefore easily accommodates itself to our ever changing mental states.

We must beware, however, of exaggeration. Some individuals (especially those suffering from some form of mental illness) manifest imagery of remarkable precision. On the other hand, sensations are not always immune to variations. If we hold a watch some distance from our ear we will notice an alternating increasing and decreasing in the sound of its ticking.

An image is "less intense" than a sensation. This is the third difference between them, confirmed by the following observations. Introspection assures us that the roar of a cannon and the crack of a small pistol are not sounds of the same intensity. Then, again, when sound diminishes progressively, there will be a moment when we cannot say whether we are really experiencing the sensation of sound, or only an auditory image. We also know from experience that images generally tend to lose intensity with the passage of time (though sometimes the opposite phenomenon occurs).

How can we distinguish imagery from sensation? How are we to know that in a sensation the object is present and in imagery the object is absent? A thoroughgoing explanation would lead us too far afield. Suffice to note that the consciousness of an external object always implies at least a virtual *judgment*, the "existential judgment." On the sensory level such a judgment does not proceed from our reason, since so-called "sense judg-

---

[38] Eidetic imagery is generally found in individuals under the age of fourteen.

ments" are found also among irrational animals. As human adults we are, of course, constantly forming *intellectual* existential judgments. But even these judgments would lack a foundation if they were not grounded in some process which furnishes us with immediate, experimental evidence of the presence of an external object. In any case, we must admit such a "sense judgment."

The elements entering into the formation of a "sense judgment" are: (*a*) Certain immediate and characteristic effects which the object produces in us by its very presence: fire burns, ice chills, the sun dazzles us. (*b*) Certain conditions essential for eliciting a sensation, for example, the activity of the external sense organ, its appropriate accommodation to stimuli, and the like. Some people will close their eyes and open them again to assure themselves that they are really seeing an object and not suffering a hallucination. (*c*) Experience teaches us that we cannot see an object through an opaque body, through a wall, for instance; we also learn that the object does not change its position to conform to ours. (*d*) The differences which distinguish sensations from images from the viewpoint of richness of content, intensity, and the like, as we have described them above.

All this explains why sleeping persons and those in certain abnormal states are subject to *hallucinations* and why even normal individuals may experience them. The existential judgment which they form concerning objects may be incorrect for some reason or other.

Hallucinations may affect any of our senses. Visual hallucinations are the most frequent and offer the widest variations. Auditory hallucinations are also common. At first they often appear as badly defined noises, whistling sounds, or murmurings not located in any object. Later they may take a more sharply determined character. Then the patient may hear the sound of footsteps, children whistling, the hushed conversation of the members of some secret society, and the like. Or he may hear insulting words directed against himself: "Beast," "Brute," or even entire sentences. The latter tell what the patient is doing, for example, "He is walking," "He is rising," or they externalize his most intimate thoughts.

Visual hallucinations may take the form of static tableaux, or they may unfold very active scenes before one's eyes. Sometimes, but rarely, they depict the thoughts of the patient in a kind of "mental photography."

Hallucinations affecting organic sensibility (kinesthetic hallucinations) are also of frequent occurrence. The patient imagines that his organs undergo changes in shape, size, and location; that someone is stabbing or burning him, or forcing him to execute various movements, especially writing and drawing.[39]

Hallucinations of active touch are rather rare, being generally associated with visual hallucinations. Those of passive touch, however (e.g., of burning, stabbing, pain, itching, pricking), are quite common. Finally there are gustatory and olfactory hallucinations; these are rare, however, and not well organized.

If we examine the attitude taken by patients in regard to hallucinations we will have a better understanding of their nature. Some accept them with absolute trust; the images seem to possess, for them, the same degree of reality as percepts. But this kind of hallucination is quite rare. More often the subject is aware of the incomplete or simply abnormal character of the hallucination. Thus, for example, the voices he hears seem to come from a distance, or over the telephone — they are mysterious, muffled, telepathetic, and the like. The patient, speaking of such hallucinations, will use expressions like: "I was made to hear." The same must be said of visual hallucinations. They often take the form of soft and ill-defined silhouettes. For this reason the patient is likely to ascribe them to the trickery of some adversary. Sometimes he doubts their reality and even recognizes them as morbid symptoms which require medical attention.

---

[39] An excellent case of this kind of drawing ("automatic drawing") is found in Pascal P. Parente, *Susanna Beardsworth, Her Life, Conversion, Mysticism,* Grail Publications, St. Meinrad, Indiana, "The Gift of Mystical Drawing," p. 76 ff. It is certainly a natural (morbid) phenomenon.

Many hallucinations are never externalized by the patient, but remain mental images; they affect the "soul" alone. Some psychologists call them "psychic hallucinations," or "pseudo-hallucinations." Among them we may include many auditory hallucinations. The subject believes he has "interior voices" which only the soul can hear. Other hallucinations present their objects externalized and definitely localized in space.

What is the cause that leads us to take a mental image for a "sensation" and fall a prey to hallucinations? Magnan and others attach great importance to the attitude of "expectant attention." The hallucination would then be a response to the subject's own preoccupations, suspicions, or desires.

This theory, however, merely explains, more or less, those occasional hallucinations which afflict normal persons in moments of emotional disturbance, and in some cases, the hallucinations of paranoid patients. The theory cannot explain the generality of hallucinations, especially those which occur when the subject is calm and which do not correspond to any particular preoccupation or desire, or those which occur during illness (e.g., typhoid fever), the hallucinations of alcoholism, of schizophrenia, of hysteria, and the like. Such hallucinations always suppose some disorder of the nervous system which may be constitutional or acquired, chronic or temporary.

It is possible, however, to induce hallucinations by simple suggestion or autosuggestion, especially during a hypnotic trance.

A hallucination often faithfully represents the experience from which it took its origin. This fidelity concerns not only the essential features of an event, but also circumstances of time and place. Such stereotypy and periodicity are especially characteristic of hysterical and hypnotic hallucinations.

Some hallucinations do not betray themselves by any particular external sign. Others, on the contrary, express themselves in lively mimicry, gestures, and speech.

This short explanation of hallucinations should demonstrate quite clearly the inadequacy of the *first* criterion cited by many writers in favor of the supernatural character of Theresa's visions. Neither the feeling of passivity which accompanies her visions, nor their vivacity, immediacy, externality, or fidelity suffice to distinguish them from natural visions, or hallucinations.

A second criterion often cited to support the theory of the supernatural is that Theresa's second vision of the passion came to her while she had a splitting headache, while she lay motionless and apathetic, "without thinking of anything." In this case, it is alleged, her vision must have come from without. From where? From God.

This criterion is equally valueless. Every psychologist knows what is meant by "thinking of nothing." Theresa Neumann was thinking of *nothing important;* she was not exerting any conscious effort to direct the course of her thoughts to any practical end. If we do not cease thinking even in our sleep, how can we admit that our psychic life should suffer a complete interruption in our waking state? To carry out a task without "attention" does not mean we are completely unconscious of it.

But is it really true that the second Friday vision took Theresa by surprise? Was there absolutely no preparation for it? We doubt it, for Theresa testifies that during the Lent of 1926, when she was very ill, she did nothing but repeat the words: "Jesus suffered much more." Moreover, it is well known that she had a particular devotion to the passion of Christ. When she would hear the story of His sufferings, in school or in church, she could not restrain her tears. The Way of the Cross was her favorite devotion (*die liebste Andacht*). During recess periods she often went to the church with a companion to meditate on the "bitter passion and death of Jesus Christ."[40] We can reasonably suppose that during her long illness she frequently recalled the passion and death of Christ. Deprived of her sight, she could devote herself to her meditations with little distraction. Theresa's temperament was suitable to meditation, for she was in the habit of considering the same topics over and over again. She would reread a story a hundred times with undiminished pleasure. Such a disposition was a great help in

[40] L. Witt, *Konnersreuth im Lichte der Religion und Wissenschaft,* I, p. 19.

remaining constantly in the presence of God, a devout practice cultivated in her by Father Naber. Bearing in mind her ardent devotion to the sacred passion, we can easily understand how it could form the habitual object of her contemplation. This being the case, we cannot accept the theory that she experienced her visions of the passion "without having been prepared in any manner."

A *third* criterion for the supernatural character of Theresa's visions is based on the alleged fact that during her visions "the natural spiritual powers, the memory and imagination, are entirely paralyzed."[41] They are like a *tabula rasa,* since "she forgets all knowledge of her catechism which she knows so well in her ordinary state. . . . All the details of the passion of Christ are, as it were, entirely erased from her memory."[42] She does not realize that Christ has been crucified, since in the intervals between the various acts of the passion she asserts most emphatically that He will not be killed.

Despite this complete obliteration of her memory and imagination, Theresa faithfully recounts the story of the passion. The only possible explanation, we are told, is that Theresa's imagination receives its images from another source, from an immediate, supernatural operation of God. The paralysis of the imagination and the memory is purposely produced by God in order to "sidetrack all natural images from the soul so as to make it entirely receptive for the taking over of the supernatural pictures."[43]

The weakness of this hypothesis is obvious. A subject who, under the influence of hypnotic suggestion, believes that he is a ten-year-old child, has also "forgotten" his actual age and social status. This fact is so well known that we need not dwell on it here. Such a phenomenon does not imply any "paralysis" of the memory or imagination but a simple distraction which inhibits the subject from using his knowledge in a conscious manner. Theresa's ignorance of the catechism during her visions can be

---

[41] Teodorowicz, *op. cit.,* p. 430.

[42] *Ibid.,* pp. 437, 440.

[43] *Ibid.,* pp. 430, 440–443.

accounted for in a similar way without having recourse to a supernatural intervention of God.

We are referred to the *contents* of Theresa's visions as a guarantee of their miraculous causation. We are told that her visions "are in full harmony with the gospel truth. . . . They never offend against the dignity, the sanctity, and the religious tone of the gospel spirit of truth."[44] They are said to be in perfect conformity with scriptural science. "Her complete knowledge of the topography of Jerusalem might vie with the most exact map of any general's staff . . . she drew with her finger in the air . . . with the most exact turns, the road along which she thought she could lead our Lord to help Him escape." Once she said: "If you should lock me in there [in the temple] I could find a way to get out." Finally, Theresa knows many details concerning the scenes of Christ's passion which are not to be found in any historical document.[45]

What answer can we give? First of all we may well doubt whether Theresa's visions "are in full harmony with the gospel truth." According to St. Matthew's Gospel, Jesus came to His disciples in the garden "and found them *sleeping*" (26:40). "And he said to Peter, 'Simon, dost thou sleep? Couldst thou *not watch* one hour?' . . . And he came again and found them *sleeping* . . . and they did not know what answer to make to him" (Mk. 14:37–40).[46] Yet Theresa tells us: "I saw three Apostles, but they were *not* lying down or *sleeping* as they are usually pictured, but rather as leaning on stones, and were entirely powerless."[47]

But even if we would concede to the Konnersreuth apologists that Theresa's visions are in perfect accord with the gospel narrative, we could conclude merely that the hypothesis of a divine origin is *not excluded a priori* — a merely negative con-

---

[44] *Ibid.*, pp. 442, 443.

[45] *Ibid.*, pp. 444, 446–449.

[46] Cf. also St. Luke: "And rising from prayer he came to the disciples, and found them *sleeping* for sorrow. And he said to them, 'Why do you *sleep?*'" (22:45, 46.)

[47] Von Lama, *Theresa Neumann von Konnersreuth*, p. 47.

clusion. A positive argument would have to show that a divine revelation *alone* could explain the agreement in question. This would be a formidable task, for many details of her visions could have been drawn from sermons, catechism lessons, spiritual readings, and from her frequent conversations with theologians.[48]

We are likewise assured that Theresa's complete knowledge of the topography of Jerusalem might vie with the most exact map of any general's staff. "Even the smallest byway is not hidden from her eyes."[49] And the proof: "She drew with her finger in the air for Bishop L. and myself. . . ." How unfortunate that she did not sketch the route with pen and paper! She also said that she could easily find a way out if she were locked in the temple of Jerusalem. This is a striking example of argumentation from *"ipse dixit."* Many an illusion might be supported by mere assertion.

Then too, Theresa gives us details which are not to be found in any historical document. It may be well for us to mention a few of these details. In his Pentecostal sermon, for example, St. Peter first pointed to the man whom he had healed. "Peter then ran his hand through his hair. . . ." When St. John heard Jesus say to him: "Son, behold thy mother," he immediately left his place and went to Mary's side. The lame man cured at the gate of the temple wished to give St. Peter all the money he had in his hat. When the Apostle refused to accept it, he threw his hat with the money into the air. When the Blessed Mother brought the Child Jesus to the temple in Jerusalem, Theresa saw that they paused in silence "before the notice whereon was written the curse on strangers who should enter the temple beyond this point." St. Peter's behavior in the episode where the Apostle tried unsuccessfully to cure the lunatic is very striking: "Now he looks upon the unhappy man," says

---

[48] St. Thérèse of the Child Jesus is supposed to have told Theresa Neumann in a vision: "I have already written that more souls are saved by suffering than by the most magnificent sermons." It is hard to believe that such a devotee of the Little Flower should never have heard these words! We must remember that Theresa was an avid reader of periodicals promoting devotion to St. Thérèse.

[49] Teodorowicz, *op. cit.*, p. 449.

Theresa, "then he stretches his hands out and above. His perplexed look is raised to heaven and then again to the scene before him."[50]

The weakness of this argument lies in the impossibility of *verifying* the *authenticity* of all the alleged details. The fact that Theresa "always repeats the same details about the appearance, form, color of hair, and movements of persons, the number and the names of the Apostles that come in this or that scene, etc." is no proof of the objectivity of these details. In fact, it is typical of the stereotypy which characterizes the "second state." The assertion that the products of the imagination "bear the stamp of unrestraint and eccentricity," that they contain "ridiculous absurdities, trivialities, ludicrousness, and abstruseness," is absolutely exaggerated. It may be true of some mental illnesses, for example, of schizophrenia, but not of all products of the imagination.

We would like to mention once again an important fact which a number of Catholic observers have emphasized (and which we have mentioned previously) namely: the things seen by Theresa in her visions are not accurately fulfilled.[51] How is this to be explained if Theresa's visions really come from God? Our difficulty increases when we learn that many of her visions depict scenes which are purely legendary, for example, details of the martyrdom of St. Agnes, St. Catherine, St. Barbara, and the voyage of Lazarus, Mary Magdalene, and Martha in a boat without sail or rudder through the Mediterranean to the south of France.[52] Are we to assume that these, too, are infused supernaturally?

Some writers answer in the affirmative, arguing that an artist sketching a landscape is not criticized for not presenting an exact picture of the scene before his eyes. They also point to the fact that the Church herself draws on legend in her liturgy.[53]

---

[50] *Ibid.*, pp. 446, 447.

[51] Cf. Chapter 5, pages 90, 92, "Cure of the Spine"; Westermayr, "Konnersreuth in der theologischen Kritik," *Augsburger Postzeitung*, No. 28, July 12, 1930.

[52] Westermayr, *loc cit.* H. Thurston, S.J., *The Physical Phenomena of Mysticism*, pp. 112–114, 127–128.

[53] Teodorowicz, *op. cit.*, p. 453.

This argument is not very convincing. When an artist paints a landscape we do not expect photographic precision. He may even make use of subjects from mythology! But a person who has a vision of some legendary occurrence is led to believe in its objectivity; nay, more, he cannot even doubt it since, according to the authors mentioned above, his memory and imagination are entirely "paralyzed," and he himself is supposed to be entirely "passive." The supernatural theory would then have to ascribe the illusion or error to God Himself.[54]

Nevertheless, such an "illusion" might be very useful for the spiritual advancement of the visionary, we are told. We might ask: Could not God obtain the same goal by other means? Is His omnipotence so limited? Moreover, *non sunt facienda mala ut eveniant bona;* the end does not justify the means.

But our adversaries do not give in so easily. Certain visionaries whose sanctity has been confirmed by God, they point out, contradict one another in details of their visions. Some saints have seen Jesus fastened to the cross with three nails, others with four nails.[55] They conclude that, despite discrepancy of detail, the visions nevertheless must have God for their author.

Those who maintain this stand forget that when the Church sets her seal on the heroicity of a saint's virtues, she does not thereby guarantee the authenticity of their visions; she does not say that they have "God for their author." Neither does she oblige us to accept them as infallible truth. We have stressed this point previously.[56] St. John of the Cross goes so far as to

---

[54] We cannot object to the Church allowing certain legendary scenes to find a place in her liturgy, for she does not oblige us to accept them as historical.

[55] Poulain, *op. cit.* (French ed.), Chap. 21, p. 342; cf. also p. 327 for other instances.

[56] An outstanding ecclesiastic, who wishes to remain anonymous, writes: "The Church, canonizing St. Joan of Arc, has confirmed the truth of her visions." This is absolutely false. Father Leczycki (Lancicius), whom Benedict XIV quotes approvingly, says: "I can mention certain persons who have been enrolled in the canon of the Saints by the Holy See and whose words and writings, received in ecstasy (*in raptibus et ex raptibus*) . . . are full of hallucination (*magnis hallucinationibus respersa*). For this reason they may not be printed." Benedict XIV, *op. cit.*, Book III, final chapter, n. 17.

forbid us to make any *research* to discover what part of a vision comes from God and what from nature.

Some writers, seeing the difficulty of the problem, admit that there is really only one criterion which can prove the supernatural character of Theresa's visions, and that is their *spiritual fruit*. Her visions must be from God, they say, because they increase the love of God in her soul.

Within limits, this is an excellent criterion, but it shows only that the visions are not of diabolic origin, that they must in some manner come from God. However, we do not know in *what manner*. The hallucinatory character of certain visions does not impugn their moral usefulness and their providential intention, notes Father Maréchal.[57] In this restricted sense, we too can admit that they come "from God." But in this restricted sense there is nothing in the world that cannot be called "supernatural." *Diligentibus Deum omnia cooperantur in bonum* — "For those who love God all things work together unto good." Yes, everything — poverty and wealth, sickness and health, disgrace and honor, failure and success. But when we inquire whether a vision be "supernatural," is *this* the meaning we have in mind? As to the *spiritual fruit* in the souls of Theresa's visitors, many of them were edified, but not few were seriously scandalized. We saw this before.

---

[57] J. Maréchal, S.J., *Études sur la psychologie des mystiques* (Paris: Alcan), pp. 210–211.

CHAPTER 9

Gift of Tongues

DURING her ecstasies Theresa Neumann not only beholds people and their activities, she also *hears* their speech. In her visions of the passion, she would, of course, hear words spoken in the Aramaic language, which was in common use in Palestine in the time of Christ. She is said to be able to hear the variant pronunciations corresponding to the place of origin of the different speakers. In the words of Von Aretin: "Despite defective pronunciation of the Aramaic words . . . my guide, Dr. Wutz (an eminent Semitist) is able to distinguish the Galilean dialect of Peter from the purer Judaean form spoken by Caiphas."[1] Dr. Johann Bauer, professor of semitic philology at Halle, asserts that "the fact of the Aramaic language [in Theresa's visions] does not admit of any doubt."[2]

Certain scholars attempt to explain this phenomenon in terms of "unconscious memory." Theresa Neumann "spent some time in a convent. She probably heard some Aramaic words there, which she repeats in her trances. . . ." This assertion is utterly groundless. Only a few scholars in Germany know Aramaic, and the good nuns with whom Theresa associated are certainly not of their number.

Others appeal to "retrospective telepathy." When a person speaks to us from a great distance, we do not hear the words at the exact moment the speaker pronounces them (because of the time lapse required for the sound waves to reach our ears).

---

[1] *Münchener Neueste Nachrichten*, Dec. 14, 1927.

[2] "Einkehr," supplement of the *Münchener Neueste Nachrichten*, No. 57, Aug. 3, 1927.

Similarly, events in the distant stars are not perceived until long afterward by terrestrial astronomers. Can we possibly believe that Theresa hears the actual sounds that were made nineteen centuries ago? If such sounds could have reached Konnersreuth they would have been spent ages ago. One might insist that the "echo" of these voices still resounds in the German mountains. But it is certainly too weak to be perceived by a human ear, as a "sound"!

Perhaps her knowledge of Aramaic is derived from Dr. Wutz. This professor, as Ewald notes, was a frequent visitor at Konnersreuth. Being of "a very lively temperament" (*temperamentvoll*), he could communicate a good deal of Aramaic to her by his questions (*hineinkatechisiert*). "It is only in this manner that we can account for the fact that Theresa suddenly began to have hallucinations in Aramaic, whereas previously she heard the words of Christ in the dialect of the Upper Palatinate."[3]

Gerlich dismisses this theory as contrary to the facts of the case. Theresa never heard Christ speaking in German. She does not understand the various speakers in the passion drama.[4]

Without subscribing to the extravagances of the theory, we must, however, give some attention to its main idea. Professor Wutz, in fact, was the first to discover that Theresa used Aramaic words.[5] He often visited her, held long conversations with her, and urged her to repeat, at least approximately, the words heard in her visions.[6] Only after long and painstaking research was he able to conclude that the language heard by Theresa was really Aramaic. He admitted to Gerlich that "it was extremely difficult to grasp even the roots of the words; and that not only in rather long sentences, but even in brief phrases."[7]

We can readily appreciate his difficulty. Anyone not familiar with a foreign language will find it difficult to pronounce even

---

[3] *Die Stigmatisierte von Konnersreuth*, München, 1927, p. 7.

[4] *Die stigmatisierte Therese Neumann von Konnersreuth*, II, Chap. 10, p. 384.

[5] Theresa herself tells us this. Cf. Teodorowicz, *Mystical Phenomena in the Life of Theresa Neumann* (St. Louis: Herder, 1940), p. 486.

[6] Teodorowicz, *op. cit.*, pp. 482, 483, 486.

[7] Gerlich, *op. cit.*, I, p. 158.

single words correctly. The difficulty increases when the foreign language has certain vowels and consonants very different from those of one's native tongue; and it becomes well-nigh impossible when the person suffers a speech defect which prevents him from pronouncing certain sounds. Theresa is faced with all these handicaps: she knows no other language but German; Aramaic has sounds entirely different from German; and finally, Theresa has difficulty in making a distinction between *d* and *t* and between *b* and *p* (she lost her front teeth as a result of her spasms).

If we add to all this the fact noted by the orientalist Johann Bauer[8] that we do not know the exact pronunciation of Aramaic at the time of Christ, nor its various dialects, we can form some idea of the herculean task facing a scholar who would attempt to discover the Aramaic language in Theresa's utterances. Such a scholar would have to be most considerate and modest in his demands, being willing to accept only vague approximations. Neither could he rely too much on his own preconceived notions as to how the words were actually pronounced in the time of Christ. Finally he would have to be of exceptional pedagogical ability in order not to *suggest* to his pupil, even by his questions, the answers he expects to hear (*hineinfragen*).

From a scientific point of view, Wutz's investigation of the Aramaic problem is *inadequate,* as a few samples of his technique will show. On one occasion the professor asked Theresa what she had heard the angels singing above the stable of Bethlehem during her Christmas vision (1926). "I don't know," replied Theresa. "Their language was so strange (*so olber*); I could not understand them at all." Then Wutz spoke the words: "Glory to God in the highest and on earth peace to men of good will" in a number of ancient, oriental languages. Each time Theresa answered: "No, the angels did not sing that way." Finally he recited the words in Aramaic. Theresa exclaimed joyfully: "Yes, that's the way they sang . . . but something is missing. . . ." By the same method Wutz learned that Theresa

---

[8] *Münchener Neueste Nachrichten,* Dec. 14, 1927.

Neumann heard the words of the angelic salutation in Aramaic during her vision of March 25, 1927.

Unfortunately this sort of evidence is no proof that Theresa really hears Aramaic in her visions. Theresa's replies to Wutz can be explained very easily by telepathy or even Cumberlandism.[9]

The "Aramaic" words spoken by Theresa herself are very few in number: *Baisebua, gannaba, gallaba, kum, as-che mag(g)era;* they were so badly pronounced that Wutz found it difficult, as he admits, to grasp the root form. According to some scholars,[10] the word *baisebua* could very well be a corruption of the German *boeser Bube* (wicked fellow; Bavarians say *Bua* for *Bube*). The word *mag(g)era* would be the *magerer* of the Upper Palatinate dialect.[11] L. Witt observes that Theresa's ability to remember and repeat words heard in her visions developed gradually.[12]

It is unfortunate that the suggestion of Professor R. Kittel, an outstanding orientalist, was not adopted. He proposed that a committee of philologists be sent to Konnersreuth to transcribe Theresa's "Aramaic" words phonetically. Orientalists would then be in a better position to study the words carefully and determine

---

[9] The following fact is frequently cited as a refutation of our theory: On one occasion Professor Wutz asked Theresa immediately after her vision (i.e., in her "childlike state"): "Do you know what this or that person said?" "No, he spoke too indistinctly," replied Theresa. "Then tell me at least," said Wutz, "how he spoke." Theresa attempted to repeat a sentence, or rather the beginning and end of a sentence. When Wutz spoke the entire sentence Theresa said: "Yes . . . you were there . . . you heard it well." Wutz then told her to repeat the entire sentence, but she could not improve on her first attempt. She learned nothing from him.

This line of argument would be decisive on the supposition that thought transference occurs only in state of complete consciousness. But, as we have already said, the mechanisms of Cumberlandism and telepathy are most effective on the level of subconscious psychic life. The fact that Theresa could learn nothing from Wutz in her childlike state through conscious reflection is no proof that she could not have been subject to subconscious influences.

[10] For example, D. Herzog, *Grazer Volksblatt*, Dec. 25, 1927.

[11] Hilda Graef is of the same opinion. She finds the words *magera, baisebua,* and *gannaba* suspiciously Bavarian. The words are Upper-Palatinate corruptions (*The Case of Theresa Neumann*, p. 88). According to D. C. Wessely, the word *mag(g)era* is really not of Aramaic, but of Greek origin (*mahaira*).

[12] *Konnersreuth im Lichte der Religion und Wissenschaft*, II, p. 11.

whether they are really Aramaic. At present we have no assurance that they are.

Before closing this chapter we would like to mention another assertion of the Konnersreuth apologists, namely that "modern languages are spoken by Theresa, too. Often in her ecstasy she speaks modern High German. She recognizes Portuguese by its sound. . . . She speaks French."[13]

"Modern High German" does not present a problem, since Theresa studied it in school, reads it, and uses it frequently in conversation with educated visitors. Her alleged knowledge of Portuguese deserves more attention. According to Teodorowicz's account, Father Greve was conversing in Portuguese with the Bishop of Petrolina, Brazil, about Theresa's stigmata while waiting in the reception room in Konnersreuth on July 16, 1928. "Unexpectedly she was heard to say: 'It seems to me I heard that language in my ecstasy.' Those around her paid no attention to her statement, thinking that she must be mistaken. Surely she could not hear Portuguese in her visions of the Passion! But she suddenly interrupted and assured us . . . very insistently that she did hear this language in her vision."[14] Father Naber then took part in the discussion and settled the matter. Theresa, he said, could be right. A year before she had a vision of St. Anthony (June 13) and she could have heard him speaking Portuguese!

This seems to us very slim evidence for her "knowledge" of the Portuguese language! And her "gift" of the French tongue rests on equally questionable grounds. It seems that she heard the dying St. Francis de Sales repeat the words: *Mon Dieu.* On another occasion (February 11, 1928) she is supposed to have heard Our Lady of Lourdes tell St. Bernadette: *"Je suis l'Immaculée Conception."*[15] Such "proofs" can hardly be taken seriously.

---

[13] Teodorowicz, *op. cit.*, pp. 472–473.

[14] *Ibid.*, p. 470.

[15] It is even affirmed that Theresa spoke these words "In the Pyrenean dialect," though no proof is offered that it was really this dialect. Again, how do we know that she never read or heard these words?

CHAPTER 10

Prophecy and Clairvoyance

THERESE NEUMANN is said to have "predicted" certain events which actually occurred later on and to have revealed hidden things. We have already mentioned some instances in Part I of the present study.

How do these assertions stand up in the light of critical scrutiny? First, we must be careful not to accept an *isolated* instance as evidence of the gift of prophecy. P. A. Poulain, S.J., and other great spiritual writers insist: "If an isolated prediction is realized, we have only the probability that it was of divine origin, even when there is question of events dependent on human free will. For the prediction might well have been made by chance and fulfilled the same way."[1]

On this basis we hesitate to accept as supernatural the prediction Theresa made to Father A. Gemelli, O.F.M., that he would be received by the pope on a certain Saturday, rather than on Thursday, as he had been expecting. Father Poulain's warning is very much to the point here, since the difference in time was rather slight and consequently the probability of the prediction being fulfilled greatly enhanced.

Second, some of Theresa's predictions are much too *ambiguous* for us to accept them as divine. When someone asked her about the possible beatification of Catherine Emmerich, for example, she said that neither the "present Pope" (Pius XI) nor his successor (Pius XII) would make any decision in her regard. But the following pope would have "much to say" (*der wird viel sagen*).[2]

---

[1] *Des grâces d'oraison,* Paris, 1909, 8 ed., p. 374.

[2] Von Lama, *Theresa Neumann,* 1929, p. 93; Spirago, *Klarheit über Konnersreuth,* p. 51.

At present we can pass no judgment on the accuracy of Theresa's prediction; we must patiently await the advent of the next pope. However, we observe that this "prophecy" is couched in very general terms, for many possible meanings can be read into "he will have much to say"!

Hellwig conducted a careful study of the ambiguous statements of certain clairvoyants. He asked a great number of persons what they thought of when they heard the phrases: "It is long and dark. One end is sharp, too sharp, the other is blunt." He received two hundred answers, all different. Only one person named the object he had in mind when he spoke the words. Hans Driesch, referring to this experiment, adds: "Almost all the statements that I have heard from German mediums belong to this category. They are too vague and consequently valueless."[3] For the same reason many of Theresa's predictions are not worthy of serious consideration.

Another prediction to which some writers allude to prove their case is when Theresa foretold that something would happen to an *automobile* which was about to start on a trip. The importance of this statement, they say, lies in its relation to a future event which no one could possibly foretell. It can be explained only as an instance of the supernatural gift of prophecy.

Such a conclusion seems too hasty. For one thing, the prediction was much too vague. If someone else had made the assertion no one would dream of calling it prophetic. But it was made by Theresa Neumann!

But let us grant that we are really dealing here with "a prediction of a future event." Must we accept it as a real "prophecy"? It is quite possible that the automobile in question was not operating properly at the time it started on its journey. Anyone cognizant of the difficulty would be in a position to "predict" an accident. We might compare such a prediction to that of a collision of two trains which simultaneously start off on the same rails toward each other from two nearby stations. An observer on a neighboring hilltop, aware of what was happen-

---

[3] *Parapsychologie* (München: Bruckmann, 1932), pp. 40–41.

ing, could easily "predict" a catastrophe without claiming the role of prophet. The future accident was already determined by the actual situation of the trains.

Theresa's prediction of the automobile accident might be accounted for in terms of "clairvoyance." Even Teodorowicz, whom no one can accuse of being hypercritical, disagrees with Gerlich in this matter, asserting that the prediction "could be explained naturally by clairvoyance through impenetrable objects."[4]

We must adopt the same reserve toward her knowledge of the character of certain people who came to her for help in their interior trials. Our experience at the Spiritualistic Institute of Paris has left us extremely skeptical on this point. What the medium usually says is so general as to be applicable to any situation. Once she said to a gentleman: "You are doing a work . . . and some people criticize you." Indeed he was painting and his work was being criticized. But the word "work" could just as well mean the writing of a book or of an article for the newspapers, and so on. Every man has his own "work" and it will usually be criticized by someone!

Masters of the spiritual life, like Schram, advise us to suspect greatly any revelation which has for its object the sins or moral faults of our neighbor; for, they argue, the visionary is then exposed to the danger of violating the greatest of all commandments, that of charity. What are we to say when the visionary makes public the hidden faults of others, or at least faults not known to those present? He is then running the risk of violating justice by robbing another of his good name.

St. John of the Cross was extremely severe in this matter: "It is true that God sometimes represents to holy souls the necessities of their neighbors, that they may pray for them, or relieve them. . . . But most frequently it is the devil that does this, and that falsely, in order that persons may be accused of sin, and afflicted; of this we have many proofs."[5]

---

[4] *Mystical Phenomena in the Life of Theresa Neumann* (St. Louis: Herder, 1940), p. 413.

[5] *The Ascent of Mount Carmel,* Book II, Chap. XXVI (English ed., p. 214):

If we are to follow the principles of the Doctor of Mysticism exactly, we would have to consider a good number of Theresa's feats of clairvoyance as "coming from the devil."[6] We cite one example narrated by Teodorowicz: "Once when only a few persons were in Theresa's room, she was in a state of ecstatic vision. . . . Suddenly she began to complain loudly. To the pastor's question of what was wrong, she answered: 'An apostate has been here. He has denied the Saviour.'"[7] Another time a young scientist (who had not impressed her favorably) entered the room. Theresa, summoning all her strength, cried aloud that someone was in the room who was living contrary to Christ. At these words the young man became pale and left the room. One day in October, 1927, she pointed to a visitor and declared aloud: "This man does not love our Lord; but our Lord does not love him either"; and she enumerated his faults pitilessly. Many other examples could be cited, and they certainly do not speak well for the supernatural character of her clairvoyance.

Before we can attribute any prediction to supernatural causes we must first prove that it cannot be explained naturally. Indeed, "the philosophers . . . explain very well the reason for which melancholics or persons near death have foretold some things which have really been fulfilled."[8] Melancholics as well as the feeble-minded (*fatui et stupidi*) are said to resemble the lower animals in their mental powers; their instincts are like those of the animal. Therefore they easily grasp the connection of certain natural causes and effects which are hid from the discursive reason. Persons near death suffer impairment of their sensitive

---

"The devil is wont occasionally to reveal, falsely, but with great distinctness, the sins of others, evil consciences, and corrupt souls, with a view to detraction, and to induce him, to whom the revelation is made, to publish the sins in question, so that other sins may be added to them. He stirs a false zeal, deluding him, in whom he stirs it, into the belief that these revelations are intended to lead him to pray for the souls of those whom he thus traduces."

[6] We can explain them naturally, however, as we shall soon demonstrate.

[7] *Op. cit.,* p. 396.

[8] Benedict XIV uses the word *"melancholici"* in the same sense as Hippocrates, to designate various mental disorders (*De Servorum Dei Beatificatione et de Beatorum Canonizatione,* Book III, Chap. 46, n. 4).

powers (*impeditae*). They are therefore more capable of recollection and can consider things calmly and with greater attention, and by this means penetrate the inner nature of things.[9]

The modern reader will undoubtedly find Benedict's theory quite naïve and summary, as in fact it is. Nevertheless, it is valuable to the extent that it shows us very clearly with what *attitude* we are to approach the problem of clairvoyance. Before acquiescing to the supernatural theory we must first consult the "philosophers" who have made a study of the phenomenon, that is, authorities in the fields of psychology and parapsychology. Benedict XIV quotes in favor of his theory the names of Plato, Aristotle, St. Gregory, and a number of eighteenth-century scholars (Valessius, Raphael de la Torre, Gaspar, Rejas, Zacchias, Father Baldellus). Were he living today he would without doubt appeal to the findings of modern psychology and parapsychology.

If we examine Theresa's feats of clairvoyance in the spirit of Benedict XIV we will find that a number of them find an adequate explanation in *Cumberlandism,* a phenomenon resulting from the motor effect of imagery. Suppose we tell a subject to hold his hand outstretched at eye level and at the same time to *think* of a *descending* perpendicular line. If we place our hand under his and exert an upward pressure we will meet resistance. We will meet no resistance, however, if we exert a *downward* pressure. Our ideas (images), therefore, are accompanied by *tendencies* to carry out the action represented by the ideas. By skillfully interpreting these overt tendencies we can often discover the *ideas* which suggest them. The so-called "willing game" is a practical application of this principle. By simply holding the hand of a person who knows where an object is hidden, the "thought reader" is led to its discovery.[10] The

---

[9] *Ibid.* Cf. Alberti, *De vaticinio aegrotorum,* 1724.

[10] Success in the "willing game" is in direct proportion to the distractions of the "guide." People who constantly make use of visual or auditory imagery pay little attention to their *motor* imagery and guide the "thought reader" very readily. Persons who are more or less hysterical make the best "guides" because of their many unconscious movements.

"rotating tables" of spiritualistic seances, the marvels of the divining rod, the replies given by Chevreul's pendulum, and the like, are all based to a great extent on the same principle. An image of movement, especially if it is very vivid, causes a contraction of the muscles normally used in executing the motion and a corresponding relaxation of the antagonistic muscles. Some individuals are such competent "guides" that the "thought reader" can interpret their movements even when following at a distance. Some "thought readers" can discover the guide's idea when there is another person interposed between himself and the guide.[11] We constantly glean a good deal of information about the characters of others in a similar way. We observe their facial expressions, their gestures, their manner of speech, their reactions to questions or to the environment, and by these means we "read" their state of mind.

Many cases attributed to supernatural powers in Theresa Neumann can easily be explained in the light of these principles. We know, for example, that in order to give information concerning certain persons she must *touch their hand*.[12] The fact that she manifests her gift of clairvoyance best in her "exalted repose" offers no problem. Reception of slight external stimuli adequate for thought reading need not necessarily imply fully conscious and controlled knowledge. It can take place on the subconscious level as well. In fact, the latter state is actually more favorable to the reception of motor stimuli. In a semiconscious state the threshold of sensitivity is sometimes lowered. For this reason persons in somnambulism or under hypnosis are often better able to "read" the thoughts of others. The exalted repose state, as we have noted before, bears a strong resemblance to somnambulism and hypnosis.[13]

---

[11] The intermediary, of course, has no idea of the action to be performed.

[12] Not all instances in which Theresa discovers information by touching a person's hand need be explained in terms of Cumberlandism. The physical contact may serve simply as a stimulus to her powers of clairvoyance.

[13] Telepathy is most effective, says R. Warcollier, in the "states of sleep." Under "sleep" he includes fainting, coma, delirium, and the moment of death (*La télépathie, Recherche expérimentale,* préface de M. le professeur Ch. Richet [Paris:

Finally, certain insights reported of Theresa Neumann can be explained sufficiently by the phenomenon known as "clairvoyance" (*Hellsehen*) and which C. Richet terms "cryptesthesia." Myers prefers the name "telesthesia." More commonly it is called "telepathy." This phenomenon is not yet perfectly understood, but various theories have been offered to account for it. Some attempt to explain it through the activity of the souls of the living (animism); others, through that of the dead (spiritism). Some prefer the radiation theory; information would be carried to the clairvoyant from objects distant in space or time through the mediation of material or psychic waves. Then there is the "excursion" hypothesis, according to which the human soul, or a part thereof, would leave the physical body for a time in order to be in the presence of distant persons or objects. Some writers favor the "whispering" theory or the "involuntary signal" theory. According to the first (advanced by Lehmann and Hansen), the receivers would respond to the unconscious whispering (subvocal speech) of their informers; according to the second, they would interpret various other involuntary signs. Each of these theories has its advantages, but none can explain all the data.[14] The fact of telepathy itself, however, seems to be well established. H. Driesch considers it absolutely certain (*ganz gesichert*). The experiments of R. Tischner, v. Wasielewski, Pagenstecher, Upton Sinclair, and many others have, in his opinion, guaranteed its reality.[15] Philosophers and psychologists, such as Boutroux, Bergson, Maxwell, C. Richet, Lombroso, Abramowski, Grasset, Binet-Sanglé, Dwelshauvers, Havelock Ellis, and the like, are far from rejecting telepathy. They maintain that individuals possess the power in varying degrees. It can be enhanced in certain psychic conditions

---

Alcan, 1921], p. 24). His view is strongly reminiscent of the theory of Benedict XIV which we described above and according to which the "melancholics" and feeble-minded (*fatui et stupidi*) as well as the dying are especially endowed with the gift of prophecy.

[14] It would be beyond our scope here to discuss them at length. We have done so in our *Psychology*, which is being printed.

[15] H. Driesch, *op. cit.*, pp. 88, 89.

which are more or less abnormal, especially in hypnosis and analogous mental states, such as the state of "absorption" and, even more so, in the state of "exalted repose."

It must be admitted that many of the marvelous occurrences in the life of Theresa Neumann lend themselves to a telepathic interpretation, such as, for example, her ability to know the contents of sealed letters and to give answers to questions before they have been expressed orally.[16] Of a similar order is the following incident narrated by Teodorowicz: "Once in a Friday ecstasy she cried out: 'Now such and such a person has arrived,' and she pointed with her hand in the direction that person was supposed to be. And it was so. Two hours later someone asked Theresa where this person might be. Without reflecting, Theresa stretched out her hand again, but this time in the opposite direction and said: 'She is there.' We looked through the window and again saw the person in front of the house and in the direction pointed out by Theresa."[17]

The same author cites the following occurrence as evidence that Theresa's clairvoyant powers are supernatural: "Once a precious relic, a tiny splinter of the true cross, fell to the floor while it was being shown to her. As it was evening and many people were taking part in the search, the relic could not be found on the dusty floor. Theresa pointed to a place on the floor and said 'There is the relic.' And it was actually found on the spot indicated."[18]

All these as well as many other occurrences lend themselves to an explanation by telepathy. The annals of the psychical sciences can recount many more similar incidents.

Some of the more zealous defenders of the supernatural character of the Konnersreuth phenomena admit, moreover, that certain instances of Theresa's clairvoyance "have their analogy in the hidden forces of the natural sphere," and that they "could

---

[16] Teodorowicz, *op. cit.*, p. 398. Psychology evidences several cases where sealed letters were read correctly by individuals who were completely devoid of any supernatural charism.

[17] *Ibid.*, pp. 412–413.

[18] *Ibid.*, p. 411.

then be explained in a natural manner."[19] The following instances
would fall in this category. On one occasion when Father Naber
returned to Konnersreuth from a journey to Berlin Theresa told
him that she had assisted at his Mass. She described the church,
she saw the priest who served the Mass, she told him of a slight
mishap — when he wished to open the tabernacle to administer
Holy Communion he could not find the key. The pastor confirmed the truth of all these details. Another time when Theresa
was in Waldsassen she assisted at the Mass read by Father
Naber in Konnersreuth. She listened to his sermon and to the
singing of the choir, saw the children and warned them with a
gesture of her finger to behave themselves. Her prediction of
the automobile accident mentioned earlier belongs in this same
class.

Nevertheless, they contend that even these facts which, considered in the abstract "could be explained naturally" must be
considered supernatural when considered in the concrete. They
offer the following argument which they consider very important:
"While the natural phenomena as a rule come after great
expenditure of thought and mental strain, the phenomena of
Theresa Neumann appear with an ease that must arouse surprise.
No strain of thought, no mental exhaustion is noticeable in her."
When the world-famous medium Mr. O. tried to read the
contents of a sealed letter "he turned the envelope this way
and that, and exerted himself to so great an extent that the
exertion was even noticeable physically."[20]

We do not think that these facts warrant the conclusion drawn
from them. That telepathic phenomena are not always associated
with strain and effort is too well known for us to insist on it.
Besides, we must distinguish carefully between telepathic communications which one tries to obtain "at will" and those which
occur "spontaneously." Mental exhaustion occurs particularly in
the former. "The will, as usually understood," notes Warcollier,
"does not seem to play an important role in telepathic phenom-

---

[19] *Ibid.*, pp. 412, 413.
[20] *Ibid.*

ena. There is no necessity for exhausting concentration such as the charlatans of 'thought transmission' pretend to exert . . . the emotional element acts independently of the will, either because it is itself the trigger which releases the telepathic movement, or because it can penetrate more deeply into the region of the subconscious than thought can."[21]

One of the most decisive arguments quoted in favor of the supernatural character of Theresa's clairvoyance is the well-known case of Archbishop Schrembs of Cleveland. "For three quarters of an hour," said the Archbishop, "she delved into the deepest recesses of my soul. She told me things that will remain locked in my breast. . . . She even spoke of the condition of my diocese. She pointed out certain things that were in connection with persons with whom I worked daily."[22]

It is unfortunate that this incident has received so much publicity. Archbishop Schrembs did not retain his enthusiastic attitude toward Konnersreuth. Indeed, a few years later, when Father Göttsches asked him at Krefeld what he thought of Konnersreuth, he made the following statement in the presence of four priests of his diocese: "I did not go there this time, and I do not intend to. The things that Theresa told me regarding the priests of my diocese were not true. I have gone to the Bishop of Ratisbon and told him that Father Naber, the pastor of Konnersreuth, ought to be transferred and Theresa herself placed in a convent. If the case had taken place in my diocese I would have ordered these steps taken immediately and I would have personally supervised the execution of my directions. I am done with Konnersreuth."[23]

Another incident cited in favor of the supernatural theory is the one in which a certain young man requested Father Naber

---

[21] *Op. cit.*, pp. 31–32.

[22] F. von Lama, *op. cit.*, p. 111 ff. Cf. Teodorowicz, *op. cit.*, p. 403. The incident took place in December, 1927.

[23] Göttsches, *Kathol. Pfarramt St. Marien*, Aachen, March 29, 1935, Wallstrasse 44. In a letter to the author, dated March 29, 1952, Hilda Graef says: "Archbishop Buchberger of Regensburg confirmed what you write in your book, that Archbishop Schrembs had been disappointed in her [Theresa Neumann]."

to ask Theresa the state of life for which he was best suited. Theresa answered that he was called to the priesthood. The young man was very much surprised and declared that he would never be a priest. Nevertheless, six months later, he entered the seminary.[24]

The weakness of this argument lies in the circumstance that Theresa's prediction was communicated to the young man *himself*. Is it not possible that the prediction brought about his decision to enter the seminary? The possibility is all the more plausible since, on the one hand, the young man was hesitant about his vocation, and, on the other, he was a firm believer in Konnersreuth.

That a prediction can have the force of a suggestion is well known. A man can die if someone convinces him that his arteries have been cut, even though only a small incision is made in the skin to permit warm blood to flow over his hand. Many suicides have resulted from "prophecies." We once knew a university professor who, when a clairvoyant predicted his death at the age of fifty-five, was deeply impressed and each succeeding year became more preoccupied and nervous. When he was fifty-five years of age his life really came to an end, through suicide. A dream, too, can act as a suggestion.

But what about Theresa's knowledge of the secrets of the human heart and of the supernatural condition of souls? "The relations of the soul to God" is something no creature can know naturally.[25]

Granting the principle that no creature can naturally know one's state of conscience, we still must face the problem of *fact*. How can we vouch for the accuracy of Theresa's statements? Take, for example, the incident of a certain nun who had left her convent and led a scandalous life in the world. When she died suddenly, without the sacraments, her anxious family asked Theresa about her fate in eternity. In an ecstasy Theresa

---

[24] Teodorowicz, *op. cit.,* p. 406.
[25] Many facts of this kind are quoted. Cf. Teodorowicz, *op. cit.,* p. 395 ff.

answered that the nun was with our Lord.[26] How can we be sure that Theresa really knew?

Another case. A pastor, who visited a sick member of his parish and heard his confession did not, however, administer Viaticum since the patient did not seem to be in danger of death. Somewhat uneasy about his decision, he asked Theresa how long the patient would live. Receiving a reassuring answer, the priest delayed the administration of Holy Viaticum. When the sick man died suddenly, the priest was stricken with remorse and reproached himself bitterly for having consulted Theresa. He even thought that she must be possessed by the devil, since her advice resulted in spiritual harm to souls. To console him, Theresa, in an ecstasy, declared that the dead man was saved.[27] Once more we ask: How can we know that Theresa's pronouncement is the infallible truth? We cannot know. What we do know for certain is that she was the occasion of a man dying without the last sacraments. This fact alone throws serious doubt on the supernatural origin of her clairvoyance. Of course, we cannot approve the conduct of the priest who asked Theresa for her opinion and was guided by it. The family of the nun deserves the same censure; we are not allowed to make inquiries concerning the fate of the dead.[28]

No creature can know the secrets of the human soul by natural means, especially whether it is in the state of grace or of sin. We admit this principle, but with the proviso: so long as the parties concerned do not themselves *manifest* such secrets by an outward sign. This proviso is fatal to a number of arguments cited by the defenders of the supernatural theory. Some of the sins which Theresa revealed were not strictly interior. During one of her ecstatic trances, for example, she said: "An apostate has been here. He has denied the Saviour." Her statement was true, but the man's apostasy was public knowledge. Another time she said to Father Naber: "Don't trust Gerlich. He is an un-

---

[26] *Ibid.*, p. 397.

[27] *Ibid.*, pp. 400–401.

[28] This is the unanimous teaching of theologians, especially of St. John of the Cross.

believer." This was also true. Gerlich merely feigned belief in order to gain the good will of the pastor, as he himself admitted.[29]

But what assurance have we that Theresa could not know such facts by means of telepathy and Cumberlandism, especially since the instances cited are very similar to others for which even the Konnersreuth apologists admit the possibility of a natural explanation?

The Konnersreuth apologists offer the following case as their most decisive argument. Wishing to give Father Naber an absolute guarantee of the supernatural origin of her clairvoyance, Theresa once told him: "That you may know that everything I am telling is true, I now tell you that a man is coming here to Konnersreuth, bringing several hundred marks in an envelope." She mentioned the exact date of his arrival, and her prediction was fulfilled to the letter.[30]

The prediction of the man bringing the money is more susceptible to a natural explanation than that of the automobile accident. In the case under consideration there was no question of a free gift to be made at some future time, but simply of the payment of a sum of money which the pastor had loaned the man a year before.[31] There is no evidence that the man's decision to pay his debt was made *after* Theresa's prediction. Why could not her knowledge be due to telepathy? Because Theresa made her prediction precisely to prove her supernatural powers, we are told. But such an argument merely begs the question. At any rate, Theresa should have offered more convincing proof.[32] What we find most confusing is that some writers who see in this prophecy of Theresa a "supernatural seal," nevertheless expressly deny "the privilege of infallibility for Konnersreuth."[33]

All that we have discussed up to now leads us to the conclu-

---

[29] Teodorowicz, *op. cit.*, p. 396.

[30] Cf. *ibid.*, p. 402.

[31] *Ibid.*

[32] The reader might well compare the difference between the evidence to which Theresa appeals here and that which Christ gave as proof of His supernatural power (cf. Jn. 11:1–46).

[33] Teodorowicz, *op. cit.*, pp. 402, 419.

sion that Theresa Neumann's clairvoyant powers are not such as to afford a guarantee of their supernatural origin.

We hold the same opinion concerning Theresa's ability to distinguish blessed from nonblessed articles and to discern genuine relics from spurious ones. It has happened that Theresa made two contradictory judgments about the same relic and declared false some relics whose authenticity was beyond all doubt. These facts are attested to by such scholars as H. Heermann,[34] Dom Mager, O.S.B.,[35] and others. Moreover, in many instances it is impossible to verify Theresa's judgment about relics, especially when there is no objective evidence for their authenticity, to what saint the relic belonged or to what part of the body.

H. Heermann suggests a very simple experiment which would settle once and for all the problem of Theresa's alleged hierognosis: present her with an assortment of religious articles, some blessed, some not, and ask her to pick out the objects which have been blessed. The experiment could be repeated at will and the question decided definitely one way or the other.

This idea was once suggested to Father Naber, in the presence of Theresa Neumann, and he rejected it emphatically: "We have never tried this method. An unfavorable result might lead to serious consequences for us." From this H. Heermann could only conclude: "This answer should help the reader to form a judgment on the above-mentioned powers of Theresa."[36]

The Konnersreuth apologists are not daunted, however. They offer further examples: "One Friday in July, 1931, after her passion bleeding," says Father Fahsel, "when she was in the state of abstraction I came closer to her and laid my finger on her hand. She reached for it and held it tight. 'You also are a priest,' she said";[37] "When she is in ecstasy and touches the fingers with which the priest handles the host, she recognizes the priestly character."[38] What natural explanation can be given

---

[34] "Um Konnersreuth," *Theologie und Glaube*, 1932, No. II, reprint, p. 7.
[35] *Études Carmélitaines*, Paris, 1933, p. 476.
[36] *Op. cit.*, pp. 7–8.
[37] Teodorowicz, *op. cit.*, p. 398.
[38] *Ibid.*, p. 408.

for such insight? They reason that the act of distinguishing the hand of a priest from that of other men is nothing of the physical order, but of the spiritual and supernatural order. No natural powers, not even the "sharpest powers of perception, with the highest developed somnambulism or spiritism" can ever directly reach the supernatural.

The above line of reasoning supposes that in order to recognize someone as a priest he must grasp the sacerdotal character directly. But such a supposition is entirely gratuitous. Manual contact puts the clairvoyant in touch with the *subject*, the possessor of the hand, and thereby permits him to derive knowledge from him, to "read his thoughts." In this way he can recognize him as a priest.[39]

To those who insist that the only reasonable supposition is that God furnishes Theresa with the necessary information, we contend that they are too quick to resort to the miraculous; the facts enumerated can just as well be explained by what the psychologists call "psychometry." The word itself, coined by Professor Buchanan, is not a happy choice, and various scholars (e.g., Richet, Driesch, etc.) have criticized its use on the ground that it may be confused with "psychometrics," the science of the measurement of psychic activities. The word as used by Buchanan signifies only that psychic power by which one can obtain certain information about a person (his character, the events of his life, etc.) through touching some object which belongs to him or with which he has at least come into contact.[40]

The facts of psychometry are so numerous and have been so carefully studied that "they can no longer be doubted."[41] Only those "who have made no study of this power" can question it, says G. Pagenstecher.[42] Its cause, however, like that of clairvoy-

---

[39] Some years ago my ecclesiastical superiors gave me permission to take part in spiritualistic seances for purposes of study, provided I went in secular attire. What was my surprise to find that I was often recognized as a priest!

[40] C. Richet believes that this definition is too restricted, since psychometry can occur in the mere "presence" of an appropriate object.

[41] H. Driesch, *op. cit.*, p. 76.

[42] *Die Geheimnisse der Psychometrie* (German translation from the English original, with foreword by Driesch), p. 22.

ance in general, is shrouded in the deepest mystery. It is very difficult to understand just what trace a person can leave on an object which formerly belonged to him. There is talk of "psychic emanations," "vital vibrations," and so forth. The phonograph record is cited as an illustration. To all of which Ch. Richet answers: "The waves which Pompey's ships cut in the sea no doubt persist in some form to this day. But how many other ships have plowed the seas since!"

To deny a fact merely because we cannot explain it would be contrary to scientific method. Of course, the clairvoyant cannot "touch" any spiritual reality in a blessed object, but we must not overlook the fact that the blessing of objects is accompanied by material actions such as gestures of the hand, the use of holy water, and the like.

We must say a final word about Theresa's "prophecies." We are assured that they are numerous. Let us consider for the moment those which are especially related to her spiritual life. During her ecstatic trances Theresa foretells the exact time when she will have future ecstasies, visions, and other events. The defenders of Konnersreuth attach much weight to these prophecies. The fact is, however, that they are utterly valueless, for similar predictions are very frequent in hypnosis, somnambulism, and analogous psychic conditions. They also are fulfilled unfailingly, just as are Theresa's. As we have shown, prediction sometimes has the force of suggestion, or better, of *autosuggestion*.

True prophecy defies all natural explanations; it always requires supernatural illumination. In the life of Theresa Neumann we have not found a single one which would qualify as supernatural. But, let us add, neither do the alleged prophecies recorded in the *Annals of Psychic Sciences* present anything more than the appearances of real prophecy. They, too, can be explained sufficiently by clairvoyance. A student dreams that he will be asked such and such a question in an examination; a man dreams that a thief will plunder his home, and the like. Or he has a strong "premonition" that such things will occur.

And, in fact, the dreams or premonitions are fulfilled, sometimes in an amazing way. Is there question here of real prophecy? Hardly, for at the time of the dream or presentiment the examination questions and the visit of the thief were *already determined* by human minds. President Lincoln cannot be considered a "prophet" because he dreamed of a funeral that would take place at his home. At the moment of his dream his murderer had already made plans to kill him. The premonitory dream finds sufficient explanation in clairvoyance.

CHAPTER 11

Prolonged Fasting

THE culminating point of the Konnersreuth problem is, as Father Leiber correctly remarks, the problem of Theresa's nourishment.[1]

How are we to explain Theresa's total abstention from food for so many years? Since Christmas eve, 1922, it is claimed, she has taken no *solid* food, and since the Feast of the Transfiguration, 1926,[2] no *liquids* except a few drops of water after receiving Holy Communion. Since September, 1927, up to the present she has ceased taking even this. Here, indeed, is the most baffling mystery of Konnersreuth.

Discussing the marvels of Konnersreuth in the preceding chapters, we always tried to find some *analogy* between them and natural phenomena. Can we find anything in nature approximating Theresa's amazing fast?

Some compare the phenomenon with the fastings of the Hindu fakirs. The similarity, however, is only apparent. A fakir can indeed abstain from food for a long time, but during this period he maintains absolute physical passivity. He avoids all exertion, physical and mental. Moreover, he lives in a warm climate which could furnish him with new energy in the form of heat. Finally, the period of his fasting is generally brief. Despite all these circumstances, the fakir loses so much flesh that he takes on the appearance of a skeleton or mummy.

---

[1] Leiber, S.J., "Konnersreuth," *Stimmen der Zeit,* Vol. 114, 1928, p. 161.

[2] According to Dr. Seidl's official report, read to the medical Congress of Amsterdam on November 7, 1928, Theresa Neumann has abstained from all solid nourishment since December 23, 1926.

Theresa, on the other hand, walks through the village and surrounding farm land, reads and answers some of the numerous letters which she receives daily, autographs a great number of photographs, receives many visitors, and endures the exhausting ordeal of her Friday ecstasy during which she loses much blood. Then, too, this has continued since 1926! No, we cannot compare Theresa's abstinence with that of the fakirs.

Others try to compare her fast with the so-called "hunger cure." Another deceptive analogy! The hunger cure requires the patient to drink a great amount of liquid.[3] Even Maria Furtner, who is sometimes mentioned by way of comparison, drank water every day during the eleven years of her total abstinence.

Still others try to find an explanation in hysteria. It is true that victims of hysteria often refuse to take food. Some abstain because they think they hear a voice forbidding them to eat; others seem to feel a lump or ball rising from their stomach obstructing their throat and preventing them from swallowing any solids. This is a nervous disorder of the esophagus, frequently found in hysterical persons. Others will not take food because, despite all their efforts, they are unable to master the complicated muscular actions involved in the act of swallowing. Some complain of lack of appetite (anorexia), loss of thirst (sitiergia), or the necessary energy or will power to eat by "reasoning" or "obedience." Still others claim that knots have formed in their esophagus which prevent the food from reaching the stomach. Others suffer severe pains and stomach cramps after eating, resulting in hiccuping, vomiting, or flatulence. Finally, there are those patients afflicted with chronic gastric ulcers, a rather common condition among hysterical patients, as Janet remarks.[4]

There have been hysterical patients whose daily nourishment was limited to "200 gr. (6.4 oz.) of milk, 100 gr. (3.2 oz.) of bread, 125 gr. (4 oz.) of coffee and a few little pieces of sugar."[5]

---

[3] "I do not believe that anyone can live more than a fortnight without water," writes W. Kroener, *Das Rätzel von Konnersreuth und Wege zu seiner Lösung. Studie eines Parapsychologen, Geleitwort von H. Driesch*, p. 66.

[4] *L'état mental des hystériques* (Paris: Alcan, 1911), p. 561.

[5] *Ibid.*

They lived for many years on this meager diet. Pierre Janet[6] testifies that Marceline, who was under observation in the physiological laboratory of the School of Medicine from 1925–1926, satisfied her daily nutritional needs with only 250 gr. (½ pt.) of milk, 100 gr. (3.2 oz.) of beer, or 250 gr. (½ pt.) of milk and 130 gr. (4.2 oz.) of broth over a long period of time. The total nourishment absorbed by her during thirty-five days (January 7 — February 11, 1926), was five kilos, 360 gr. (11 lb., 13 oz.) of bread, 9 kilos, 850 gr. (9 qt., 27.2 oz.) of milk, 4 kilos, 650 gr. (4 qt., 20.8 oz.) of coffee. The normal human body requires about 3000 calories of food per day. Marceline's diet gave her between 560–850 calories. What was even more remarkable was the relative constancy of her weight despite frequent attacks of vomiting. During the five weeks she lost only 0.14 kilo (5 oz.) — clear proof that she lost no energy as a result of her abbreviated diet. She was weighed quite often at two and a half-hour intervals. The scales registered very little difference. During the lapse of one minute, she lost only from 0.48 to 0.5 mg. (.0000170 to .000076 oz.) while normal persons lose, during the same period, from 9.1 to 18 mg. (.000310 to .000834 oz.). It was evident that her organism lost very little substance through breathing or perspiration.

Urinalysis confirmed this fact. During six weeks she excreted only 5 to 6 gr. (.16 to .19 oz.) of urea daily (in 200 gr. of urine) while a normal person voids 25 to 30 gr. (.8 to .96 oz.) a day.[7] The nitrogen content of her urine was only 6 to 7 gr. (.211 to .246 oz.) per day compared with 12 to 15 gr. (.422 to .258 oz.) for a normal person.

A basal metabolism test was also very revealing. Marceline exhaled very little carbon dioxide, an indication of a low meta-

---

[6] *Ibid.*, pp. 569–573.

[7] Another subject of Janet voided still less urea, only 1.91 gr. (.061 oz.) daily. One of Charcot's patients voided only 0.20 gr. (.0064 oz.) daily through the normal channels. Uric acid contained in her vomitings brought the daily total to 5 gr. (.16 oz.). Richet's hysterical subjects emitted only 3 to 5 gr. (.096 to .16 oz.) per day. Madeleine, studied by Janet, voided only 3 to 4 gr. (0.96 to .128 oz.). Cf. Janet, *Névroses et Idées fixes*, Paris, 1924, Vol. II, pp. 521–523.

bolic rate. On the other hand, she absorbed an unusually large amount of oxygen, as if the organism was using it to replenish stores of nourishment.

It has been scientifically established that hysterical patients can live, work, and maintain their weight on a very small amount of food. This fact did not escape older writers. Benedict XIV treats of it at length, and his words merit close attention.

He poses the following problem: How are we to distinguish long *natural* fasts from long *supernatural* ones? Those who have studied this question, he says, list a number of decisive criteria (*summopere advertendas*). We must determine: first, whether the fasting was undertaken in order to confirm some article of faith; second, whether the person practiced heroic virtue; third, whether the person who fasted was nourished by Holy Communion alone.[8] Some scholars,[9] he adds, claim that any single one of these marks would guarantee the supernatural origin of a long fast. They attribute the prolonged fasting of the saints to a miracle, and that of other people to natural causes.

Having listed the views of the theologians of his time, the Pope gives his own opinions on the subject. He insists, first of all, on the necessity of making careful inquiry into the fact itself to discover whether the person in question *really* abstained from eating and drinking during the *whole* time. This inquiry must be extremely serious and exact (*admodum severos*).[10]

Once the fact of a long fast has been established, we must find out whether the fasting began with some *illness* (*an jejunium a morbo incoeperit*), for "not only physicians but theologians as well admit long natural fasts in sick persons."[11]

---

[8] *De Servorum Dei Beatificatione et de Beatorum Canonizatione,* Book IV, P. I, Chap. 27, n. 13.

[9] He quotes here Cardinal de Lauraea and Pignatelli.

[10] Benedict gives some instances of this exactness. The hermit Blessed Nicholas of Flüe is said to have fasted 22 years. The Congregation of Rites, nevertheless, did not accept his fasting as miraculous for, though he was closely observed by some people during a period of time, he could have eaten food brought to him by unknown persons or have drunk water. Finally, he could have eaten herbs, or earth "as the worms do" (*ibid.,* n. 14).

[11] Benedict XIV asked the Academy of Bologna for their opinion on long fasts,

If the fasting did not begin with an illness, we must next examine whether the person *felt well* during his period of fasting. If he did, we must proceed to inquire whether, during this period, he neglected other obligatory *pious* works. If *all* these conditions are verified, we must consider the fasting miraculous.[12]

We may sum up Benedict's criteria as follows: the fasting must not have begun with an illness, nor have caused illness; it must have been undertaken with a good intention and must not have impeded the fulfillment of moral duties. The last two criteria are to assure us that the long fast was really the work of God and not of the evil spirit.

If we follow the Pope's method rigorously, we would immediately rule out a supernatural origin of Theresa's fast, for her fasting did commence with an *illness*, with a natural impossibility of eating. After the shock of the fire (March 10, 1918) Theresa was afflicted with persistent nausea. She could not retain solid nourishment, but rejected it immediately. She lived on liquids and barley mash. In 1922 she was stricken with a throat ailment which prevented her from swallowing anything. For twelve days she was forced to abstain from Holy Communion. Dr. Seidl is supposed to have told the family that the muscles of her esophagus were paralyzed. Theresa suffered sharp pains in the pit of her stomach, gastric hemorrhages, and vomitings of blood. She had recourse to a charlatan, Frederick Heinzl of Neustadt, who succeeded in giving her temporary relief. At this time an abscess also formed in her throat, which broke and drained into her stomach. Vomiting followed immediately. For the next three months she could take only liquids through a straw. After a short period of relief her digestive troubles reappeared. It was then that Theresa said she had lost her appetite for food. After the Feast of the Transfiguration of Our Lord (August 6, 1926), her entire nourishment consisted of a small amount of tea or coffee and some raspberry juice.

---

whether they might last for months or years (*ibid.,* n. 16). Their answer may be found in the seventh volume of his works.

[12] *Ibid.,* n. 15.

At her mother's insistence she attempted to take some solid nourishment, but had to reject it immediately. Since Christmas, 1926, we are told she has taken no nourishment at all, solid or liquid. Professor Mayer, who visited Konnersreuth at the beginning of Theresa's fast, heard her mother advise her: "If you keep on fasting you will die of starvation. Eat with all your strength!" But Theresa was physically unable to comply.

Benedict XIV agreed with the Academy of Bologna that in such cases fasting may last for years without supernatural intervention. He cites the case of a girl from Gratianopolis, who did not eat or drink for four years. But, since her fasting owed its inception to a "violent illness" which made eating and drinking impossible, the physicians declared that it was natural. The illnesses which facilitate long natural fasting are, according to the Pope and the Academy, various nervous and psychic disorders, but especially hysteria.[13] This opinion is in perfect accord with modern science, as we have shown above. Father H. Thurston, S.J., lists a number of persons who lived many years "without any food."[14]

Let us now consider the case of Theresa Neumann. During the two weeks when she was observed by the four Franciscan nuns, she took only three Hosts and drank only three spoonfuls of water. During the same period, she voided 50 cm. (1.6 oz.) of urine and one spoonful of feces. Her weight dropped from 110 lb. (as of Wednesday, July 13) to 102 lb. (by Saturday, July 16), rose again to 108 lb. (Wednesday, July 20), dropped to 105 lb. (Saturday, July 23), and finally rose to the original 110 lb. (Thursday, July 25). During this period she maintained normal humidity of the mouth; she did not sleep more than ten hours. Yet she was strong enough to work.

It is true, as L. Witt remarks, that Theresa's voice always

---

[13] *Quo ex genere sunt multae earum aegritudinum quae cerebrum et nervos infestant. . . . Omnium vero diutissimae mulieres ex utero laborantes (op. cit., 7 App., ad I, P. IV, n. 4, p. 536).* As we observed previously, *ex utero laborantes* would now be classified as *hysterical* persons.

[14] "Living Without Eating," *The Month,* Sept.-Oct., 1931; *ibid.,* Mar. 1931, pp. 243–244.

sounds tired: "she speaks like someone who has a weight on his chest, though many people do not notice it easily, or do not notice it at all."[15] But this may be the effect of her long suffering rather than of fasting. She never completely recovered her health.

When the laboratory analysis revealed that her excrements showed signs of "hunger" products, some claimed that Theresa's fasting is due to the fact that *she eats herself!* But if this were true there should not be a particle of Theresa's body left by this time. After her long abstention from fluids, her copious bleeding during her Friday ecstasies, the elimination of urine, her organism (which is composed of four-fifths fluids) would long ago have been completely desiccated. How can a human being abstain from food for many years and maintain the same bodily weight?[16] How can we explain the sudden increase of weight which takes place in the days following Theresa's ecstasies? *Ex nihilo nihil!* There must be *some* cause, and if that cause is not natural, it must be supernatural.

The dilemma is so clear that the only possible answer is in a theory of imposture. "Before I accept a revolution in the order of nature," writes Dr. Wolfgang, "I would prefer to hold that there is something lacking in the controls exercised over the somnambulist [Theresa], that she takes more food in a semiconscious state than while awake."[17] An unconscious fraud, or a miracle — these are the only alternatives. But we are taking "unconscious fraud" not exclusively in a *psychological* meaning, but also, and even principally, in a *moral* one. Theresa Neumann, for different reasons (e.g., the glory of Christ, the conversion and edification of the souls, and so on) can sincerely believe that there

---

[15] L. Witt, *Konnersreuth im Lichte der Religion und Wissenschaft,* I, pp. 156–157.

[16] Total abstinence from food causes a fatal loss of weight, through the consumption of fat and, in part, of muscle tissue, as well as by loss of bodily heat. A child dies when it loses two tenths of its weight, an adult when he loses four tenths. (This is true in total abstinence. In relative abstinence it is possible to lose up to 50 per cent.) A man can live on water alone for about 40 days. Terrence MacSweeney died (1920) after a hunger strike of 74 days. Others have succumbed after only seventeen days.

[17] *Voss Zeitung,* Berlin, Aug. 19, 1927.

is no moral fault in affirming that she takes no food, as she eats really very little . . . almost nothing.

We cannot give serious thought to the so-called "fluid theory," and Vampirism, for they do not explain anything and are wholly devoid of any scientific foundation.[18] Nor can we accept the obsolete medical theory quoted by Benedict XIV. The physicians of his time thought that a man might live naturally for a long time without any food because they supposed that the only function of food was to compensate for the loss of the "humid" element consumed by the "warm" element. Modern biology has proved that organic life is based on combustion and therefore requires fuel. Breathing alone cannot possibly supply sufficient fuel for metabolic processes. "I cannot and will not believe that it is possible," says Wolfgang, "to live without adequate food and drink. I cannot and will not believe that a person could fast, even for two weeks, and at the same time walk, suffer . . . and excrete."[19] All living organisms breathe, and in breathing give off carbon dioxide.[20] The weight of the carbon exhaled by a normal person in the course of a year is greater than that of his entire body. From what source does the human organism receive its carbon? Science proves that it comes from the food we consume. In breathing, the human body gives off water vapor. According to Ewald, the amount of water lost in this manner amounts to almost 400 gr. (12.8 oz.) a day, or more than 146 kilos (146 oz.) each year. The principal source of this water content is, of course, the liquids which we drink.

We are forced to conclude that the individuals mentioned by Father Thurston in his article did not really live for years "without any food." We must suppose that they took at least a little food, without the knowledge of their acquaintances, and perhaps without knowing it themselves, that is, in some somnambulist or autohypnotic condition. In their normal state, however, they were physically unable to swallow anything without experienc-

---

[18] Cf. Dr. Reissmann, *Tag,* No. 263, Nov. 3, 1927.

[19] *Op. cit.*

[20] This is true even of plants. Cf. Paul Siwek, *The Philosophy of Evil* (New York: Ronald Press Co., 1951), pp. 37–38, 110–111.

ing nausea and pain. Some of them could not even move themselves in bed and did not feel any need of eating or drinking.

Let us apply these facts to the case of Theresa Neumann. She breathes; therefore she gives off carbon dioxide. This was scientifically proved on October 5, 1927, by C. Isenkrahe and Dr. Miller in the presence of Father Naber. Her body also loses some of its fluid content through exhalation.[21] Now how is the carbon and liquid restored to her body? Does she do it in some way similar to what we have suggested in regard to the individuals mentioned by Thurston?

Such an assumption is usually ruled out by the fact that Theresa Neumann was subjected to a close scrutiny in her home by four Franciscan nuns for two weeks in 1927. But some serious doubts have been raised about the accuracy of the observations made at that time. When Theresa's urine was analyzed on the two Fridays of the observation period, it had all the characteristics of "hunger urine," excreted by a person abstaining from all food and drink, or eating and drinking very little. But the urine analyzed on the Friday nine days after the observation period was perfectly normal. It was the same as that of a person who eats and drinks. Then, too, the urine taken on a Friday only two days after the observation period ended presented an interesting transition stage between the "hunger urine" and normal urine. Here are the pertinent statistics for the four analyses:

	During Observation Period		After Observation Period	
			Two Days Later	Nine Days Later
Reaction	very acid	acid	acid	alkaline
Nitrogen	1.28	2.24	1.139	0.482

---

[21] It is regrettable that they did not measure the precise amount of carbon dioxide and water.

Salt	0.657	0.84	1.08	1.02
Density	1025	1024	1033	1014
Acetone	very strong	strong	weak	none
Color	not given	not given	dark	light

From these data some scientists have drawn the following conclusion: Theresa Neumann ate and drank little or nothing during the observation period. Normally, however, she takes food and drink.[22] Dr. Seidl attempted to account for the lack of acetone in the last analysis by the fact that the samples had been left in open containers. Dr. Heermann, however, attaches little importance to this circumstance. "I have made a series of experiments with a specialist who devotes himself entirely to this study. The experiments proved that the acetone in the urine of a fasting person remains, even in an open receptacle, for several weeks. . . . But even if Dr. Seidl's supposition were correct, we must account for the other significant differences between the urine sampled during, and outside of, the observation period — the disappearance of acid, the diminution of nitrogen and the increase of salt (this latter despite increasing clearness of the urine), and, finally, the light color characteristic of normal urine."[23]

It may be said, of course, that we do not know how physiological functions operate in stigmatized persons. However, we do not deem it important to know their operation; we would like an explanation of the fact that, when Theresa is *under observation*, she excretes hunger urine, and when not observed, normal urine. This difference demands an explanation.

Theresa's family was asked (in 1929) to submit samples of her urine at regular intervals for medical analysis. The family

---

[22] Cf. Deutsch, *Ärztliche Kritik an Konnersreuth*, pp. 45–53.

[23] In *Theologie und Glaube*, 1932, No. 2. Some defenders of Konnersreuth try to deprive the argument of Heermann of its value by saying that he is not a "specialist" for this kind of problem. They obviously did not remark that he made the experiments mentioned "with a specialist who devotes himself entirely to this study."

answered that she had ceased to urinate![24] Another marvel?
Possibly, but it is strange and disquieting that this marvel
should occur at the precise moment when things were getting a
bit suspicious.

Another strange circumstance must be noted here. Dr. Ewald
detected a definite odor of acetone in Theresa's breath in the
course of the scrutiny we mentioned above. He never detected
this odor afterward. What could be the reason? A very simple
explanation would be that Theresa no longer fasted after the
observers left.

The ability of Theresa to regain lost weight is of great importance, according to some scholars. Dr. Heermann notes that it
occurs during the two or three days after her Friday ecstasy,
that is, when no one is paying particular attention to her. On
other days of the week she is the center of interest, she is closely
watched, and she loses weight. This is another coincidence that
might be studied. Dr. Heermann recommends a very simple experiment. He would ask Theresa to sit, or lie, on a special
scale for twelve hours.[25]

This experiment was, in fact, attempted. With the special
authorization of the Bishop of Ratisbon, Dr. Seidl was sent to
study Theresa's weight variations. But her family refused to
admit him. Why? Was there really something to hide?

Even the nursing Sisters who were commissioned by the
Bishop of Ratisbon to observe Theresa day and night for two
weeks (July, 1927), were seriously hampered in carrying out
their task. The members of the household never ceased placing
obstacles in their way. Theresa herself abetting them strongly,
as may be seen from the following incident. One day
the nuns were discussing in a subdued voice the difficulties which
Theresa's acquaintances and relatives were making for them.
Theresa, who just then was in a state of "absorption," began

---

[24] Nevertheless, Rev. Fahsel, a great apologist of Konnersreuth, says that Theresa
Neumann ceased to urinate in 1930. "There was then an urine," notes Prof.
Waldmann, "but not for examination" (in his letter to the author, July 9, 1952).
[25] *Op. cit.*

to complain of terrible pains in her head and limbs. Suddenly she heard a Voice telling her that she would have to endure these sufferings to atone for the faults of the nursing Sisters who had manifested themselves unworthy of the great task committed to them. The nuns, it seemed, had made some unkind remarks about Father Naber, about Theresa, and about a gentleman of their company. To calm Theresa the Sisters asked pardon if they had really done anything wrong. Thereupon Theresa relaxed and listened once more to the Voice. She then told the Sisters that their faults had been pardoned, and at the same time Theresa's pains disappeared.

The difficulties inherent in any examination of inedia in the subject's own home have been well described by the great pathologist Virchow: "For seventeen years," he declared in one of his Berlin lectures, "I was a prison doctor and came to learn that even in the best organized infirmaries one cannot be too well on guard against feigned illnesses; I learned that, despite all precautions and the closest surveillance, fraud in the matter of nourishment can be committed . . . and that it is very difficult to detect all the tricks and subterfuges employed."[26] For this reason he attaches no value to the observations made on the fasting of Louise Lateau. By the same token the reality of Theresa's long abstention from food and drink has been seriously questioned, and it has been recommended that a more accurate observation be held in some Catholic sanatorium.[27]

The proposal for a new examination met with great sympathy among the Catholic clergy. Unfortunately, it was rejected by the Neumann family. We quote here an official document of the Bishop of Ratisbon, dated December 10, 1937. "In 1927 Theresa Neumann, by order of her bishop, was subjected to a fortnight's observation for the purpose of determining the reality of her fasting. The results have been published. Ten years have elapsed since then. During all this time, as she herself affirms,

---

[26] Heermann, *op. cit.*

[27] *Crefelder Zeitung,* Sept. 25, 1874. Quoted by Deutsch, *Où en est actuellement l'affaire de Konnersreuth,* Paris, 1937, p. 32.

she has taken no food, and, for several years, no liquids. Some doubts, however, have been expressed about the accuracy of her statements. Are they true or are they the result of imposture or of an illusion? These doubts can be settled only by a new, medically controlled observation. That undertaken in 1927 could reveal merely the situation as of that time, but cannot confirm or deny in any way the fasting of the years that have since elapsed. For this reason the bishop of the diocese requested the Neumann family to agree to a new observation. The entire Bavarian hierarchy, and on August 4, 1937, the Holy Office, concurred in this wish. Theresa Neumann declared herself willing to submit to the examination. However, her father refused his consent, or laid down conditions that were unacceptable.[28] This being the state of affairs, the ecclesiastical authorities disclaim all responsibility for the alleged absolute fasting and for the authenticity of other extraordinary phenomena at Konnersreuth. . . ."

---

[28] In *"Memories of Konnersreuth,"* written in 1930 by a Hungarian priest, we find a striking illustration of the role played by Theresa's father in the Konnersreuth affair. A certain German prelate heard some physicians state that a person who would abstain from all food and drink for four weeks would suffer complete desiccation of the kidneys and eventually die. He begged the Bishop of Ratisbon to order a new observation of Theresa. The bishop sent him to the pastor of Konnersreuth. The latter, in turn, referred the matter to Theresa, who said she would ask our Lord what was to be done. Jesus told her: "The answer rests with your father." The prelate then went to Theresa's father. He had hardly uttered a sentence when Mr. Neumann shouted: "Get out of here!" (*Schaun's, dass Sie hinauskommen!*), and stormed so loudly that the whole village could hear him. Was this really Christ's answer?

Father Maréchal, S.J., was also convinced of the necessity of certifying whether Theresa's fasting is really absolute, as she asserts. If the contrary should ever be proved, this alone "would be decisive, for it would show a persistent course of conscious or unconscious dissimulation." He made this statement in a letter to the author dated October 15, 1933. In this same letter he expressed his surprise that he had been numbered among the "partisans" of Konnersreuth: "Lacking any personal observation and sufficient documentary proof, I do not feel entitled to pronounce, or even to entertain, a definite opinion on the case of Theresa Neumann."

A number of Catholic scholars have complained of the opposition raised by the "Konnersreuth Circle" against any attempt to conduct a serious study of the phenomena. Cf. Dom Mager, O.S.B., *Études Carmélitaines,* Apr., 1933, pp. 50, 106; Apr., 1934, p. 222; "Stand der Konnersreuther Frage," *Katholische Kirchenzeitung,* May 5, 1932; Father G. Wunderle, "Wie steht es heute um Konnersreuth?," *Fränkisches Volksblatt,* Würzburg, June 2, 1932.

It is certainly regrettable that Theresa's family,[29] in opposing the wishes of the Church, has not permitted light to be thrown on the most important of all the marvels of Konnersreuth.[30]

---

[29] In December, 1951, Theresa received an invitation from the Heidelberg clinic to be examined there under most favorable conditions. This invitation was sent to Konnersreuth by the bishop. After six months, having heard nothing from Theresa Neumann, the clinic withdrew its invitation.

[30] Rev. Piwinski reproaches us for suggesting new investigations concerning the fasting of Theresa Neumann. One of his principal arguments concerns the result of the investigations made by Dr. Hohn. He refers to the book of J. Teodorowicz, published in 1933. What a pity that my distinguished critic did not see the later publications, notably that by Dr. Deutsch, on these investigations. In the light of these new theories, the value of Dr. Hohn's investigation is very doubtful (cf. J. Deutsch, *Où en est actuellement l'affaire de Konnersreuth,* 1937, p. 14; *Ärztliche Kritik an Konnersreuth,* p. 48 ff.).

CHAPTER 12

Conclusion

IT MAY be well, at the end of our study of the Konnersreuth phenomena, to cast a retrospective glance at the road we have traversed; a difficult road, no doubt, for we have had to encounter obstacles of all kinds, such as the reticence of documents, facts insufficiently verified, and the like.

Our aim, however, was to follow the road just as it lay before us. We have endeavored to face the problems squarely and according to the method laid down for us by those great teachers *quorum laus est in Ecclesia.*

For this reason we did not begin our present study with a discussion of the personal holiness of Theresa Neumann or her mystical life. Actually there is no necessary or intrinsic connection between a saintly or a mystical life and the sort of problem which has been the object of our study. One can be a saint, yes, a great saint, without the gift of miracles, without enjoying any exemption from the laws of nature which oblige us, under penalty of death, to take nourishment. Similarly one can attain the very heights of mystic contemplation without bearing the visible marks of Christ's passion, without experiencing visions, prophecies, or even ecstasies. On this point all modern Catholic authors are in agreement.[1]

---

[1] "Ecstasy may be a concomitant of Catholic mysticism, but it is not of its essence, and this for the reason that ecstasy is not so much a thing, as the effect of a thing on the body and surface of consciousness." Neither ecstasy nor visions "are ever sought by true mystics" (A. J. Francis Stanton, *Catholic Mysticism,* Herder, 1939, p. 39). "Ecstasy belongs to the concomitant manifestations of the mystical life and not to its essence. Let the reader take the fact well to heart" (Hieronymus Jaegen, *The Mystic Life of Grace,* London, 1936, Eng. trans., p.

The theory which holds that ecstasy is the "measure of value"[2] for the extraordinary phenomena of the spiritual life, or as "an absolutely necessary condition for their genuineness,"[3] is, in our opinion, definitely incorrect.

Occasionally we come across the following line of argument: We must accept Theresa's visions, clairvoyance, abstinence, and the like, as supernatural because she herself possesses solid Christian virtues and authentic mystic states, even though they be the lower ones.[4] Such reasoning is vitiated by the logical error known as the *"fallacia accidentis."* There is only one reliable method of studying these phenomena, as the *Dictionnaire de Théologie Catholique* tells us, just as there is only one reliable method of examining miracles. That method is to take them one by one and discover whether, considering all the circumstances, we can explain them in a natural way, or whether we must ascribe them to the special intervention of God. Possibly such a procedure will not bring us certainty — it is not always easy to recognize a miracle — but in that event we must have the courage to admit our doubt.[5] In any case we must show ourselves more rigorous than lenient in conducting such an examination in order not to furnish unbelievers with a pretext for ridiculing the faith. We must learn to resign ourselves to slow progress.[6]

"Empirical psychology," writes Father Pinard de la Boulaye, "is in its proper field when it attempts to study those religious phenomena which are explicable by natural causes."[7] The *Dictionnaire de Théologie Catholique* tells us: "In these matters we must be ready to revise our judgments according to the

---

114). Ecstasy "is distinct from mystical operations, just as one fact is distinct from another fact which occasioned it" (A. Saudreau, *The Mystical State*, p. 99).

[2] Teodorowicz, *Mystical Phenomena in the Life of Theresa Neumann* (St. Louis: Herder, 1940), p. 170.

[3] *Ibid.*, p. 430.

[4] In the higher stages of the mystical life, imaginative visions occur rarely or not at all. Theresa experiences a great number of such visions. Cf. F. von Lama, *Konnersreuth en 1928*, French trans. by A. Desguigues, Mulhouse, 1930, pp. 29–31.

[5] *Dict. de Théol. Cath.*, cols. 2653–2654.

[6] Cf. St. Thomas Aquinas, *S. Th.*, I, q. 46, a. 2; *Dict. de Théol. Cath.*, cols. 2649–2650.

[7] *L'étude comparée des religions*, Paris, 1925, Vol. II, p. 336.

light afforded by the undeniable progress of the psychological sciences, and to cease considering supernatural some facts which up to now we have believed such."[8]

How happy we should be if, like so many other students of Konnersreuth — we could conclude our present study with a *Constat!* — "It is certain that the Konnersreuth phenomena are supernatural." Unfortunately we are not able to do so at present. All the extraordinary phenomena seem amenable to a natural explanation, except Theresa's continuous fasting, and this has never been proved factual. Will our doubts be finally resolved some day when Theresa, bowing to the wishes of the Church, submits herself to a new examination in a Catholic hospital? Perhaps. Meanwhile, we must be cautious of premature pronouncements.[9] We would do well to imitate the policy of watchful waiting adopted by the Catholic Church, for we know that she is "the Church of the living God, the pillar and mainstay of the truth" (1 Tim. 3:15).

---

[8] Col. 2649.

[9] If the examination alluded to will one day furnish us with new material which cannot be explained *naturally,* we shall then study it in the light of "moral" or "mystical" criteria in order to decide to which "supernatural cause" the phenomena in question are to be attributed: to God or to the devil. To do so *now* would be contrary to our *method,* which we have traced in the Preface of this book.

Index

223

Printed in the United States
106855LV00004B/266/A